Jo Ramirez

MEMOIRS OF A RACING MAN

Jo Ramirez

MEMOIRS OF A RACING MAN

FOREWORDS BY **SIR JACKIE STEWART** AND **ALAIN PROST**

SECOND EDITION

Haynes Publishing

First published in hardback September 2005
This paperback edition, containing new material, was published in February 2010

A catalogue record for this book is available from the British Library

ISBN 978 1 84425 861 1

Library of Congress control no. 2009936971

Published by Haynes Publishing, Sparkford,
Yeovil, Somerset, BA22 7JJ, UK
Tel: 01963 442030 Fax: 01963 440001
Int. tel: +44 1963 442030 Int. fax: +44 1963 440001
E-mail: sales@haynes.co.uk
Website: www.haynes.co.uk

Haynes North America, Inc.,
861 Lawrence Drive, Newbury Park, California 91320, USA

All photographs appearing in this book are courtesy of the author unless
otherwise credited. Front cover image courtesy of LAT.

Page layout by Dominic Stickland

Printed and bound in the UK

CONTENTS

FOREWORD
BY SIR JACKIE STEWART OBE

This book is written by a man who represents a group of people in the world of motorsport that I describe as the only true professionals in the business.

I can really only comment about the period of time that I have had the privilege of knowing Jo Ramirez. This mild-mannered and gentle Mexican entered my life in the halcyon days of the Ken Tyrrell era. Ken was a remarkable man in a modest, mostly quiet but truly determined fashion, resulting in an amazing amount of success. He achieved success by choosing to have around him top-class people. Through some hidden skill of his own, Ken could see from the interviews that he conducted, a potential that would allow those people to rise above what they probably perceived as their own true potential. Jo Ramirez is such a man. The rise and rise of Jo you will read about in this book, but I count myself very lucky to be one of the people who shared a part of this man's professional career.

As Jo progressed within the sport, with his eyes wide open, allowing him to learn through observing others, he developed and polished his skills to enable him to move with effortless style and dignity through the world of Grand Prix motor racing and the industry that developed around it. I witnessed a fair amount of that in his role within the Tyrrell team during a time when we experienced some incredible highs and such desperately cruel blows – from the highs of the team winning World Championships, to the horrific loss of life in the accident that took François Cevert away from us.

François's accident had a devastating effect on the whole of the Tyrrell team and particularly on Jo – François's mechanic at the time. On that weekend, Ken Tyrrell and I chose, out of respect to François, to withdraw the team from the event. Many months before I had decided firmly to retire after the final race of that 1973 season, the US Grand Prix at Watkins Glen, which would have been my 100th Grand Prix. So, as the records show, I only competed in 99. François, although he never knew it, would have been the number one driver in the Tyrrell team in 1974. I have every confidence that, supported by a combination of the direction of Ken Tyrrell and the dedication of Jo Ramirez, François Cevert would have gone on to become a very proud French Formula One World Champion.

Jo Ramirez is now retired from active participation in Grand Prix racing, but he has never left the sport completely. He serves as a Trustee for the Grand Prix Mechanics Charitable Trust, of which I am Chairman. His contribution is substantial. His access to people within the sport is still well respected and always welcome. There are not too many mechanics, engineers or administrators who 'come through the mill' and write a book about their experiences. I am sure that those who read this book will learn a great deal, and by so doing admire the man who wrote it. A man who has worked with some of the greatest racing drivers in the world, including Graham Hill, Bruce McLaren, Dan Gurney, Niki Lauda, Alain Prost, Ayrton Senna, Mika Häkkinen and David Coulthard, and in a great many of the top categories of motor racing outside of Formula One, including Le Mans, CanAm and TransAm. What a life he has led, and what characters he has been exposed to. All of these experiences have provided Jo Ramirez with stories to tell and that is exactly why he has decided to write this book.

FOREWORD
BY ALAIN PROST

I met Jo during my first test of the McLaren Formula One car in France, and I was feeling pretty nervous. Jo was working with a small team and was borrowing some tools from the McLaren boys. I had worked long and hard to get to Formula One and that is where I wanted to be, and therefore I was eager to meet as many people in the business as possible. From then on our paths crossed several times, but it was not until 1984 that we had the chance to work together at McLaren.

Jo was one of the greatest enthusiasts of the sport that I have ever come across, and he devoted himself totally to McLaren. His sense of humour, enthusiasm and electricity were a great motivation for the whole team. He arranged everything for the drivers, making our lives easier, many times above and beyond the bounds of duty. He was not impressed when, in 1984, Niki Lauda beat me to the championship by half-a-point, even though I had dominated the year.

In the first year with Ayrton Senna, Jo always kept the balance between the two sides by cracking jokes in both corners and making the most of the humorous aspects. During the second year, when relations between Ayrton and I deteriorated, Jo, who was close to Ayrton, as they could speak and swear in the same language, remained completely impartial. He never took sides, and even after I left to go to Ferrari he tried very hard to heal the rift between us.

Jo was very close to joining me at Ferrari, but was dissuaded by Ron Dennis. He was an important part of the chemistry at McLaren, so important that no wonder that McLaren has been less competitive since Jo left. I wish him all the best in his retirement, although I would love to see him back in the pit lane in any capacity or team, because there is no more fun and warmth in Formula One these days – the sport needs men like Jo.

INTRODUCTION

Those of us who, in life, have had the pleasure of not knowing the meaning of a hard day's work – and I believe that I'm among the minority of lucky ones who discovered that they could actually be paid for indulging in their hobby – can live our lives enjoying every day. I didn't ever want to stop, but as I was approaching 40 years in motor racing I realised that, pleasant and enjoyable as it was, I wasn't getting any younger and the demands were getting greater.

Throughout the latter part of the last century, Formula One was changing more and more – which isn't unusual in any sport at the top level. The important thing is to be able to change with it and accept the changes (which I believe are called 'progress', although in certain areas they were far from it). Although I still had a few years of work left in me, I began to feel that I wasn't enjoying it as much as I always had. I found it more difficult to change at the same rhythm as the sport, and therefore decided that it was time to move on.

During the last few years of my career in motor racing innumerable friends and fans from all over the world asked me if, one day, I'd write my memoirs. Although it was nice to be asked, I never thought that I'd really have the time. I'm sure that during our lives there have been times when all of us have felt the need to share some of the things that happened to us; but having the discipline to actually write these anecdotes down is another matter.

Ken Tyrrell always said to me, when something interesting happened, "Have you written it in your diary?" "No, Ken, you work me too hard, I haven't got the time." I remember Ken once said to François Cevert, "If you keep a diary, one day it will keep you!"

Mind you, if I'd kept a diary throughout my racing career it would be as large as the *Encyclopaedia Britannica*; but maybe, with the good things still stored in my memory, plus a rear-view mirror to look back at my past, I'll be able to put together a reasonable book.

At times I was full of enthusiasm at the prospect of writing a book, but at other times I felt that perhaps I wasn't prepared enough to embark on such a new challenge. When you're working in Formula One you're 100 per cent involved in what you do and you don't have time to prepare for your future. No wonder they call retirement one of the three most important events in your life, along with birth and marriage!

By the time I left McLaren I knew I wanted to live part of the time in southern Spain, where the weather is a bit milder and drier, and I'd already bought some land in Andalucía, near Málaga, and the foundations of the house had been started. Bea and I were to sell our home in Berkshire in order to pay for the Spanish house, and then move to a very small but practical property in a village where we had previously lived very happily. Our daughter Vanessa, who was in her late 20s, was a senior nurse at London's Great Ormond Street Hospital looking after children with heart problems, and lived in a flat of her own in Muswell Hill.

Bea always loved this little village south of Oxford called Dorchester on Thames, and she always said that whenever and wherever I decided to retire – be it in Mexico, France, Spain, Italy or Brazil – she wanted to keep a base in Dorchester, so we bought this small house there. But it needed completely refurbishing, which along with supervision of the Spanish house meant that I had my work cut out.

I'd planned to contract expert tradesmen to do a lot of the jobs, but in the prevailing economic situation after 9/11, and seeing my own pension shrinking faster than a candle, I could no longer afford this luxury and I had to do the work myself. When you've built Formula One cars there's nothing that you cannot do, or at least tackle, and I've always found it very rewarding working with my own hands, relaxing and soothing; but naturally it all takes time. On the plus side you can do things exactly the way you want, without having to allow strangers into your own home, and your bank manager does not get to know. So the chances of me ever having the time to write my own book diminished daily.

2002 was the first season that I was out of the sport, and what a boring season this was! I was asked by Atlas F1 to write a column for their website after every Grand Prix. My column would appear the week after the Grand Prix, and therefore I didn't have to talk about the race, but just gave a quick résumé of how I saw it, then talk about any other experiences that happened to me at any time in my life during that particular event, plus general chit-chat about my life after Formula One.

I'd agreed to do this as I saw it as a kind of discipline in order to fulfil a commitment, as well as to get me in the frame of mind for writing – and, of course, as a way of shaking up my memory, to remember things before I forgot them. The result was that I enjoyed writing the columns: they kept me in touch with what was happening in Formula One, and they gave me that sense of having to do something for someone else which you no longer have when you retire completely!

One of the things that came out of these columns was a question from one of the long-standing collaborators of Atlas F1, writer of many books Karl Ludvigsen. I met Karl in the 1960s, when I was working with Dan Gurney, so he has been aware of all my different jobs since then. He asked me when (not if) I was going to write a book. I said to him that perhaps I'd left it too late, as I felt I should have been writing it by then and have it out at the end of that year, before people forgot my name.

He told me that it was never too late, and was kind enough to put the question to his readers. As a result I was bombarded with dozens of e-mails saying that they would always buy a book written by me about my racing experiences. Needless to say, I was pleasantly surprised and this gave me the confidence to take the bit between my teeth and get on with it.

Last year when I read the first page of Murray Walker's book *Unless I'm Very Much Mistaken* (incidentally, I'm very proud to count myself among Murray's friends – he wasn't only the voice of motorsport but one of its greatest ambassadors), I noticed that Murray mentioned one of the all-time characters of the sport, Rob Walker (no connection between the names). Rob was the one with the money from the Johnny Walker whisky family and was the mentor and sponsor of the one and only Stirling Moss.

When the two Walkers met at one of the many motor racing gatherings, Murray asked Rob: "When are you going to write your autobiography?" Typically unassuming person that Rob was, he said, "Oh no, I couldn't do that. It's one thing to reminisce with a bunch of old chaps like this but another to put it all in writing. I'd just dry up if I tried to put it all on paper." Murray said: "Rob, if you don't do it and go to your grave with everything you've said and done still in your head you'll be committing a crime against motor racing. You must do it."

This, together with the comments of my family and some of the many racing fans that through the years you get to know, as well as many Mexican and South American enthusiasts who often asked me how it came about that somebody from a third world country found his way into the high-profile world of Formula One, made me feel that perhaps it would be selfish on my part not to share my wonderful life with any motor racing nut who'd be interested. After all, I've had so much out of the sport that it's time to give something back. I therefore made it my New Year's resolution to start the book.

To some people, writing a book might seem something of a personal indulgence, but I didn't see it that way at all. A personal satisfaction, yes: a chance of living my life again, travelling down memory lane. I've enjoyed doing it. If any reader has a quarter of the fun reading it that I've had writing it, then it will have been worthwhile.

I've met many people in my life and probably most of them are mentioned in this book. Some have been an inspiration in one way or another, and some have been very important in my career. One who has been both is Ron Dennis from McLaren, where I spent the last 18 years of my working life; therefore you'll be hearing a lot about Ron in this book. I've probably known him for about 30 years: for 12 years he was my friend and for 18 he was my boss.

On my last day at McLaren (Friday 26 October 2001), Ron wasn't going to be at the factory because he was due in Germany on business. But he called me into his office the day before to say he was sorry that he was going to be away – something which I appreciated very much, because at the time he was so frantically busy that one hardly had a glimpse of him, let alone a conversation with him, so I was grateful that he remembered.

For the first half of our short meeting he was great – warm, calm and sincere, as he always was with me in crisis times – saying that the McLaren doors would always be open for me at Woking or at a race meeting. Whenever I wanted to come I'd be more than welcome. He then made pleasant comments about how far we'd come together: we had difficult times together, we fought together, we laughed together, we cried together, we lost together, we won together, and we got pissed together. Then during the second half of our conversation, he told me he'd heard that I was intending to write a book. "As you know," he said, "I've always given you good advice, and my advice to you is – don't bother, don't do it, you'll not make any money from it. Whoever you collaborate with will take you for a ride and you'll be sorry you've done it. You look at the world through different eyes to the rest of us and it won't be what the public wants to read..."

I have to say that I was I little bit taken aback by all this, and said to him that so far he'd only read what other people had written about me, but nothing that I'd written myself, and surely he shouldn't pre-judge me? "During all the time that I've devoted to McLaren, you never trusted me to talk to the press, but I've never for one minute thought that you need be concerned or in any way worried about a book written by me. Of course, you're right, the truth hurts. But, equally, the truth can gratify, and surely for any wrong decision you've made, you've also made dozens of perfect ones that have given the team the success we enjoyed. Therefore readers would have to weigh the balance and judge for themselves. The success of the team speaks for itself, and you have to trust me to carry on enhancing the McLaren legacy."

I must admit that Ron's sudden advice about not writing this book fuelled my desire to do it, as I'd be certain to sell another copy!

The last hurdle that you have to mount once you've written a book is to think on an eye-catching title. One of the mottoes I always had was that the problem with Formula One racing was "So many women, so little time", and the Marlboro girls always said that if I ever wrote my memoirs I should call it that. However, I've kept it clean. It might have given the wrong impression...

ACKNOWLEDGEMENTS

Every book I've read, seen, or browsed through always has a page for the Author in which he or she thanks all the people who helped them with their book; but since this is an autobiography I should really be thanking all of the people who helped me throughout my life. That would be so many that it would take up more pages than the first chapter, and I'd still be afraid of leaving someone out. But it's thanks to all of you, and you know who you are, that I was able to have such a fabulous life in this fascinating sport.

A MILLION THANKS
Special thanks go to my family and all my friends in Mexico, and fans throughout the world, who've nudged me into finally writing my story; to my wife Bea, who stood by my side through the ups and downs of my selfish motor racing life, and corrected and proof-read the first edition of this book; and to my daughter Ana Vanessa, who for many years had to do without a father while I played race cars somewhere around the globe.

CHAPTER 1

SOUTH OF THE BORDER

I was born on 20 August 1941 in a suburb of Mexico City called Colonia Napoles. My father had bought the land a few years earlier and had only just finished the house by the time the family started to arrive. Although at the time he was criticised by his friends for having bought a piece of land so far from the city, today it's almost in the city centre.

I come from a large family – five brothers and three sisters, which in those days wasn't uncommon. Two other children who died in infancy would have made us a family of ten, so perhaps my parents were trying for a football team, or maybe the lack of television had something to do with it. But I suppose that the main reason was the fact that Mexico was a very Catholic country and the influence of the Church was very strong.

My father came from a very wealthy family; my grandfather was one of the owners of Mexico's biggest department store, El Nuevo Mundo, and with only one sister my father had grown up accustomed to having everything. He had the best education that money could buy, and in his early 20s he always had the latest motor car available and hadn't a care in the world about his future, as he'd have inherited his father's business. He couldn't have guessed that my grandfather would develop an early onset of what we now call Alzheimer's disease, which affected his brain. Before his immediate family found out the extent of his illness, his business associates had taken the company out of his hands.

For my father, who was used to having everything on a silver plate, it was a bitter blow, as he now had to start working for a living. It was a blow from which it would take him a few years to recover, but the one thing that he learned from it was that no matter how much money he made, or whether or not he'd ever reach the financial status of my grandfather, he'd never hand out 'blank cheques' to his own children, and each one would have to make their own way in the world.

He suffered so much from his experience that he was determined that none of us would ever find ourselves in the same situation, therefore he never gave us anything unless we proved that we'd earned it. He wanted us to find out the value of money the hard way.

Despite this, we never suffered the lack of anything essential. We lived in what was then a very nice part of Mexico City and the eight of us had a decent education. We weren't by any means rich and at meal times it was the rule that everybody ate what was put in front of them – there were never any leftovers, and the dog was always disappointed. This is something that has stayed with me my whole life, since I don't recall ever having left food on my plate – as a child because it was all I was given, as a boy because it was all there was, as a young man because it was all that I could afford, and now because it has become an ingrained habit!

Unlike many children born every second all over the world, I was born with a definite desire in my life, and there was no question of what I'd be doing when I grew up. My wife has always maintained that I was born with four wheels rather than legs and arms! From my earliest memory cars and engines were my passion. There weren't many luxuries at home and therefore very few toys, and I remember that I used to play in my room using shoes as race cars. Whenever I had a toy it was always something to do with cars, and they always lasted me well past their guarantee date!

I was the third child in the family: my sister Ana Elena was the first, followed by my brother Fernando two years later, and then me hot on his heels the year after that. Then there was a big gap because of the children who didn't survive (one boy and one girl), before my brother Paulino came along, six years after me. There always existed a gap between 'the big three' and the rest – Maria Dolores, three years after Paulino, Luz del Carmen four years after that, and Jose Antonio, another three years later. By that time we all thought that enough was enough and Mum would take a rest, but no, two years later along came Javier.

I fought with my parents over Javier's name, just as I had when Jose Antonio was born, as I wanted one of them to be called Juan Manuel, after my hero Juan Manuel Fangio; but I lost both times – obviously my parents didn't share my obsession! Javier arrived just a few months before I was due to leave the country, and we therefore never really knew each other, except for the times when I visited Mexico. However, strangely enough we've formed as big a bond as I enjoy with Jose Antonio, to whom I am godfather.

Naturally, my brother Fernando and I always went to the same schools, but he was mad about football, while career-wise he was set to be an architect from a very early stage, as he was very artistic and a very good scholar. My sister Ana Elena, meanwhile, developed a great talent in the swimming pool. She was a member of the Chapultepec Club Aquatic Ballet – the same club where Olympic diving champion Joaquin Capilla learned his craft.

With my closest brother and sister being so good, both in school and out of it, I became somewhat the black sheep of the family. Although I loved my school days, I was never a brilliant scholar. I wasn't as bright as my brothers and sisters and I had to work harder, but I managed to get to university with middle-of-the-road marks.

I chose the only course that would be closely associated with something to do with wheels, Mechanical Engineering, but two years down the road I found myself becoming more and more disillusioned, as nothing about it was related purely to cars, let alone racing cars. I knew then that I wasn't going to have the patience to finish the five-year course. At the same time I was working hard in a part-time office job that I got through my father's government connections, and saving money to go to Europe. I also took a correspondence course in Automotive Mechanical Engineering from a college in Los Angeles, which at least gave me a diploma and the basic knowledge to distinguish between a carburettor and a rear axle!

At the end of 1961 I was all set to leave for Italy the following spring, but I was petrified of telling my father, as I knew that he'd not only disapprove but would disinherit me and cut me out from the family tree completely! As I've said, I was already the black sheep of the family, and this would have put the final nail in my coffin lid. To say that my father was very strict would be the understatement of the century, and for me to leave home without finishing university was something that in his opinion would be out of the question. He would take it personally, and would have felt betrayed. I just didn't know how to approach him. I thought that perhaps the best thing to do was just to go, and face the consequences later.

I spoke with my mother, and asked her to intercede on my behalf. My mother – and I'm sure that everyone who knows her would say the same thing – really *is* the best mother in the world. First of all, she was a saint to put up with my father, because although he wasn't an ogre he was very strict and set in his ways, and was a harsh disciplinarian, though a good father in all material ways. My mother was and still is a warm person. I've never heard her be spiteful or condemn anybody, and she always sees the best in people. But probably her best attributes have always been her character and sense of humour; my brothers and I agree that we have never known her to be in a bad temper.

Mother did smooth the ground before I spoke with my father, who tried everything to convince me to finish my university course, and at least go to Europe with a degree under my belt even if he couldn't persuade me to stay at home. Although he didn't have my obsession, my father was himself a lover of cars, and perhaps, deep inside, he understood my desire to follow my instinct.

While I was at school I used to spend all of my weekends wherever there was any racing. I followed the karting brigade, and every now and then I had a chance to drive. It was there that I met Ricardo and Pedro Rodriguez, and became particularly friendly with Ricardo, who was similar to me: Pedro was very reserved, quiet, serious, and introverted, while Ricardo was an extrovert with a good sense of humour, always ready to laugh.

Of course, Pedro and Ricardo came from a very wealthy family. Pedro Rodriguez senior, 'Don Pedro' as he used to be known, owned several businesses and was well connected with the government, so that his products were those the government chose whenever it needed the particular items he manufactured. He therefore never lacked sales.

In Europe and the United States there were all sorts of different versions of where and how Don Pedro came by his money: it was said, for instance, that he was the strong man of the Mexico City police force, and that he was the right-hand man of President Lazaro Cardenas in the 1930s, and therefore had the necessary connections to make a huge profit from property and land in Mexico City and Acapulco. It was even suggested that he owned the biggest chain of bordellos in Mexico City. I didn't bother to find out which was true. As far as I was concerned, he was definitely investing his money the right way – in Ricardo's driving talent – and that was all that mattered.

Don Pedro had been a motorcycle racer in his youth, and was a great racing enthusiast who wanted his sons to shine in the sport. He therefore started them early, on motorcycles and in karts. By the time they were in their teens they were already driving big powerful race cars – Ricardo raced a Porsche RSK Spider, while Pedro had a Chevrolet Corvette and a Ferrari Testa Rossa, even though they weren't old enough to drive on public roads.

I remember one particular weekend when Ricardo went to California with his RSK Porsche, to drive in a couple of races at Riverside race track. When he got there with the family he was, naturally, not allowed to drive on the Californian roads, so Don Pedro did the chauffeuring. When they got to the circuit and met all the other drivers – people of the calibre of Ken Miles, Richie Ginther and John von Neumann – they took one look at this Mexican boy and had wry smiles on their faces. Well, Ricardo may have been just a boy, but he went on to win both the Saturday and Sunday races.

OK, the Rodriguez brothers had money and the best equipment, but there was no doubt that they were good, especially Ricardo. He was a born racer who didn't have to work at it – it all came naturally. He had a talent for speed and was completely fearless. In short, he had all the ingredients of a World Champion. On another occasion I saw him driving in six different races on a Sunday at the Mexican Autodromo Magdalena Mixhuca, now renamed the Autodromo Hermanos Rodriguez. The first race was for small saloon cars (which he won in a Renault Dauphine), then there came a race for bigger saloon cars, then sports cars, and so on to the main event, Formula Junior. Ricardo proved his versatility by winning all of them.

The respect which Ricardo and Pedro earned within the racing fraternity grew more and more all the time, and their fame started to spread not only in Mexican racing and sporting circles but also in the social pages. They always drove the latest American or European cars and went out with all the high society girls.

They were born and bred in Polanco, a very upmarket part of Mexico City, but somehow Ricardo often associated with girls from the Colonia Napoles, where I lived. I often used to see his metallic gold Oldsmobile parked outside my house when he was dating one of my immediate neighbours, and he finally married Sarita Cardoso, who lived just two blocks from my house and whose mother was a close acquaintance of my own.

It was in this same gold Oldsmobile that Ricardo used to practise and taught me how to drive in the wet. We used to go out when it was raining late in the evening, or even at three or four in the morning after parties, and drive flat out along the Avenida Reforma, one of Mexico's leading roads, which was very wide and in those days was empty at night. The trick was to go round the roundabouts as fast as possible without losing control, he used to tell me: "In the wet you have to go as fast as possible in the straight, brake late but smoothly without upsetting the car, then when you start turning touch the steering wheel only with the tips of your fingers. Never make any sudden or sharp movements, and when the car starts going sideways the first indication you'll have will come from your arse, because that's the closest part of your body to the road. That's when you must start to correct the steering wheel again with the tips of your fingers, without any jerky movements."

It was easy for Ricardo to say that, but how I managed not to park the Oldsmobile up a roadside tree I'll never know. However, it was advice that whenever I drove fast in the wet I always put into practice, remembering Ricardo laughing his head off as the gold Oldsmobile created one of the original 'Mexican Waves' in the Avenida Reforma as we swooshed around in the rain.

Ricardo and Pedro had a string of successes in the late 1950s, both in the USA and in Europe. Ricardo's talent was recognised by Luigi Chinetti, the American Ferrari importer who owned the North American Racing Team. In 1960, at the age of 18, Ricardo was second in the Le Mans 24 Hours, co-driving NART's Ferrari Testa Rossa with André Pilette. Then in 1961 he and Pedro were third in the same car at Sebring, led at Le Mans until the engine failed, and were second at the Nürburgring, before winning the Paris 1000km at Monthléry with Chinetti's Ferrari 250 GT – a victory that they would repeat in 1962 sharing the NART 250 GTO.

Ricardo's fame started to spread outside Mexico and his face was in most of the leading international magazines, such as *Sports Illustrated*, *Life*, *L'Europeo*, *Oggi*, *Paris Match* and many others. Enzo Ferrari, who'd been following Ricardo's progress, was eager to see him driving one of his red cars and offered him his first Grand Prix drive in the Italian at Monza in September 1961.

There have been few very young drivers in Formula One: Mike Thackwell was the youngest, then Ricardo, and then Chris Amon, none of whom had turned 20 when they started their first Grand Prix. More recently there have been Eddie Cheever, Fernando Alonso, Jenson Button and Rubens Barrichello. But Ricardo was perhaps the most impressive of them all, and maybe his debut reflected the history of his short and tragic Grand Prix career.

Ricardo qualified his 'sharknose' Ferrari 156 on the front row, second to teammate Wolfgang von Trips by a mere 0.1 of a second, and well in front of the other Ferrari drivers, Phil Hill and Richie Ginther. At the time, Ricardo had asked himself in disbelief why the other Ferrari drivers asked him which gear he was using in the Lesmos or the Parabolica? "They asked me, but I've never been here before. This is my first time in a Formula One car."

In the race, Ricardo's fuel pump packed up after only 13 laps, and fortunately he wasn't involved in von Trips's fatal accident, but nevertheless it was the first time that death had come close to him and he was shocked, remembering how at lunch von Trips had told him to have only a light meal before the race, otherwise he'd be bound to throw up with the G forces in the Parabolica or the Curva Grande. Von Trips, a German aristocrat, was a very good friend to Ricardo, and had it not been for the crash he would undoubtedly have been the 1961 World Champion. Although Enzo Ferrari was devastated by his death, in the long term the Scuderia would benefit in the American market, as Phil Hill became the first American Formula One World Champion.

It was in the latter part of 1961 that I confided to Ricardo my intentions of coming to Europe in the new year, hoping to find some work in Italy, as I was getting more and more frustrated at university. He told me that I was mad, as he knew that I hadn't sufficient means to keep myself in the event of failing to find a job. But he saw that I was determined to go ahead with my project and agreed to give me a helping hand, introducing me to the right people once we met in Italy.

Through the connections of a very good friend of mine, Roberto Ayala, who used to race saloon cars very successfully, I got a free ticket from Mexico to New York in February 1962. I then visited Thomas Cook and bought a ticket to sail to England aboard the original *Queen Elizabeth*. Believe it or not, this was then the cheapest way of crossing the Atlantic (the turning point, when flying to Europe started to become more affordable, came later in the decade). Of course, crossing by boat would take six days, but I had all the time in the world and I was looking forward to the experience. I paid $200 for an inside shared cabin in Tourist class. Having arrived two days prior to the ship's departure, I also took the opportunity of making a short visit to New York city.

I'll never forget the day we sailed – it was really done in style, with a big band playing at the dock, and the gap between the port and the ship covered by millions of coloured paper streamers from the different deck levels of the massive vessel. Champagne was, of course, the order of the day as people laughed and cheered in anticipation of the holiday of a lifetime. For those of us on our own it was a mixed feeling, but nevertheless a wonderful one, with one or two obligatory tears. Just at that moment I discovered that a large group of Mexican people were aboard, so in the end I wasn't a forlorn figure – particularly as I met up with a mother and daughter from Guadalajara with whom I fell in love, not knowing whether I was more in love with the mother or the daughter, or just in love with the whole prospect of the voyage and the start of my new life.

Just as we were leaving the docks, we could see in the next berth the new ship *France* arriving after its maiden voyage, and although it looked fantastic it seemed dwarfed by ours. As the Statue of Liberty said goodbye to us we could appreciate the wonderful Manhattan shoreline, with all its great buildings slowly getting smaller in the distance.

It was time to check my cabin. I found that my cabin-mate was a young Australian touring the world, and I lucked out again, as we hit it off in spite of the fact that neither of us spoke the other's language. It was a great opportunity for me to start learning English! The two of us used to filter our way clandestinely from the Tourist section to Cabin and First Class, to see how the other half lived, but we found their parties boring and we used to bring anyone nice back to Tourist, where the parties were always swinging.

As we disembarked at Southampton I remember thinking of the *Queen Elizabeth* as a big floating building, and feeling sad that this wonderful six-day party had come to an end. Today I bitterly regret not having kept any souvenirs of the voyage. Little did I know then that, 35 years later, I'd be invited by the magazine *Autosport* to cross the Atlantic in the other direction aboard the *QE2* in time for the 1997 Canadian Grand Prix, as part of a forum alongside the likes of Murray Walker, Alan Henry and Nigel Roebuck. We gave a series of talks about Formula One to a group of punters who'd bought the package tour. Needless to say, I'm now one of the few people who can proudly claim to have travelled on both the original *Queen Elizabeth* and the *QE2*.

I walked to Southampton station and took the first train to London, where I was going to stay with some friends from Mexico for a few days. It was while I was with them that I was lucky enough to meet Stirling Moss, who walked into the same restaurant in Kensington where we were having dinner. I couldn't believe it! I was seeing one of my heroes for the first time in the flesh, and I wasn't going to waste the opportunity: I had to talk to him. I had another glass of wine and gathered my courage, trying to think what I was going to say, and convinced that he was going to snub me for disturbing him. On the contrary, he was very kind, and even invited me to join him at his table when I told him I was a friend of Ricardo and was going down to Sicily to meet with him for the Targa Florio. Sadly, a few weeks later Stirling suffered the horrendous accident at Goodwood that ended his career, but from which, thankfully, he fully recovered some months later. Nowadays he and his wife Susie have become very good friends of mine.

After a few days in London, I travelled south to Italy and reached Modena, where I put my case in storage so that I could then travel light, as I'd have to hitch-hike my way to Naples in order to take the ferry down to Sicily for the Targa Florio. On the ferry I had the opportunity to meet some of the gentleman racers who were travelling with their cars to the Targa, and naturally I scrounged a lift with them as far as Cefalu, the small Sicilian town that was the centre of the race. Once in Cefalu I met up with Ricardo and Sarita, who'd just arrived from France, where Ricardo had finished in second place at Pau. Through him I met the whole Ferrari team: Eugenio Dragoni was the racing director and new team manager; Mauro Forghieri was the new technical director; and Signore Becchi was the chief mechanic, who was known to everyone simply by his surname. The other drivers were Olivier Gendebien, Willy Mairesse, Giancarlo Baghetti, Lorenzo Bandini and Phil Hill.

Ferrari had brought a couple of 250 GTO Berlinettas for the drivers to get used to the gruelling and tortuous 72km circuit, saving the V6 mid-engined 246 'Dino' cars for the practice sessions and race. I then had the pleasure of accompanying Ricardo on a quick lap around the Targa, and he let me do one lap – as long as I stopped to change over again before the pit straight, so that the Ferrari personnel would never find out. I don't know which I enjoyed more, being driven by Ricardo or the experience of actually driving, for the first time, a full-blooded powerful sports car that was to become my all-time dream car.

Ricardo's drive was a real eye-opener, as it was the first time that I was a passenger in a proper race car driven by a Grand Prix driver on normal – or perhaps less than normal – roads in the Italian countryside. It was a mesmerising experience. For the first few kilometres I grabbed a firm hold on anything I could and I had my balls as a bow tie, but soon I started to relax and enjoy the sheer ease with which Ricardo handled the power and controlled the car. Later in my life I had many more opportunities to drive with other champions in other superb cars, but the first time is always the most memorable.

In practice, Phil Hill, the World Champion, destroyed the only 248 V8 experimental car that Ferrari had brought. Although it seemed to have been a mechanical fault (jammed throttle), Hill, who was luckily unhurt, was told by Dragoni to relinquish his drive, and his co-driver Gendebien joined Rodriguez and Mairesse in the first car – the 246SP which would end up winning the race, with Baghetti and Bandini finishing second in a similar car. It goes without saying that I was more than delighted that on my very first race with Ricardo in Europe he won, and I became his talisman for the rest of the year.

Next day Ricardo and Sarita left for Modena, while I went back on a ferry to Naples and up to Rome, where I was hoping to catch up with Piero Taruffi and Umberto Maglioli, both of whom I had met in Mexico, thinking that perhaps they could guide me somewhere. Although my first introduction to the Ferrari team hadn't been a bad one, I wasn't putting all my eggs in one basket, and wanted to explore other avenues that might open up for me. I went to Milan to knock on the door of Gianni Restelli, the manager of the Autodromo di Monza. I'd been given his name by a friend of a friend in Mexico, and I was hoping to find out if there was any kind of an opening there. By then, needless to say, the $300 with which I'd left Mexico were shrinking fast and I was getting very worried about whether or not I was going to make it.

While in Milan I spent some time with Lorenzo Bandini and Giancarlo Baghetti, who were both Milan residents. Lorenzo had a car agency and workshop, while Giancarlo came from a very aristocratic family and was the epitome of the gentleman racer, although he's the only driver in history to win his very first Grand Prix, at Reims, in July 1961. Giancarlo told me that while in Sicily I'd made a good impression on Signore Dragoni and Signore Forghieri and that I should go openly and speak to them. He thought that something could come out of it, and suggested that I should go with him to Holland in his Ferrari for the next Grand Prix, an offer which I gladly accepted.

At the Zandvoort circuit Dragoni was very honest with me and said that it would be impossible for Ferrari to employ me without any qualifications or a work permit, but that he'd help me with accommodation and food at race meetings in exchange for labour. I was as happy as a sandboy, and no matter how much or how dirty the work was, whatever they gave me to do helped me learn the ropes and the language of living in this new world that I'd dreamt of for so long. In the race Hill and Baghetti finished third and fourth for Ferrari, while Ricardo had a massive accident with Jack Brabham's Lotus 24 while dicing for third place.

After Holland, Baghetti and I drove to the Nürburgring for the 1000km sports car race. This wasn't without drama, as near Koblenz, in heavy rain, Giancarlo and I almost disappeared with the lovely Ferrari under a big lorry. I thought the accident could have been avoided and I was disappointed by the very little, if any, avoiding action that Giancarlo took. As a result the front left-hand wing of his pride and joy was severely modified.

The Nürburgring was one of the places that I most wanted to visit. Its name was as synonymous with racing as Le Mans or Monza: a circuit of 22.8km with 180 corners was nothing but a big challenge, and when we arrived we just had to go round, even though the rain was still pouring down. I have to say that I was never very impressed with Giancarlo's driving – he was very brave, but lacked finesse, and it was easy to understand why he won his first ever GP at Reims, which is a flat-out circuit where balls are more important than brains. I decided that one lap was enough, and while Giancarlo was taking round one of a dozen Italian *tifosi* from the hotel lobby, I went to try to find a room.

Phil Hill had only just arrived together with Dan Gurney, to whom he introduced me, and the four of us had dinner at the Sporthaus Hotel. Gurney was also from California and a good friend of Hill, so I spent a long time talking to him. Dan was very fond of Mexican people and Mexican food, and later on he was to become one of the key people in my racing career, for whom I worked for five years in F1, Indianapolis, TransAm and CanAm racing in Europe and the USA. Without a doubt one of the best bosses and friends I've ever had.

For the race, the Rodriguez brothers were to drive the 2.5-litre V8 'Dino'. Ricardo wanted to be the one to finish, so Pedro had to start. I tried to convince Ricardo that it would be better if it was the other way round, as Pedro was always nervous at the start while Ricardo was much quicker and could then give the car to Pedro in a good position. Ferrari management didn't care who started; their only stipulation was that Ricardo must drive if there was a period of rain. It's interesting to note how Ricardo was recognised as being the good driver in the rain, but later on Pedro was to become one of the greatest 'rain masters' of all time.

Pedro made a lousy start and then tried his hardest to recoup the lost time – until he left the circuit. More often than not Pedro used to spend more time off the circuit than on it, and whenever there was a crash it was Pedro at the wheel. Even Ferrari were noticing and showing unhappiness about this, but Ricardo always stood by his brother and would much rather drive with him than anyone else. Pedro in turn had an unshakeable admiration for his brother's talent and they raced together, not against each other.

1962 was perhaps not the best year for Ferrari and therefore not for Ricardo or myself. Although they'd been World Champions the year before, Ferrari had lost Carlo Chiti and five other key men, which is why it was the first year for Eugenio Dragoni and Mauro Forghieri. The 1962 car was practically identical to the 1961 car, but the work continuity was non-existent. In addition the Scuderia was handicapped by a series of industrial problems in Italy caused by labour unions, which slowed the progress and development of the cars so that they missed some races.

One of the races that Ricardo missed was Monaco, and we never really found out the reason. He was told that the organisers wouldn't accept a fourth entry from Ferrari as they already had Phil Hill, Willy Mairesse and Lorenzo Bandini, and there were only 16 cars in the race. Maybe Ferrari only had three cars, but of course Ricardo was bitterly disappointed; he'd been looking forward so much to this race, especially since he did so well at Pau, which was also a street circuit. Maybe *Commendatore* Ferrari wanted to teach him a lesson if he thought that Ricardo had caused the accident in Holland, as a way of stopping his youthful enthusiasm from getting the better of him. However, we'd no cause to disbelieve the reason that was given, as in previous years there had always been only 16 cars starting at Monaco.

Ricardo wasn't the only one to be disappointed: there was also a whole bunch of Mexican fans who'd made the trip to see Ricardo race at such a famous circuit, including Sarita, Don Pedro, and Pedro junior with his wife Angelina. And although I still reckon that Ricardo would have put on a better show than Bandini or

Mairesse, Ferrari still finished second and third with Hill and Bandini – and I had more time to visit the Casino!

I suppose that for someone who's never been in the Monte Carlo Casino, especially someone coming from way south of the border, there's always some kind of mystique about the place that can only be got rid of by actually being there and being able to say afterwards, "Been there, done that...". So I *had* to go and gamble my very hard-earned money on the tables – and is it ever true that there's such a thing as beginner's luck! I could do no wrong. I had only to scoop the money into my corner and leave the Casino considerably richer than I went in. After having a wonderful weekend almost in the style of the Monaco regulars, I couldn't resist the temptation of returning on the Monday, only to lose all my winnings plus a lot more that I could ill afford. All I had left were the memories of a lion's weekend and the lesson to stay away from gambling tables. To this day I've never gambled any of my money again.

The next Formula One race was at Spa-Francorchamps, one of the most wonderful circuits in the world (and it still is, although in a shorter form). This time Ferrari had entered four cars and it was the turn of Bandini to step aside. Ricardo drove like a veteran for a podium position behind Jim Clark's Lotus 25 and Graham Hill's BRM P57, until two laps from the end when his pit gave him a signal to let Phil Hill – who was in fourth place – go by, as he was the reigning World Champion and had to accumulate points! Ricardo was on Hill's gearbox as they crossed the finish line. Forty years on, nothing has changed at Ferrari...

The labour union problems at Ferrari were getting worse, with a general strike on some days each week, so the team could only send one car (for Phil Hill) to the British Grand Prix, and no cars at all to the French. In the meantime I was almost on the breadline and was forced to go to Milan, where, thanks to Bandini and Gianni Restelli from Monza, I met a Formula Junior constructor, Wainer Mantovani, who was in need of cheap labour and didn't care whether or not I had a work permit.

Wainer produced lovely Formula Junior cars, all handmade at his factory in Milan, but his workshop was a big mess and he was a real slave-driver. He knew I was in desperate need of work and very keen to learn, and that it would be difficult for me to find work elsewhere, so he assumed I'd be happy to work 18 hours a day. This I did, but the money was so little that there was no way I could afford a place to live and I had to sleep on the factory floor. I was aware that Wainer was taking advantage of me, but he was also giving me an ideal opportunity to learn the hard way. The guys in the workshop were great, because they were all very enthusiastic and every day they gained more and more confidence in me and gave me more difficult tasks.

After several weeks of hard work without a single day off, friends of mine from Milan invited me out for lunch on a Sunday, and I thought that I'd rightly earned some time off and left the shop at midday. Signore Wainer wasn't amused, and next morning he gave me a big rollicking for having taken the afternoon off and terminated my 'employment'! I was understandably resentful at this harsh treatment, but I wouldn't have missed the experience. I thoroughly enjoyed working with the mechanics and what I learned in those few weeks was invaluable.

Eleven years later, when I was with Tyrrell, I was Jackie Stewart's mechanic at Monza when we clinched the World Championship. One of the first people to come to the pits to congratulate me was Wainer Mantovani. Never being the sort to harbour a grudge I didn't push his teeth down his throat, but shook his hand and appreciated the fact that he'd been keeping track of me!

After I was fired, it was time to get back to Modena, and everyone was very pleased to see me, including the staff at the Palace Hotel where Ricardo and Sarita had their permanent suite, and they offered me the small room that I'd had before, even though I was still in debt from my earlier occupancy. Whilst in Modena, Ricardo and I took long bicycle rides every morning, as Ricardo loved his food and had a tendency to put on weight, something the *Commendatore* always used to tease him about. In those days no drivers were keep-fit fanatics as they are now.

The French GP had gone by without Ferrari's participation, and there'd been only the one car at the British, but a full team of four cars was despatched to the Nürburgring for the German GP. Baghetti was going on a small private plane belonging to a rich friend and was taking Ricardo and Sarita with him, but as there was no room for me and it was too late to arrange any other free transport I was obliged to stay in Modena, much to my chagrin. Ricardo was the only Ferrari driver to finish, in sixth place, in a very wet race. He was the best Ferrari qualifier despite driving the oldest of the four cars.

While I was in Milan, Ricardo and Pedro went to Le Mans for the 24-hour race, where they put on a very brave show indeed, as they shared the lead with Hill and Gendebien (the eventual winners in a 4-litre V12 330LM) until the early hours on Sunday, when their smaller 2.4-litre V6 246SP suffered incurable transmission problems.

The brightest note of the month was when Juan Manuel Fangio, my all-time hero, came to Modena to visit his old friends at Ferrari. When I'd met the great man in Milan earlier in the year, with Ricardo, he said that on his way to Modena he was going to contact me to introduce me to the Maserati bosses, and, true to his word, he left a note for me in the hotel. That was the type of man he was. I met him at the Real Fini Hotel and he took me to meet *Ingegnere* Giulio Alfieri, who agreed to take me on if I managed to arrange a work permit with the help of a letter from them.

CHAPTER 2

THE ITALIAN JOB

With a firm work offer from Maserati and a letter in hand, I set off to organise my work permit. Everyone had told me that it was a very difficult task, and that only a few people managed to get through the complicated Italian bureaucracy, but I hadn't come this far to give up now, and after a few trips to Bologna and Rome to talk to the relevant people my permit came through, and I was an official Maserati worker by October 1962.

My last F1 Grand Prix with Ricardo was at Monza in September, but unfortunately this year wasn't like 1961, when Ferrari had been competitive. The Ferraris didn't figure anywhere near the front of the grid, and in the race only Mairesse and Baghetti finished – fourth and fifth – of the five that took part. Following this race Enzo Ferrari withdrew his team from Formula One for the rest of the year because of the Italian labour disputes that had stopped the development of the cars. This left his drivers free to race elsewhere for the rest of the season, and in this way Ferrari unwittingly contributed to Ricardo's premature death, as he took the opportunity to sign with Rob Walker's Lotus team for the Mexican Grand Prix – his home race – since Stirling Moss hadn't been able to take up the drive following his Goodwood crash.

Enzo Ferrari wasn't very pleased that Ricardo was going to drive for Lotus, because he still wanted him to drive for Ferrari in 1963, but he understood Ricardo's desire to drive a competitive car in his country's first Grand Prix. Little did the *Commendatore* know that Ricardo had plans to drive for Walker or for his friend Count Giovanni Volpi de Misurata, who was forming the new Scuderia Serenissima team for 1963.

After Monza we returned to Modena, but only for a few days,

since Ricardo was offered $10,000 plus tickets to return to Mexico for a Formula 3 race. Ricardo, and especially Sarita, were compulsive shoppers and just didn't have enough bags to put it all in after a few months in Europe, so I got a complete new wardrobe, since the only things of Ricardo's that didn't fit me were his trousers. In this way I acquired lots of shoes, shirts, and jackets, as well as his bicycle, one of his yellow helmets, and his goggles, gloves, and race suits.

I took Ricardo and Sarita to Milan, where we were joined by Bandini and Baghetti, with their girlfriends Margarita and Pupa, and had dinner at a popular *trattoria*, where we all signed our names on the wall around a Ferrari *Caballino Rampante* badge (I often wonder if they're still there). From there we went to the airport for our sad farewells. Ricardo and Sarita had been more than just friends: they were like brother and sister to me, and I knew I was going to miss them terribly. As they departed, Ricardo said that if he could make a deal with Rob Walker for 1963, or with Count Volpi, there would definitely be a place for me on the team.

Alf Francis was the man who ran the Walker Team for Rob, and he'd been Stirling Moss's head mechanic for a number of years. He was a very self-confident and opinionated man of Polish origin, but really knew his job. I met him on numerous occasions when he came to Modena looking for parts; he used to like his drink, and neither I nor my New Zealander friend Bob Wallace could keep up with him in the bar. Alf wrote the first book ever written by a race mechanic and made himself very famous, especially to foreigners like myself who wanted to follow in his footsteps. For us, Alf's book was a bible, and I still treasure my copy.

The Lotus 24 arrived late for the Mexican Grand Prix and was assembled in a hurry, as Ricardo was eager to drive in the first unofficial trials, in which a friendly duel for fastest lap began between him and John Surtees. Unfortunately, Ricardo didn't come back.

I was working at Maserati when a colleague told me that he'd heard on the radio that Ricardo had had an accident, and soon afterwards two more people told me that Ricardo had been killed. At this I ran like crazy to the Palace Hotel to see if they had any news, and I called Franco Gozzi, the press officer and right-hand man of Enzo Ferrari, with whom even now I have a great friendship. He couldn't confirm any news to me, but as I was sitting in the lobby drinking strong coffee the hotel secretary called me, shouting, "Ramirez, there's a phone call for you." Fearing the worst, she burst into tears.

It was my friend, Roberto Ayala. He'd been at the trials and had witnessed the accident, which happened exactly at the Peraltada corner. He said: "Joaquin, Ricardo lost control at the entrance of the Peraltada where there's an undulation right across the track. It's difficult to know what happened, but it could have been a chassis failure. He hit the outside guardrail and then bounced back into the inside one, where he was thrown out against the rail and practically cut in half. I helped to get him into the ambulance. He was conscious but in deep pain, crying: 'I don't want to die, please don't let me die!' But all of the paramedics' efforts were in vain, and he died on the way to the hospital."

The telephone call wasn't much longer than that. I couldn't say a word. It was as if my whole world had ended. I was ill for two days, shivering and shaking, without the will to do anything. I never thought that I'd take the death of someone who wasn't one of my own family so hard; but then, Ricardo had come to be like one of my family. He was always such a good friend, there whenever I needed him, always happy, always ready for a joke. He won the affection of all his fellow drivers because, although he was quicker than most of them, he was of a very simple nature.

Ironically, his death had taken place in Mexico, preparing for the Grand Prix that he most wanted to win, in front of the people who idolised him, on the track that he loved and where he'd spent most of his brilliant but short career. Destiny had been too cruel to him. He shouldn't have died, he should have won the World Championship one day and brought it to Mexico, as was his dream.

I clearly remember every one of the moments that we spent together, celebrating the victories with joy and taking the defeats with serenity. I remember seeing his eyes full of tears on the eve of the Dutch Grand Prix once he realised that the British cars were far superior to the Ferraris, but there were happy times as well. At the prize-winning party after winning the Targa Florio, everyone surrounded Ricardo and Sarita dancing the twist. Then it was all happiness. There were moments of desolation too, when he was unable to participate at the Monaco Grand Prix, and of sadness when a carburettor failure forced him out of the Italian Grand Prix, and he'd embraced Don Pedro and Sarita with damp eyes, saying: "It isn't important, the important thing is that I'm here with my old man and my old woman!" Sadly, only for a couple of months more…

I heard that the Rodriguez family were devastated. He was the favourite son of a family that adored him and never thought that anything could happen to him in a race car. They followed his career with the same anxiety as any family with a son in a dangerous job, but their anxiety was somehow different. Chronometers in hand, they checked his lap times and were only restless when he was slow; then his mother would stand up in the pits, waving a white handkerchief and shouting: *"Mas aprisa, Ricardo"* ('Faster!'). And then Ricardo would do his fastest lap.

They never, ever, for one minute thought that anything could spoil the party. Nothing could ever happen to Ricardo. Only Sarita seemed to be a bit concerned every time Ricardo jumped into a race car, as if anticipating, perhaps, that he wouldn't be coming back. But Ricardo had no fear, he didn't know what fear was: he was destined to win, and if he didn't win then it was because the car had broken down or it wasn't up to winning. Maybe we all felt a bit responsible. I remember making all the preparations in Monza for a cocktail party at which Javier Velasquez, the Mexican organiser, invited all the drivers to the first Mexican Grand Prix. In retrospect, it felt as though we'd been preparing for Ricardo's death.

Don Pedro was a man who would tear himself into a hundred pieces for his sons, and he was immensely proud that Ricardo made the Mexican flag wave in places where they hadn't known what it looked like before, and caused the Mexican national anthem to be played where it had never been heard. But Ricardo's attempt to raise the Mexican flag amongst his own people, and have the anthem played to those to whom it meant most, failed, and the Mexican racing fraternity will mourn him forever.

Ricardo never made it to his 21st birthday. He lived only a short time but achieved considerably more than millions would during much longer lives. He was one of those privileged men born with the ability to do something better than the rest of us. For him, controlling a fast race car came naturally, he didn't have to work hard at it. He was one of those geniuses of the steering wheel born every ten years or so: Nuvolari, Clark, Stewart, Prost, Senna, and now Schumacher. Who knows how far our Mexican champion would have gone, a young man who had everything in his favour – except the necessary protection to survive a 150kph crash at the entrance of the Peraltada corner on 1 November 1962.

I wish I'd had the means to go to Mexico to accompany him to his last resting place and see him resting in peace, and to be with both Sarita and Don Pedro, as I never knew which of them adored him more. Those of us who were among his friends will always miss him, and even now Mexico has yet to realise the magnitude of its loss.

I have to admit that it took weeks and even months for me to come to terms with Ricardo's absence, not only as a friend but professionally. He'd have had a great influence on my immediate future. Life at Modena continued as normal, but the Palace Hotel wasn't as happy a place as it had been. By then I was renting a room in the centre of town, but my post still went to the Palace and my friendship with the hotel staff continued as before.

That winter Alf Francis came to Modena, as he was planning to open a factory there to build gearboxes for racing cars. After having dinner together, we stayed in the bar until the early hours reminiscing about Ricardo and the reasons for the accident. Alf was really shocked – it was the first time that a driver had been killed in one of his cars.

That December saw the presentation in Bologna of the new Formula One team Scuderia Serenissima, formed by ex-Ferrari personnel who'd left the company due to the troubles in Maranello. It was headed by engineer Carlo Chiti and financed by a consortium of top Milan industrialists, whose vice-president was Count Giovanni Volpi de Misurata, the great friend of Ricardo who'd been hoping that he'd join Phil Hill and Giancarlo Baghetti to drive the team's cars. However, following Ricardo's tragic death Count Volpi sold his shares, saying that he didn't want to take part in supplying the means for young men to meet a premature end. Such was the impact of Ricardo's death on the Italian racing world. The team then changed its name to ATS (Automobile Turismo Sport).

It was some consolation for me that my working life at Maserati began to get better and better; I was learning a lot, and they were happy with me and my willingness to work all the hours that God sent. After a few months, once I'd worked in all the departments under my different bosses – Corrado Manfredini, Gino and Guerino Bertochi – my wages were doubled and I was given the opportunity to go into the racing department, which was a very small one. They only raced one car, in the new long-distance endurance series for prototype sports cars, under the direction of a young engineer called Gian Paolo Dallara.

When I met Dallara, I had the feeling of meeting a new friend – a very clever and open young man who has since created one of the most successful racing car factories in the world. His cars are sold and raced in every corner of the globe, dominating in almost every category in which they're entered, and I'm so pleased with his deserved success, since Gian Paolo was a key person in the early days of my career. I couldn't have had a better teacher: he has clearly raised the standards of many racing leagues.

If you lived in Modena in the 1960s, sooner or later you were bound to meet everybody in the racing world, since so many companies there made bits and pieces for race cars that the place became a compulsory stop for the racing man. One of the people that I had the fortune to meet was Tony Settember, a Filipino-born man in his late 20s who'd lived most of his life in California. We got on like a house on fire, both of us having the same likes and dislikes, the same tastes and hobbies. Tony was forming a small team on a shoestring budget – 'Scirocco-BRM' – and he asked me to join him because he was hoping to get Pedro Rodriguez to drive the other car.

We arranged to meet in Monaco for his second race. I was there, but Tony wasn't, even though he was on the entry list. It turned out he hadn't managed to make it to his first race at Silverstone either, and I was happy that I hadn't taken the plunge of leaving Maserati and joining him. Tony and his team eventually raced in the Belgian Grand Prix and at other events, with Ian Burgess as a second driver, but he later vanished from the face of the earth. I felt sorry that he didn't have better luck, as he was a real character and a very sincere friend.

The 151 V8 car we raced at Maserati was financed by the Paris Maserati concessionaire and was therefore not a full-blown factory effort. Still, it was a good place to learn, as we were only two or three mechanics under the direction of Guerino Bertochi, the legendary mechanic of Juan Manuel Fangio, and I had the opportunity to see at first hand the trick that Guerino always played with his drivers. He'd fit a duff spark plug in one of the cylinders, the driver would go out and complain that the engine wasn't running smoothly, and Guerino would open the bonnet, look around the exhaust pipes, and remove the offending plug and replace it with a good one conveniently ready in his pocket. The driver would then go out again and return delighted with the engine, convinced that Guerino was the greatest mechanic in the world.

Our 4.9-litre Maserati was the fastest car in a straight line at Le Mans, and André Simon was in the lead for over an hour, holding off the Ferraris which dominated sports car racing at the time. But soon after Lloyd 'Lucky' Casner took over from Simon the car broke its rear axle, and that was that.

Just under a year after I'd joined Maserati, Gian Paolo Dallara was offered a job to build the first Lamborghini, and he offered me a place within the new organisation. Although I wasn't planning to make a career at Maserati, I was working on racing cars, and I felt bad about leaving them so soon as they'd been extremely good to me. However, the challenge of building a complete new car – engine, gearbox, chassis, and bodywork – even if it was only a road-going sports car, was very appealing. The promise that they'd be racing within a couple of years, and the opportunity to continue working with *Ingegnere* Dallara, convinced me that this was the way forward.

When I left Maserati after 13 months with them I also left a lot of good friends behind, but the future looked rosy. Dallara had been busy selecting some of the best people available in Modena. These included my New Zealand friend Bob Wallace, who'd worked for the Scuderia Camoradi when they were racing Giulio Alfieri's famous 'birdcage' Tipo 61 prototypes, and for Maserati; Achille Bevini, a brilliant young draftsman recruited to pen the engine; and Francesco Cazaniga, who was to build the engines. A brand new factory was constructed in Sant'Agata Bolognese.

The boss, Ferruccio Lamborghini, was a self-made billionaire, owner of Europe's premier tractor company as well as factories producing air conditioning systems, and was one of Italy's richest men. Tired of having troubles with his Ferrari, he'd decided to produce a better car than those of Enzo. He was full of character and more like a friend than a boss, just like one of the boys. He had a very refreshing way of approaching problems and maybe that's why he'd been so successful. I just hoped that he'd continue to enjoy the same success with the sports car named after him.

The experience of working for him was certainly an eye-opener, and one I wouldn't have missed for the world. I learnt a hell of a lot in every way and about every part of the new car, and I was lucky enough to be able to drive a lot of the test mileage, but these were perhaps some of the hardest months of my life. Finishing a car for a major automobile show like the one in Turin, where we presented the first Lamborghini, wasn't an easy task, especially when, at the same time, you're building the factory, the engine test-bed, and the production systems. Neither Ferruccio nor any of us enthusiastic car madmen imagined that it would be so hard. As a result, every one of us working on the project was on edge from overwork, and relations became tense to say the least. I could see that a racing programme was certainly not on the immediate agenda.

Ferruccio himself was starting to realise that perhaps his dream was a little bit too ambitious. All the profits from his other businesses were being eaten away rapidly by the car factory, and his anxiety and frustrations were passed on to the rest of us, which didn't help. His demands were far greater than the means available to us and he generally became very unreasonable. Dallara was the first to finally throw in the towel.

Fortunately, Lamborghini didn't accept his resignation. If Dallara had left at this critical time the whole company would have collapsed, and Ferruccio knew it, but his threat to go was, perhaps, what was needed in order to make the boss understand that enough was enough. As a result things improved, and common sense prevailed for the time being. However, I knew that things didn't bode well and I could see that Lamborghini would never go racing – the economic situation in Italy wasn't at its best, with Fiat, Alfa Romeo and even Ferrari and Maserati having car parks full of unsold vehicles. It was going to take some time for Lamborghini Automobili to succeed, or even to survive, and I didn't need to be a rocket scientist to see that Italy was no longer the heart of motor racing: that had now moved to England.

While the situation at Lamborghini was starting to go sour, I was busy sending letters to all the racing teams, hoping that someone would have an opening for me. The other opportunity that I was given was to work for John Mecom in the USA. I'd met John in Modena a couple of years earlier when he came to buy Ferrari. Yes, he was that rich! He was one of the biggest oil producers in Texas, if not *the* biggest, but was a very down-to-earth man and a fanatical racing car enthusiast, who, seeing an opportunity to buy Ferrari when the company was weak in 1962, had tried to cash in on it. But of course, Fiat wouldn't allow Ferrari – the jewel in the Italian automotive industry crown – to fall into foreign hands, and they had duly come to Ferrari's rescue.

Mecom came back to Modena in 1964 on his way back from Africa and Persia, where some of his petroleum wells had been expropriated: this had resulted in the loss of several million dollars, but he didn't seem too bothered by it. We took the opportunity to invite him to Sant'Agata to visit the Lambo factory, which he did, and he appeared very interested and impressed, especially with the engine test-bed. We also showed him (without Ferruccio's knowledge) all the drawings of the first Lamborghini prototype sports car racer.

He liked everything he saw, but having just lost several million dollars perhaps he wasn't in the spending mood. Not that Lamborghini was ready to sell yet, but I'd have just loved for him to buy the know-how and create Lamborghini Racing. Perhaps if we'd had something more tangible than just clandestine drawings he'd have been more impressed. We had dinner at Modena's smartest venue, the Real Fini, and stayed with him into the small hours as he waited for news of his Chevrolet Corvette Stingray cars, racing at the Sebring 12 Hours; but none of the three finished.

As we said goodbye, he asked me to keep in touch, and said that if I ever had a change of heart I'd be more than welcome on his team in the USA. Flattering though it was, I didn't think that my future was in the USA: I'd come to Europe to make a career in international racing, and going to the USA would have only been a stopgap move, and not the real thing, although the money was very tempting. I might have gone there if something more positive had been offered, since I wouldn't have had to start from the beginning all over again.

Going to England, on the other hand, I knew I'd have the same problems that I'd had in Italy, as no team would be prepared to get involved in arranging a work permit, and because of my very limited knowledge of the language I'd have had to start right at the bottom. I had the feeling that I was better than that, but if I wanted to get back into racing that's what I'd have to do. My only card left in Italy was, of course, Ferrari, and I always kept in touch with engineer Mauro Forghieri; but Ferrari was only just recovering from its bad years, and although they were doing well in the 1964 championship with John Surtees, Fiat was now involved and everything was more complicated.

So the decision was made: I'd go to England. I told Gian Paolo Dallara what I was intending to do and he was very sympathetic and gave me lots of encouragement. I then had to find the right moment to approach *Cavaliere* Lamborghini, and that wasn't going to be easy. He took it really badly; he invited me to dinner and promised me the earth! He offered me his car, six days off, an all-expenses paid trip to the next Grand Prix in Austria to feed my racing bug, and a 40 per cent increase in wages, and if that wasn't enough I should name a figure. I told him again that it wasn't the money: I just wanted to be involved in racing.

I left Lamborghini at the end of July 1964, just as we delivered the first production car; the second was going to Switzerland and the third to England. I told Ferruccio that if the English customer had any problems, he could always contact me, and he really liked that idea, saying, "Great, we can say that we have a concessionaire and service centre in England." He offered me half a million *lire* commission for any car that I could sell in the UK, and told me that the Sant'Agata doors were always open if things didn't work out for me. Needless to say I was moved and flattered by all his efforts and I knew that I was leaving a lot of friends in Italy.

The next choice was to either drive my little Fiat 500 to England or to sell it and go by train. I had a lovely Autobianchi known as a 'Bianchina', white, semi-convertible, good-looking, reliable and a lot of fun. I'd already seen a lot of Europe in it, so she ended up taking me to England rather than me taking her. One of my girlfriends, bilingual Brenda Vernor, an English teacher in Modena, asked me to give a lift to one of her pupils, and being a request from Brenda I couldn't say no – she was one of my first girlfriends in Modena and we'd had a lot of fun together. Although a passenger would reduce the luggage space she'd help with the expenses, and it would perhaps make things easier with the British Customs.

Brenda later became the girlfriend of Mike Parkes, the Ferrari driver and race engineer. After he was sadly killed in a road accident, Enzo Ferrari gave her a secretarial job and she went on to become the *Commendatore*'s personal assistant and the only woman on the racing team.

CHAPTER 3

RULE BRITANNIA

So there I was, trundling north along the Italian *autostrada* in my Autobianchi, absolutely petrified at the thought of passing through the British immigration system, which was renowned for being the worst in Europe. The process then was that they checked the passengers during the boat-trip across the Channel: my passport was taken away and I went through two hours of agony. Finally, on arrival at Dover, and after a million questions because the officer was puzzled by so many passport stamps in and out of Italy, I was allowed in – but only for one month: he'd obviously smelled a rat!

This naturally put the pressure on me to find a job, so it was a race between this and the breadline as to whether or not I'd have to return to Italy. I began knocking on doors the next day, starting with Lotus, Brabham and Cooper. My next choice of team was BRM, but their factory was in the north of England, so I decided to go first to Ford, who were near London. They were planning a big Le Mans programme and had answered a letter I'd sent from Italy, although not 100 per cent positively. The Ford racing company was called Ford Advanced Vehicles (FAV) and was headed by the legendary Aston Martin team manager John Wyer, with John Horsman – also ex-Aston Martin – as his first officer.

I met John on a wet Tuesday morning and was immediately aware that the pressure was on. There were people rushing in all directions and it wasn't difficult to feel the sense of urgency about the place. John seemed to like me and was impressed that I'd come all the way from Italy even though his letter wasn't encouraging, but he was concerned about the work permit and the implications for the company of employing someone without the regular paperwork. I told him that all I needed was a letter from his company saying that it was specialised work and that they couldn't find a British subject to fill the vacancy, and that I'd undertake to follow it up with the Home Office. In addition he didn't have to pay me until he found out if I was any good. It was that, I think, that prompted him to give me a try. I was at work the following day.

The work permit took a few months and several trips to London but it eventually arrived. The most pressing item on the Ford team's agenda at the time was a week's testing at Monza in Italy, which was very much in my favour as I was able to serve the company additionally as an interpreter, and they were very appreciative. However, it was a disastrous trip: it rained non-stop and we crashed both cars through stupid mistakes. One of the cars, driven by Sir John Whitmore, went straight on at the Curva Grande at 200kph with the throttle stuck open! Miraculously he only suffered minor cuts. One positive result of the testing was that the company took on board the reason for the accidents. This was nothing less than the complete and utter exhaustion of the workforce, which had been working for weeks with an average of only three hours' rest a night, so new working practices were then put in place.

On our return to England my immediate boss, Des O'Dell, left to be chief of the competition department of the Rootes group in Coventry, and two mechanics were sacked, but we were joined by others – one of whom was Ermanno Cuoghi, a charismatic Italian who became a very good friend. In later years Ermanno went on to Formula One with Brabham, to become Niki Lauda's personal mechanic, before eventually returning to Italy and joining Ferrari. During his 'retirement' Ermanno was very involved in the formative years of the latest Formula One phenomenon, the Spaniard Fernando Alonso.

Ermanno and I rented a small house in Old Windsor and we let out rooms to some of the other mechanics who came and went through FAV: Malcolm Malone the chief mechanic, Vincent Higgins, a mad Irishman but an excellent mechanic, and many more. It was a great feeling to have one's own house and not to live with strangers in hotels or rented rooms any more.

From 1965, our participation in US races was stopped and

Carroll Shelby's Shelby American Inc – best known for the Cobra – took over the running of the cars in California, with the UK force just building them. The GT40, designed by Len Bailey, was to become one of the classic cars of all time. However, we were kept just as busy, as we still had a European racing schedule with drivers like Graham Hill, Bruce McLaren, Richard Attwood, Jo Schlesser, Masten Gregory, Chris Amon, Richie Ginther, Bob Bondurant and Sir John Whitmore.

While I was in England I took the opportunity of going to every big race meeting that took place, especially Formula One events. I was also a small contributor to two racing magazines in Mexico and Argentina, therefore I couldn't miss the traditional Race of Champions at Brands Hatch, where I was able to say hello to some of my old friends, like John Surtees and Mauro Forghieri of Ferrari. I also spent some time there with Dan Gurney, who was racing for Brabham. He drove one of the best races of his life from an eighth-place start, chasing down Jim Clark's leading Lotus 33 until he was just inches behind and forcing him to make a mistake at Bottom Bend and crash. Gurney then led until an electrical problem put him out.

For all the magic that Jim Clark had, his Achilles' Heel was that he wasn't too good under pressure, especially from the people that he feared; and being as honest as the day is long, he always said that Dan Gurney was the most underrated driver of his generation, and that in a good car Dan was the best he ever raced against. Clark shared this weakness with today's Michael Schumacher – both of them fabulous drivers, tremendously fast, but liking to be away at the front on their own, and falling apart on the rare occasions that they're put under pressure.

One of the first appointments of the year was the traditional Le Mans test in April, always very interesting with all the new cars for the year and a little less pressure than during race week. It was good to see all my old friends from Ferrari and Maserati, and among them was Lloyd 'Lucky' Casner, American owner of the Scuderia Camoradi, which was testing the 'birdcage' Maserati prepared by Bob Wallace. 'Lucky' was a great guy and we used to spend very amusing evenings in Modena – he was a great raconteur, and it was always a pleasure to bump into him from time to time. Not long after I'd been chatting with him the practice was stopped, and I heard over the tannoy that a Maserati had crashed at Mulsanne straight.

'Lucky' had run out of luck: he left the circuit at 300kph, taking several trees with him, and was killed instantly. It was a dreadful feeling. One minute you're talking and laughing with a friend and the next he's gone forever. It's very difficult to handle, and I was starting to believe that perhaps it's never worth getting close to a racing driver as they could so easily be gone without ever having the chance to say goodbye. John Whitmore was also very shocked, as was everybody, and the rest of the testing was a very sad and subdued affair.

For the race itself in June 1965, the great attack by Ford was on the cards. Carroll Shelby and his large entourage arrived with four cars, two 7-litre Mk2s and two 4.7-litre GT40s, supported by all of us from Ford Advanced Vehicles with our own GT40 plus another from Ford France: in all there were probably more than a hundred people. In those days this was unheard of, but it demonstrated Ford's commitment to conquering the hardest and most popular race in the world. The cars were quick, but we weren't confident that they would go the distance – 24 hours is a long, long time.

But the word from the top was to go for it in order to make the Ferrari P2 drivers try too hard and perhaps break their cars early. If we weren't going to win we had at least to make an impression, and this was the way it went. FAV's GT40, which was driven by Sir John Whitmore and Innes Ireland, went out with a broken engine in the sixth hour, so I and the rest of our crew were transferred to help with the American effort. All the fastest cars failed to finish, including the Ferrari prototypes. They had to rely on outdated cars to win at Le Mans yet again, with a 1–2–3 led by Luigi Chinetti's NART 250LM.

Soon after, the supreme command in Detroit halted the Ford racing programme, but we knew that this couldn't last. They'd spent millions, but they'd no illusions that it was going to be easy: they just needed to regroup and plan a better and more systematic approach, and Ford Advanced Vehicles were given instructions to build 50 cars in order to be able to homologate the GT40 with the FIA as a Group 4 GT racing car, rather than a prototype. I was very happy working at FAV, but I wondered if it was time to move on, even though I'd been promised to be included whenever the cars were racing.

One afternoon the boss sent me to the Forte Hotel at London Heathrow to give some transmission parts to Dan Gurney, who was leaving for the States, and I was happy to do this as I always kept in touch with him. We had dinner at the hotel and he asked me how I was getting on at Ford. He let me in on his plans for the future. He had a racing car business in Santa Ana, California, called All American Racers, formed by Gurney and partner Carroll Shelby with backing from Goodyear Tyre Co, who were fed up with Firestone always getting more than their fair share of wins in America.

AAR was already building and racing successful Eagle Indycars, but now Dan wanted to build and race his own Formula One car, as he'd worked out that the same chassis, with just a few modifications, would serve for both type of races, thereby saving some money. This convinced Goodyear to sign the deal for a serious American Grand Prix effort with the participation of Mobil as well as lots of American fans who'd sent cheques towards the cost of the Eagle effort. He'd be building the chassis in Santa Ana but the engines would be built by Harry Weslake in Rye, Sussex, and the team would be based in a new extension built at the back of the Weslake engine factory. He was going to need good people to staff the project.

He said that the project was running on target, although final sponsorship was still to be sorted, but that he hadn't signed with any team for next year as he was sure to be racing his own cars. He finished by saying that if I was interested my place was booked and we should remain in contact, since as soon as the first chassis was sent to the UK I'd be needed in Rye. I left the Forte Hotel as happy as a sandboy, the thought of being back in Formula One, working with the driver I (and maybe Jim Clark too) believed to be the best in the world, was what the Godfather would call "an offer you can't refuse".

Back at Ford, my bosses had also realised that I wasn't going to stay happily in Slough building GT cars, and they suggested to me that since they'd rather see me stay with the Ford family I should leave to join Alan Mann Racing, who'd be racing the first GT

Group 4 cars leaving Slough. I couldn't at the time reveal my plans with Gurney, so I just said that the 1965 season was about to end and I was happy to stay the winter at Ford building cars.

That winter a significant event took place that would change the rest of my life. I was invited to a party by Alan Gordon, one of my colleagues at Ford, who said: "I want you to meet my sister-in-law, she's a very pretty blonde girl, a stewardess with British Airways, who's learning Spanish. I thought that perhaps you could improve your English and she might pick up some Spanish from you."

Alan was right, Brenda Helen was a very pretty girl, very intelligent, with a wonderful personality and great conversation, and she was the world's best listener. She had a wonderful way with people, which perhaps was part of her job, and a tremendous facility for languages, something seldom found in British people. She spoke Italian, French, German, and Spanish, and was learning Russian, because for every language she spoke she'd get a little flag on her uniform and a pound a week more in wages. She was a fascinating girl who left more than an impression on me and we became very good friends.

In February 1966 Ford sold two Group 4 GT40s to a Canadian racing team called Comstock and they sent me to look after the cars, which were going to compete in several minor races and two big ones, the Daytona 24 Hours and the Sebring 12 Hours, which meant that I was going to be away for several weeks. The feeling of being my own boss was absolutely great. The first stop was Toronto, which was under ice, and here I was greeted by Paul Cooke, who was in charge of Comstock and with whom I got on fine. He had a good knowledge of how to run a team and was the most extraordinary driver on ice that I've ever seen. By all accounts he should have been driving one of the cars, but the drivers were Eppie Weitzes, the Canadian champion, George Eaton (of the Eaton Department Stores family), and a promising young driver from Vancouver called Bob McLean.

At Sebring we couldn't keep the temperature of the cars down: they boiled every time we were out, and there was no way we could run for 12 hours like that. I therefore did something drastic that I'd always been tempted to do in Europe but my bosses wouldn't hear of, because it would spoil the look of the coachwork.

I cut and enlarged the front radiator air intake, and although I knew that I was going to have my knuckles rapped the cars ran at 80°C, and they didn't look ugly, just mean!

Everything was running well and a third of the way into the race, after three stops, we were still first and second, but disaster was soon to strike. After the last stop for fuel, Bob McLean lost control and hit a barrier. The car exploded like a grenade, we saw the smoke without knowing who it was until we heard on the speaker system that the Ford No. 18 had crashed. I ran like a madman to the corner, but was stopped by an official. The car was an incredible ball of fire, fed by 140 litres of fuel that had only just gone in. Bob was trapped helpless in the blaze, and by the time the fire was out and I could get close to the car all I could see were his charred shoes.

I burst into tears. It was the first time that a driver had died in one of my cars and that was something I'd never really anticipated. It was a horrible feeling and no matter how many people came to tell me that it was only the excessive speed with which Bob had tried to take the corner that caused the accident, nothing could make me feel better. Bob, who'd had a wonderful sense of humour, was the quickest of the Comstock drivers, and Canadian motorsport had suffered a great loss. I asked Ford if I could return to England as soon as possible after putting things in order in Florida; they agreed, and I returned in time for the Le Mans test. But I needed some time for myself after such an experience, and I spent some of it with my new stewardess girlfriend. This helped me back towards a sense of reality.

The Le Mans test was, as always, an interesting experience. This time the attraction was to see our cars that had been sent to Shelby and were now returned super-modified as 7-litre Ford Mk2s. One of the things that brought a smile to my face was to see that the Shelby Mk2s were using the same modification to the front radiator air intake that I'd initiated at Sebring, so I was on the right track, as these were the cars that finally won the Le Mans race for Ford.

Another unfortunate tragedy for Ford at the test weekend was the death of Walt Hansgen, who aquaplaned on a wet track and crashed very heavily in the Holman & Moody entered Mk2. I didn't have direct dealings with him but I knew him as a kind and modest man who drove for John Mecom before he was contracted to Ford.

I met up with Dan Gurney again at Le Mans, who told me that everything was in place for the Eagle Formula One project, and that very soon I was going to get a call from the newly appointed team manager, Bill Dunne. The call arrived in April as I was going south to Rye.

Once again I went through the painful process of saying goodbye to all my colleagues, and I have to say that I was astonished and overwhelmed at the way that 'Captain Cool' (as we used to call John Wyer) made his farewells. From the outside we always saw him as a calculating and hard person, but inside he was a very warm and human person.

Like most racing bosses, he always insisted on an immaculate and tidy factory. I remember him doing his weekly walks through the workshop and asking: "What are those engine parts doing there, and those suspensions? What about that bodywork gathering dust? If you're not using them, throw them away." The amount of perfectly good parts that went on the rubbish heap was sinful and I wish I'd had a place to store them. In hindsight, I should have moved heaven and earth to find such a place, as I could have built a couple more GT40s, which are now worth hundreds of thousand of pounds.

John Horsman was also very kind. He didn't say goodbye, just "Until we meet again," which made me feel that perhaps I was leaving something behind that one day I'd come back to.

CHAPTER 4

WHERE EAGLES DARE

At the end of April 1966 I started work at Anglo American Racers in Rye, Sussex, the Formula One base for Dan Gurney's All American Racers, whose headquarters were in California. I was going to have a room in a big house that the company had rented for Bill Dunne, the team manager, with enough guest rooms for Dan Gurney and anyone that needed to come from the USA base. The chief mechanic was Tim Wall, an ex-Brabham mechanic who'd looked after Dan's cars, a very quiet and taciturn man but with a world of experience and a solid engineering background. The other mechanic was Mike Lowman, also with racing car experience and the best welder/fabricator that I've ever come across in my career. The designer was Len Terry, an eccentric and individualistic Brit, but a nice man to work with. Len had probably made more racing car drawings than any other British racing car designer – and he was also the fastest pencil in the west!

This was the small group of people who were going to help Dan Gurney to realise the American Dream. Later on we were joined by a couple of machinists and Rouem Haffenden, a local mechanic from Rye. The monocoque chassis was built in California, to a standard that hadn't quite reached Europe, by an Australian craftsman called Pete Wilkins. Our cars were much admired by the whole F1 fraternity and soon afterwards the British took up some of Pete's techniques, copying being the sincerest form of flattery! The car was called the Eagle, a patriotic and American name, and the nose carried a strong but subtle resemblance to an eagle's beak. Dan's father also designed a very smart oval badge bearing a large 'G' with an eagle's head inside.

The Weslake 3-litre engine was made next to our factory in Rye, or

50

rather our factory was based in a purpose-built extension of the Weslake Engineering factory. One of the most skilled and helpful workers at Weslake then was someone who would become one of the biggest names in the sport, Patrick Head, co-founder and designer of the Williams Grand Prix Engineering Formula One team.

The engine wasn't going to be finished during this first year, and we therefore used a 2.5 Coventry Climax enlarged to 2.7 litres. Tim Wall knew these engines like the back of his hand – which was just as well, as it was an old engine and there weren't too many around. Tim performed miracles in keeping them going, often taking the head off between practice and race to fit a new head gasket or regrind the valve seats.

We made our Grand Prix debut at Spa, where Dan was not classified as a finisher, and then finished fifth at Reims for our first World Championship points. It was interesting to see how, on circuits with lots of corners where power wasn't so critical, Dan's driving was a great asset. At Brands Hatch we qualified in the front row, but we didn't collect any silverware on the Sunday. We then came fourth in Holland and seventh in Germany.

By the time of the Italian Grand Prix at Monza the Weslake V12 engine was finished, although perhaps not race-ready, and it was decided to take it and use Monza as a test, but it only completed eight laps, having qualified on the last row! We took it again to Watkins Glen and entered Bob Bondurant in the Climax car, but neither of them finished. In Mexico City, Dan switched back to the Climax car to finish fifth, and that was the sad balance of our first season – frustrating, but nothing to be ashamed of with a new car, new team, and very underpowered engine. In fact all of us felt that we'd accomplished one hell of a lot in our first year.

After Mexico we went to California to visit AAR's headquarters and drove to Indianapolis, where we were supposed to test next year's Indy Eagle, but when we got there temperatures were below zero and, with the race track frozen, all we could achieve was a few laps with Dan in the rent-a-car at 200mph (but only on the speedometer, as the wheels were spinning like crazy).

Back in the UK, I moved to a small rented house in picturesque Church Square in Rye and started to feel very much at home in this quaint corner of England. A revised Weslake V12 engine was about to be completed, and we started testing that December at Goodwood. The car was very quick indeed, but we decided not to take it to the first Grand Prix of 1967, in South Africa on 2 January, but instead took the Eagle-Climax, and this was good news for Pedro Rodriguez who ended up winning his first Grand Prix with Cooper-Maserati. I remember that the organisers didn't even have the Mexican national anthem to play on the podium, so they played the Mexican Hat Dance (*Jarabe Tapatio*) instead!

The spring came, and our luck came with it: we won the Race of Champions at Brands Hatch, with Dan in first place and Richie Ginther in the second car coming third. We also collared the hundred bottles of champagne for pole position. In the race we'd been 1–2 until just three laps from the end, when Richie's car slowed down and was overtaken by my friend Bandini, while Pedro came fourth after a tremendous race. What a great feeling! We were winners at last and had a competitive car for the coming Grand Prix season. We had a team dinner where Bill Dunne wanted to finish the hundred bottles of bubbly, but none of us who'd spent three days without sleep could keep our eyes open as it was!

The European season was due to start in Monaco on 7 May, and suddenly – panic! Brenda and I wanted to get married, and it had to be either before Monaco or at the end of the season in November, so we decided to go for it if we could find a church and a priest within ten days. Everything was such a rush that most people thought a *bambino* was on the way!

We were married in Oxfordshire on 15 April. We also managed to get a honeymoon in, although Brenda always maintained that it was nothing but a busman's holiday – I was allowed to take some time off, but only on the understanding that we went to the Cote d'Azur and found a suitable garage in which to work and keep the cars during the Grand Prix! In those days, Monaco didn't have a paddock and the teams didn't have the sophisticated, ubiquitous transporters that they have today, so all the teams did their work in rented garages around Monaco. I managed to find a place in Cap d'Ail that we shared with Brabham. That done, we drove to Milan to see the 1000km race at Monza, and then went to Modena to visit all my old pals. Somehow we also found time to visit the Lamborghini, Maserati and Ferrari factories...

We returned to Rye in time for me to leave for the Monaco Grand Prix, where unfortunately we didn't continue our momentum from Brands Hatch. Our garage was about 10km out of Monaco and I used to drive the Eagle F1 racer to and from the garage after each practice through the streets and roads of Monte Carlo and the south of France. Can you imagine doing that nowadays? We qualified seventh but went out with fuel system problems.

The 1967 Monaco Grand Prix was yet another tragic race for me. As we'd gone out early I stayed to watch the race, rooting for Bandini, who was going strong until the late stages when he had a horrendous crash after the tunnel, by the bottom chicane. It looked to me as if he just lost concentration. The car, after bouncing off the guardrails, burst into flames, and the rescue team took forever to get him out. How he managed to survive for two days after that I'll never know. I was with his wife, Margarita, the next day, but I prayed that God would take him as survival would be nothing more than a living death.

We had to wait two more races before we finally took our first and only Grand Prix victory, which came in Belgium. Spa-Francorchamps is probably one of the most fantastic race tracks in the world, a real drivers' circuit, very fast; no other circuit in the world will push your whole stomach against your rib cage with the G forces in the downhill curves. It was also one of Dan's favourite circuits. Before the race I went to the airport to collect Dan, who'd won at Le Mans with A.J. Foyt the previous weekend in a Ford Mk4 but had returned to the USA for Ford's celebrations. We were on our way to the hotel in the company Ford van when he decided to take me around the circuit practically on its door handles! I gathered that he knew the circuit pretty well and was ready for Sunday.

Dan was indubitably one of the greatest racing drivers that I ever had the pleasure to work for, but he was a great fiddler. He never stopped making changes to the car, but he was such a good driver that he just drove that little bit harder to prove to us that whatever he'd changed was better – even if afterwards he asked you to put it back as it was! In Belgium, where the pits were on a downhill gravelled surface, he stood at the door of the transporter looking down at the car and said to me, "Joaquin, that right-hand wheel has far too much toe-out. Bring it in one quarter of a turn at least."

The race wasn't without a few dramas. The starting grid was downhill and Dan didn't want to overheat the clutch by keeping the car in first gear with his right foot on the brake as well as operating the throttle. He asked us to put something on a rear wheel to stop the car rolling, but it didn't work, and when the start was given he was in neutral and started late. He got to Eau Rouge, the first corner, in eighth place, but he was fifth by the end of the first lap. Clark led in his Lotus 49 but then stopped to change spark plugs, and Jackie Stewart took over in his BRM P83. Dan came into the pits to warn us that the fuel pressure was coming down, but then everything clicked. Dan passed Stewart and led for the last eight laps, which must have been the longest eight laps in his life, with vivid memories of 1964 when he was leading but ran out of fuel in the Brabham on the last lap. This time he made it to the chequered flag, to the tremendous relief, cheers and tears of the whole team.

It was on the slowing down lap that realisation dawned on Dan that he'd won. All the people, workers and fans were waving at him, and he waved back with the indescribable feeling of, "By God, we've done it!" And then to see the Stars and Stripes waving on top of the podium, and to hear the US national anthem playing, was a special moment not only for the driver and the team but also for the millions of fans around the world who'd been rooting for us. There was no champagne on the podium this time, like there'd been at Le Mans the week before, so Dan just threw flowers at the crowd. He was absolutely ecstatic.

The first half of the American Dream was achieved exactly a year since our first race. It was the first Grand Prix won by an American in an American-built car, and set a new record for the fastest Grand Prix in history (at just under 146mph). With the Le Mans victory the previous week, I guess this was the best week of Dan Gurney's racing career, and he was deservedly euphoric. As for me, it was my first Grand Prix win too. Did we celebrate! Today Belgium, tomorrow the world!

For the next four Grands Prix we ran a second car, which Dan offered to Bruce McLaren who'd had problems with his own. Little did we guess then that McLaren would take up a big chunk of my life or, sadly, that Bruce would never see the success of the team that he created.

The German Grand Prix at the Nürburgring was going to be the next one that Dan wanted so much to win, another real drivers' circuit, 22.5km, 185 corners. This time we went round in a rented Mercedes-Benz, which sadly returned minus tyres – two laps at the Nürburgring averaging 14 minutes per lap doesn't do the tyres a lot of good. We led the 15-lap race from lap four to lap twelve and achieved a lap record, but then a driveshaft gave up when we were 42 seconds in front. This was as big a disappointment as winning in Belgium was a pleasure, but motor racing is like that, except that the disappointments are much more frequent than the victories.

The rest of the races were more of the same, running at the front but not finishing, except for a third place in Canada. In Mexico, Dan qualified third and was behind Clark on the grid. Jim was normally very good at starting, but this time his engine coughed, he almost stalled, and Dan rammed him from behind, maybe giving him the push he needed. But disastrously Jim's Lotus exhaust had gone through the Eagle's radiator, and Dan was out with overheating on the third lap! I'd have loved to have done well on my home territory, but it wasn't to be – maybe another time. Jim was so sorry and sincerely apologetic to Dan after the race; this was the kind of man that Jim was.

It was a great shame that Jimmy was no longer with us for the 1968 season. Colin Chapman sent him to a F2 meeting in April at Hockenheim, where he wasn't even dicing for the lead when he left the track and hit a tree sideways at 140mph and was killed instantly. He was a great man, honest and unassuming. I remember him playing cards with the boys in the P&O boat across the Channel when all of us used to drive to the races. I'll never forget his driving – one of the most exciting things that I've ever seen in my racing life was to watch Jimmy drive the Lotus Cortina as a guest driver at Brands Hatch, where he was about one or two seconds a lap quicker than the regulars who drove them every week, people like Frank Gardner, Jack Sears and Sir John Whitmore. He used to come down the Bottom Bend left-hander with the inside left front wheel on the grass but a foot in the air, the right front wheel on the apex just brushing the grass, with the left rear doing the same and the car balancing with the right front tyre almost out of the rim and everybody thinking he was going to roll it! But no, he kept on like that, lap after lap. What a great maestro he was.

If there's one thing that I thoroughly miss from motor racing these days, it's to see these magical drivers, phenomena of the steering wheel, driving normal cars which people can relate to. Could you imagine Schumacher or Senna driving a road or sports car in competition? The last time this happened was in May 1984 when, at the opening of the new Nürburgring circuit, Mercedes-Benz decided to launch their new Mercedes 190 saloon car and organised a 15-lap race, inviting some of the old names of the past together with the stars of the present. The result was a fabulously mixed grid with names like Phil Hill, Moss, Hermann, Brabham, Surtees, Hulme, Scheckter, Hunt, Jones, Lauda, Prost, Rosberg, Laffite, De Angelis, Reutemann, Watson, and the newcomer to Formula One, but F3 champion, Ayrton Senna. Ayrton was the only one amongst them who hadn't won a Grand Prix, and was invited only because Domingos Piedade, the AMG boss, was one of the men who helped his career and was a firm believer in his talent. For Ayrton it was a big vote of confidence, like being accepted in the establishment. It was the first time that Prost and Senna met, and most of the other drivers had never heard his name. Besides being a wonderful social occasion and a good publicity stunt it was a good race, although some of them decided to make it just a fun run and went grass-cutting instead of keeping their cars on the road. Ayrton was probably the one who took it the most seriously, as he was the only one that needed to prove a point against the *crème de la crème* in such a high profile event. He left everyone else speechless at his aggression and the way he attacked the kerbs, winning the race and his rite of passage easily.

In the winter of 1967–8 it was decided to move the AAR factory and do our own engines. This was a very brave move, motivated perhaps by our own enthusiasm, or maybe there was no choice. Either way we hadn't done our sums properly. We found ourselves well out of our depth and miles behind schedule; we didn't make the Spanish Grand Prix in May 1968, and we were even late for the Monaco. I had to stay behind to finish the last engine, which I then had to take to another test-bed as ours wasn't ready. The only dynamometer we could find was Peter Westbury's in Dorking, Surrey, but this was only intended for F3 engines, so we had to adapt the F1 Weslake engine, which, with its exhaust, completely filled the little room. The fuel and oil were fed by gravity in a very agricultural and primitive fashion.

We couldn't run the engine more than 4,000–5,000rpm, which was fairly useless, but at least we could see that it was running well and had no leaks, and enabled us to give it a little running in! I could only run it for four or five minutes at a time, as the room got too hot and filled with fumes. I couldn't have the door open, as the rest of the workers in Peter's factory would object to the noise, so I ran it in stages and stopped every so often for a breather. I did this a few times until, unfortunately, an oil pipe touched the red-hot exhaust and the whole thing lit up like an incandescent red balloon, trapping me in the corner of the room.

For a second I had visions of being burned alive, but before I started panicking and saying my prayers I leapt on top of the dynamometer and jumped across the wall of fire in the direction of the door. Luck was on my side and the door wasn't locked: it flew open as I hit it and I fell on the floor with the fire following me. By then the rest of the workers had realised what was happening and got to work with the fire extinguishers, and I escaped with minor burns and a cut on my chin.

While someone took me to hospital to have a few stitches, someone else retrieved the engine and cleaned it up, and on my return we changed some of the damaged wiring, put the engine in the van, and rushed it out to Blackbush aerodrome, where a Cessna plane was waiting to take us to Monaco. When we got to the airport we realised the engine was, in fact, a little too big for the plane, so we had to take the seats out, and even then the engine just barely fitted. There was no way at all that there was room for me as well, but after the ordeal I'd been through I wasn't too bothered.

And this wasn't the end of the saga! When the plane reached the south of France the pilot was told that the airports were on strike and there was no way they could land at Nice, so they went instead to a small airfield near Cannes. It was getting dark – and the airfield had no lights. Dan had to find enough friends with cars to come to the airport and park along the sides of the runway with their headlights on so that the Cessna pilot could see to land! Only winning the race would have been enough to compensate for this little epic, but Dan was out on the ninth lap.

The only consolation was that the next month the Eagles finished 1, 2 and 4 in Indianapolis, with Gurney second behind Bobby Unser. This was one of the goals that Dan Gurney and his partner Carroll Shelby had in mind when they created AAR – to build a car capable of winning the biggest car race in the world. Also, we mustn't forget that it was Dan who personally invited Colin Chapman of Lotus and the Ford Motor Company to the Brickyard in an attempt to get them together to build a car for the Speedway. This had been accomplished in 1963, when Jim Clark finished second, with Gurney seventh after an embarrassment of pitstops. In 1964 they were let down by their Dunlop tyres, but in 1965 Clark had finally won, though Dan's engine broke its timing gear while running second.

AAR's success at the 1968 Indy was just as well, because in the UK the Eagle was flying very low. We had to withdraw from the Belgian and French Grands Prix, and though we raced in Holland, Britain, Germany and Italy it was without success. The only memorable thing about these events was that, at the Nürburgring, Dan wore the Bell Star enclosed helmet for the very first time – he was the pioneer of the all-enclosed helmet, which every driver has used ever since. Although he only finished ninth in the race at the Nürburgring, Dan always considered it one of his greatest drives. In the most dreadful conditions, with rain and fog, he got up to third at the beginning and then had to trundle seven miles to the pits with a flat tyre. After rejoining in nineteenth place he carved his way back up to ninth with similar lap times to Jackie Stewart, who won arguably his greatest race in Ken Tyrrell's Matra-Cosworth.

On the subject of things pioneered by Dan, he was also responsible for the introduction of the popular 'Gurney flap', which still bears his name: Dan was the first driver to bolt that small reversed lip on the top of the rear wing, which every team in the world has since used in different sizes to provide extra downforce with minimal aerodynamic disturbance. He was also the one who started the tradition of spraying champagne in the winners' circle, which is now the 'rule' at every motor racing event. In 1967, when he and A.J. Foyt won the Le Mans 24 Hours, Dan was handed a magnum of Moët et Chandon and in the spirit of the moment he thought it would be a good idea to spray all the photographers, drivers, and the whole top entourage of the Ford Motor Co, including Henry Ford and his wife.

Little did he knew that from then on it was to become the norm. After the celebrations, Dan gave the autographed bottle to his friend Flip Schulke, a *Life* magazine photographer, who made a lamp with it. A few years later Flip, suffering from ill health, sent the bottle back to Dan saying that he really ought to keep it. Dan took the lampshade off and the bottle is now in a glass case at AAR headquarters and will probably finish up in a Ford or Moët et Chandon museum. The lampshade is at Dan and Evi Gurney's house in Costa Mesa, signed by all the racing people who have visited their home. In the year 2000, I was honoured to be asked to sign it, alongside names like Mario Andretti, Ronnie Peterson, Jim Clark, Graham Hill, James Hunt, Carroll Shelby, Parnelli Jones, Phil Hill, Wolfgang Porsche, Teddy Yip and many others.

After the Italian Grand Prix, it was decided to withdraw our Eagle from the last three races of the 1968 season, and a deal was struck with Bruce McLaren for a third McLaren M7A car, entered and run by AAR. Can you imagine a deal like this in today's Grand Prix circle? Not in a million years. Dan was fourth in the USA but had to retire in Canada and Mexico.

And this was the bitter end of the short-lived, small but enthusiastic American team, though we could at least say that we'd won one non-championship Formula One race and one Grand Prix. That winter we had to close down the team and try to sell the project. Probably the saddest thing was to see Gurney out of Formula One, which was very upsetting for all American fans. There have been other American efforts in Grand Prix racing since, but no one ever achieved what Dan Gurney did at Spa in 1967; and because of the way in which the sport has changed I can't see another American effort on the cards in the near future.

We were all offered jobs in California, running TransAm,

CanAm and Indy cars, and some British teams also offered us jobs to stay in Formula One. When decision time arrived the other three mechanics and I decided that the American offer was an opportunity we had to take, not least through loyalty to Dan and the company.

California was really the easiest place to live. We rented an apartment within a day of arriving – fully furnished, heating, air-conditioning, garage, tennis court and three pools. In 1969 Dan ran a Lola in the CanAm, a series of races across the United States and Canada for big sport cars which that year was dominated by the McLarens of Bruce and Denny Hulme, with Gurney occasionally running third.

While we were running these CanAm cars, our engine shop in Santa Ana was preparing a new engine based on a big American block with cylinder heads prepared by Gurney with Weslake technology. It proved a very successful project and we even sold one of these engines to Moises Solana in Mexico. He was delighted with it and wanted to buy one of our chassis for the new Formula A, and we were in talks with him about it. I was on the phone with him daily, until I heard that he'd been killed at a race at Avandaro circuit in Valle de Bravo. There was a lot of controversy about his accident, and I felt dreadful once again for Mexico, as we'd lost another excellent sportsman. In addition to driving cars, Moises had been an accomplished 'Jai-alai' (Fronton) player, and I'd often accompanied him to his games whenever I was in Mexico.

Working for Gurney in California was certainly very diversified: one day we were running CanAm, the next a USAC Indycar or a big Ford saloon. Throughout 1970 I was the mechanic/fabricator of AAR's TransAm team, running a Plymouth Barracuda on behalf of Chrysler in a series of races across the USA and Canada in which most of the manufacturers were represented: competitors included the Ford Mustang, Dodge Road Runner, Chevrolet Camaro, Pontiac Firebird and American Motors Javelin, as well as a few private racers.

The races were great, the competition was intense and very professional, with drivers of the calibre of Gurney, Swede Savage, Parnelli Jones, George Follmer, Sam Posey, Mark Donohue, Ron Bucknum and Jim Hall. Our contract with Chrysler was to run two cars, but later they cut it down to just one. Dan was very upset, but he decided to pull out himself and leave his young protégé, Swede Savage, in the remaining car. Swede was a great guy and we all got along just fine. In fact, when I started the series I wasn't at all convinced whether or not I was going to like it and I was tempted to say yes to an offer from John Wyer, who by then had a contract with Porsche running 917s with Gulf sponsorship for Pedro Rodriguez and Jo Siffert. However, I decided to give the TransAm a go.

I'm glad I did, as it turned out to be one of the greatest series I've taken part in. Our own team gelled perfectly and the race tracks, the locations, AAR's eastern base in Michigan, and the whole *camaraderie* amongst all the teams was nothing short of fantastic, although the competition was so close that sometimes the mood of a TransAm meeting was very uptight: the slightest mistake in pit work or strategy could lose races. Without a shadow of a doubt, this was a fabulous year for me.

But 1970 didn't pass without claiming more important victims. Early in June, as Bruce McLaren was testing his latest CanAm car at Goodwood, the rear body came off and Bruce lost control with fatal consequences. McLaren Racing and Goodyear offered Bruce's CanAm drive to Dan, which he accepted, and along with the deal were three Formula One races, the Dutch, French and British GPs. At the time this sounded exciting, but it did nothing for Dan's reputation, because the 1970 McLaren M14A wasn't at all competitive. The Dutch Grand Prix was the scene of another tragic loss: while the motor racing world was still in shock from losing Bruce, Piers Courage's De Tomaso-Ford crashed and caught fire, and it was a long time before the flames were put out, with fatal consequences for Piers. It was also François Cevert's first Grand Prix.

Then, at the Italian GP in Monza, Jochen Rindt crashed his Lotus 72 and became the first posthumous Formula One World Champion. Dan was very much affected by Jochen's death, as much as he had been by Jim Clark's.

On the positive side, 1970 was proving to be a great year for Pedro Rodriguez. He won the Belgian Grand Prix, as well as sports car races at Daytona, Brands Hatch and Monza, and he acquired the reputation of being the 'King of the Rain'. Finally, Don Pedro's dream was starting to be realised, at least with one of his sons.

Back in California, my wife Bea was very homesick and wanted to return to England, but as ever wasn't putting me under any pressure. I told her that as soon as Dan retired we'd return home. There weren't many firm plans for AAR for 1971 except for the USAC Indy racing series. Dan decided to race in the last round of the TransAm series at Riverside and then hang up his helmet forever. As he got out of the car he shouted, "I made it alive!" Since he'd started racing, 59 of his colleagues had died, but when Jimmy Clark went Dan realised that he could only do it for a couple more seasons. I think Jochen's death must have been the last straw.

Almost in the same week I received another letter from John Wyer and John Horsman, now JW Automotive Ltd, asking me to return, and this time I couldn't refuse. Dan, as always a real gentleman and friend, said that if he couldn't keep me, he was happy to pay for some of my trip back. AAR sent back all my tools and household goods and JW paid for our return trip via Mexico.

Dan's last helmet, which he wore at Riverside, was left in the cockpit after the race and, when he went back for it, it had disappeared and he was devastated. Despite several announcements on the loudspeakers, followed by radio and newspaper appeals asking the offender to return the helmet, it was never seen again – until a few years ago, when it was returned anonymously to AAR with a note just saying: "Sorry"!

Two Christmases ago a parcel arrived at my home from Dan Gurney's AAR workshop. It was a black Bell Star helmet, which he wanted me to keep among my collection. I'm not ashamed to admit that tears came into my eyes. What a wonderful Christmas present.

CHAPTER 5

ATLANTIC CROSSING

While we were in California, I was earning well and Bea had a job in a real estate company: they thought it was a great asset to have a girl with an English accent at the other end of the phone, although Bea always told them it wasn't she who had an accent, but them! We used to bank my money and live on hers, so that on our return to the UK we could buy our first house with cash and this we did, in Maidenhead, only a few miles from JW Automotive.

So 1971 saw me back in Slough: same place, different cars. It was great to see a few familiar faces again: Ermanno Cuoghi, Peter Davies, Johnny Etheridge, Alan Hearn, Ray Jones and many others. We were to be racing the beautiful and sophisticated 4.9-litre flat-12-engined Porsche 917 with sponsorship from Gulf Oil, in the 11 races of the 1971 FIA International Championship of Makes. The team had already had a successful season in 1970 and everything seemed to point to another good year.

The drivers were Pedro Rodriguez and Jackie Oliver in one car and Jo Siffert and Derek Bell in the other (Pedro and Siffert were also Formula One BRM teammates that year). The management was the same: John Wyer and John Horsman, with David Yorke as team manager, and they all thought that one Mexican in one car was sufficient, so I was assigned to the Siffert/Bell car.

In the first race – the 1000km event at Buenos Aires – we came away with a 1–2, with Siffert/Bell ahead of Pedro and Jackie. The second event, at Daytona, was one of the most enjoyable and satisfying races of my life: after leading for 18 of the 24 hours, Jackie Oliver came into the pits with one of our cars stuck in fifth gear, and although we had a significant lead it wasn't a dead certainty that we could fix the problem, as the rules forbade changing the gearbox. One could change all the insides, as long as the case was left intact.

As soon as the car came to a halt we started a frantic transmission rebuild in the pit-lane. The gears and cogs were red hot, almost welded to the main shaft, and there was practically no way to separate them. By applying lots of heat with a welding torch and using pulleys, levers, hammers and a lot of patience we finally managed to release them, although it left the shaft pretty scratched. Then we threw in the new gears, filled up with oil, closed everything up and hoped for the best. We'd taken one-and-a-half hours to repair the box and we'd lost the 43 laps that we were in front: we were now nearly three laps behind the new leader. This time it was Pedro's turn. We strapped him in and he took off like a man in a hurry. We waited anxiously for his first lap, and as he went by he put his thumb up and we all leapt and shouted as if he'd already won the race!

Obviously, we hadn't won the race yet, but the team had cleared its biggest hurdle and now it was up to the drivers. No sooner had Pedro completed his first lap than the skies opened, and there was no better driver than him in the rain, so he soon started carving off the seconds and in the last hour we took the lead back from the Ferrari 512S of American drivers Ronnie Bucknum and Tony Adamowicz and won the race. It was an extremely rewarding team victory, and next morning the headlines read: "Gulf mechanics rescue win for JW and Porsche".

I'd managed to scrounge a few days' holiday and I was due to go back to Mexico for a quick visit to the family and friends, which I was looking forward to enormously. However, in a 24-hour race mechanics don't get any sleep, and they get very little the night before, and after winning we celebrated late and I got to bed like a dead parrot and completely slept through the alarm clock. My flight was at 1300 hours and I was about 250 miles away from the airport. When I finally came to life it was just about nine o'clock, and in the naivety of my youth – and feeling cocky after having won the race the day before – I decided that in the Shelby-prepared Ford Mustang I had on loan it would be easy to average 100mph on the Sunshine State freeway all the way to Miami and catch the plane. Wrong! Although I was doing OK for the first 100 miles, a police car hidden behind a bridge picked me up and followed me at 130mph! Whoops! I stopped, and two cops with guns in hand ordered me out, hands on the car roof, big search, handcuffs, no questions asked, into the police car, and straight to jail without passing Go!

I felt terrible. I'd never before been treated like a criminal. I had to deposit all my belongings, had my fingerprints taken, and was put in a cell surrounded by very seedy-looking characters; it was the most horrendous experience. The jailer, though, was kind enough to send a telegram to the family telling them of my misfortune.

I waited there for a few hours until the judge arrived, and I think that my guardian angel was looking after me because the judge turned out to be a hell of a nice person, who had a long conversation with me, listened to my story, and accepted my humble guilty plea. He weighed it all up and decided that, taking into consideration the car that I was driving and the freeway, perhaps I wasn't endangering anyone else, and he let me go with a $140 fine. Although this was a lot of money in those days, at least I was a free man, and what a relief that was! I had to wait until the Wednesday for the next flight to Mexico City, which meant two nights in Miami – but at least they weren't spent in jail. Needless to say, I've never done any speeding in the USA since then.

Back in Europe, we had three bad races. One of the vivid memories I have is of Jo Siffert at Brands Hatch in the BOAC 1000km race; he came in for a regular pitstop, but one of his front wheels refused to come off. The steel wheel nut had seized with the aluminium hub and we lost some laps fixing the trouble, while Siffert, a true racer, jumped up and down in the cockpit hitting the steering wheel and shouting, "Leave it, leave it, send me out!" Of course, by then the nut was halfway off, but he just wasn't listening. Eventually we got it sorted and sent him back out.

For the Targa Florio, we were running the 908 Porsche, the smaller open car, more suited to the Piccolo Madonie circuit than the 917. But because of the length of the circuit (72km) it was decided to also take three 914 Porsches – the fast rally cars – in order that the drivers could get acclimatised and learn the circuit in the same way that Ferrari always did. I won the jackpot of driving one of the cars down, along with Derek Bell and Arnold Stafford, Arnold being the man in charge of organisation and logistics. It was a very enjoyable drive through France, Germany, Switzerland and Italy. Derek and I were really hammering down, stopping every so often to wait for Arnold, until I managed to spin my Porsche in Italy. Derek decided to slow down a bit after that, as he'd have felt responsible if one of us smashed a 914.

Down in Sicily, it was my good fortune again to be driven round the Targa circuit, this time with Pedro, almost ten years after I'd gone round with Ricardo in the GTO Ferrari. As we were driving back to the pits he asked me, "How do I rate against Ricardo?", and I replied, "Do you really want me to tell you?" "Yes, of course," he said, knowing how close I was to Ricardo. I decided to wind him up and said, "Six out of ten!" "Good," he said, "I still have room for improvement."

The race was another disaster. Pedro spun and broke two wheels on the first lap and Brian Redman had an horrific accident due to a steering failure: the car was destroyed and caught fire, and, typically for a long circuit like the Targa and 30-plus years ago, it took some time before Brian, who'd suffered bad and painful burns, could be attended to. The next day we had to nurse him all the way to the airport and back home, and even now he still bears the marks on his face from that day in May 1971. When we went back to recover the wreck, all that was left to collect were the metal parts of the engine – the camshaft and rods, the flywheel, etc. The rest was completely incinerated.

For Le Mans we always stayed at the Hotel de France in La Chartre-sur-le-Loire, John Wyer's favourite place, and we worked on the cars in their large garage. However, the hotel was about 40km from the circuit and we used to drive the 917 cars down to the track early in the morning and then back again after practice. This particular year Siffert had a small incident at the end of the last practice which prevented him from bedding-in his last set of brake pads for the race. I remember telling him, "Don't worry, I'll bed them in tomorrow when I drive the car to the circuit." Next morning I went to the circuit accelerating and braking and generally having fun – those cars used to accelerate like a jet, and when you put your foot on the brake they just stopped without weaving at all. However, that was when you realised why these guys earn a lot of money: it takes special men to get the best out of these Porsche 917 beasts. When I arrived at the track I found, to my amazement, that I'd only scrubbed the pads, and they still weren't quite bedded properly. Luckily the brakes were fine, though 'my' car didn't finish the race.

As he was coming down the Mulsanne Straight at more than 200mph Pedro had split the oil pipe that ran all through the inside of the car. He was covered in hot oil, as was the inside of the windscreen! He managed to coast the car into the pits and we repaired the pipe and sent him off again with dry overalls and a fresh helmet, but unfortunately the engine had ruined its bearings.

Sadly, the next race, at the Osterreichring in Austria, was to be Pedro's last victory, but he won it in style. He started in pole and was leading from Ickx by 23 seconds after the first quarter of the race, when he stopped with a damaged battery. We lost three laps fixing it and then David Yorke put Richard Attwood (the second driver) in the car for the minimum time required by the rules so that Pedro could resume the chase and win.

Two weeks later, on 11 July 1971, he lost his life in a Ferrari in an unimportant non-championship Interserie sports car race on the Norisring street circuit in Nuremburg, Germany. That was typical of Pedro: he loved racing and would race anything that he could get his hands on. He had recently moved, with his girlfriend Glenda Foreman, to Bray in Berkshire, which was very close to Maidenhead, where I lived, and that weekend he and Glenda were due to come to my house for dinner. Pedro called me a few days before to tell me that Herbert Müller had offered him a drive in his Ferrari 512 at the Norisring, so perhaps we could get together another weekend? I assured him that this was fine and wished him luck in the race.

I was busy at home and never heard the news of his death until I saw David Yorke on Monday morning. What an unbelievable shock it was. The cause of the accident was never clear, except that Pedro was leading under pressure from a Porsche 917 Spyder driven by, of all people, Leo Kinnunen, who'd been his regular co-driver the previous season at JW Gulf. He'd just passed a slower car driven by Kurt Hild when the Ferrari hit a wall and burst into flames. It was difficult to extinguish the fire and get Pedro out. He died from multiple injuries on the way to the hospital.

With Pedro, the last chance for a Mexican World Champion had gone, although we kept hoping that it wasn't lost forever. Pedro had matured so much in his last years and was ready to win races regularly. After his brother Ricardo's death, he didn't race professionally for a few years and devoted most of his time to his import car business. However, he discovered during the occasional races he entered that, away from the shadow of his brother, the more gifted of the two – against whom he was always measured – he became more confident, relaxed and unquestionably quicker. He raced three Mexican Grands Prix, in 1963–64–65, the first for Team Lotus and the other two in Ferraris entered by Luigi Chinetti. He was then asked to replace Jim Clark in the Lotus 33 at the 1966 French GP in Reims, after Jim was hit in the face by a bird. Even without a proper practice, he got up to fourth in the race before an oil pipe broke. He then got a drive in Mexico, where he got up to third but went out with gearbox problems.

He was rewarded for these performances with a contract with John Cooper/Maserati for 1967, and won his first Grand Prix at the season's opening event in South Africa (this was the occasion when the organisers played the Mexican Hat Dance instead of the Mexican national anthem). He raced that year alongside one of the fastest drivers of the time, Jochen Rindt, and there wasn't too much difference between them. In fact, Pedro finished sixth in the championship, better than Rindt's 11th place.

Pedro was a loner and never made friends with his fellow drivers. He always said: "When another driver knows you better as a person, socially, he'll have a better idea of how you'd react fighting inside a racing car, when you're racing wheel to wheel, so I'd rather not make friends among drivers."

He was also a fatalist and didn't have much time for Jackie Stewart's safety crusade, which he didn't approve of, condone or endorse. This, and the fact that he was a very hard driver, didn't make him popular with his colleagues, but he was nevertheless respected, especially in a wet weather race where he was a master – probably the best of his time. His Le Mans win in the Ford GT40 and the incredible drives in the Porsche 917 at Brands Hatch, Daytona and the Osterreichring were staggering, and he'd have won the wet 1971 Dutch Grand Prix in the BRM P160 but for a fuel pump problem. He relinquished first place there to the Ferrari 312B2 of Jacky Ickx, the other great master of the rain, and between the two of them they lapped the entire field. His other

Grand Prix win was at Spa in 1970, in a BRM P153.

Pedro loved England, the people and their way of living, and became very Anglicised. He drove a Bentley Continental car, always wore a deerstalker hat, and probably had as many or more followers among the British public as in Mexico.

At the end of that year, on 24 October 1971, I went as a spectator to the Rothmans World Championship Victory Race at Brands Hatch, organised after the Mexican Grand Prix was cancelled. This was a non-championship event but it was well represented by many teams and was dedicated to Jackie Stewart and Ken Tyrrell, this year's champions. It was an unusually sunny and warm autumn day and the British public were delighted with the opportunity to see these wonderful cars again.

My main reason for going was to contact Ken Tyrrell, in the hope of getting employment with his team; but I also wanted to say hello to some of my friends racing or working in F1. Jo Siffert was very happy, sitting in pole position with the BRM, and I was chatting to him as he got into the car on the starting grid. I probably got the last ever picture taken of 'Seppi', as his close friends called him. This had been his best year in F1, winning the Austrian GP and finishing fifth in the World Championship.

He got away badly and was running fourth when, on the 15th lap, his car hit an earth banking and immediately burst into flames. It was an awful scene. When the other cars got to the place where the accident happened they had to stop, as the flames and smoke were obscuring the track. The engines were switched off and an ominous silence told the public that a fatal crash had taken place.

Hopefully Jo was killed on impact and didn't suffer much, although his friends and colleagues were now suffering his loss. I felt relieved that I wasn't staying with John Wyer for the following year, as with Pedro and Seppi gone the team would never be the same again.

The world moves on and when one life goes another one starts. My daughter Ana Vanessa was born in August 1971 at a time when I happened to be at home (more by luck than judgement). I was with Bea at the time, but she suffered quite a hard and long labour, so by the time the little girl arrived I had been sent out of the room. Although at the time I would have preferred to have had a boy racer, I would not change her for the world.

CHAPTER 6

THE FAMILY AFFAIR

For 1972, the rules for sports car racing were changing from 5-litre to 3-litre engined cars, and I hadn't seen John Wyer making any preparations for the future. I therefore decided it was time to look around. I heard from Neil Davies, Tyrrell's works manager, that they were going to need to replace one man, and since they'd just won the 1971 World Championship I decided to approach Ken Tyrrell, one of the most likeable and respected people in the Grand Prix circus.

Ken ran the tightest and most efficient team in the business but, as I arrived in Long Reach, near Ockham, I couldn't believe that the World Championship-winning car had been built and run from this place. There were three sheds, three Portakabins, and a muddy yard for a parking place; the whole ensemble was enough to put off a travelling salesman. This was a good example of the saying: "The habit does not make the monk". The meeting didn't take long and I was given the job, starting in November; more importantly, I had a wonderful feeling that I was about to start some of the happiest years of my life.

Ken was the father figure of a 'family' team which was run with the basic values of life, where every member of the family pulled together. Ken's single-mindedness, sheer determination and contagious motivation were spread throughout the whole team. Everyone admired him deeply, he was a unique type of boss. He and his brother Bert had run a timber business until the team became big enough that Ken had to devote all of his time to it – hence his early nickname, 'Chopper', and the fact that the workshop was in a woodyard.

The team was very small, race team and factory employing less than 30 people. There was no room for deadwood or passengers; everyone was an expert in his own field and they all pulled their weight in great harmony, starting with the drivers, Jackie Stewart and François Cevert. Norah Tyrrell, better known as 'Mrs T', did the timing and the catering and was a great pillar of the team; Derek Gardner was the designer; Neil Davies looked after the workshops and did the buying; Keith Boshier, a real glassfibre artist, did the bodywork; and Peter Turland made the monocoques. Roger Hill and Roland Law were the chief mechanics, Roy Topp looked after Jackie's car, while I was employed to look after François's car alongside Robin Coleman.

1972 wasn't as good for the team as 1971, although we started well, winning the first race in Argentina and finishing second in the World Championship. Lotus and Emerson Fittipaldi were very strong that year, but we also had a run of bad luck. At Monaco we felt that Jackie could have definitely won since it was one of the wettest races ever, but he battled with the extra-wide Ferrari of Clay Regazzoni, spun a couple of times and then, as he was closing on Jean-Pierre Beltoise and Jacky Ickx, the spark plugs got wet; after stopping to change them he only managed fourth place. From that race on every Cosworth engine carried rubber inserts for the cylinder plugholes, specially designed and made by Roger Hill, the most meticulous and creative chief mechanic I've ever come across and a real joy to work with.

Jackie missed the Belgian Grand Prix at Nivelles because of health problems, won at Clermont-Ferrand in France, and was second behind Emerson at Brands Hatch. But the races that I particularly remember took place during the last trip of the year, to Canada and the USA. All the teams used to travel in the same plane and have pillow battles between front and back, but nowadays one top team could almost fill the whole plane! During such 'flyaway' races we used to organise tennis matches, golf tournaments, bowling competitions and a piss-up in the local bar afterwards.

This year we won in the Canadian Grand Prix at Mosport, and in between races Roy Topp won the golf tournament and I won the bowling. Then Stewart and Cevert put the gold seal on Tyrrell Team domination by finishing first and second in the American Grand Prix at Watkins Glen.

Normally, in flyaway races, we had to use some very bizarre locations for a paddock, such as a tent or an old aircraft hangar, where all the teams squeezed in like sardines as we prepared the cars. One day Ken Tyrrell was pumping five gallons of fuel into Jackie's car as he'd always done, but the improvised workshop was obviously not earthed and Ken was wearing a nylon shirt. The resulting spark sent the place up like a ball of fire! But one thing that all race mechanics have is good instant reactions, and just about one man from every team leapt to the scene with a fire extinguisher. As we were clearing up the ashes and checking the damage, good old Rob Walker, another great character of our sport, ambled up to Ken and in his inimitable BBC accent said, "I say, Ken, are you taking part in the end of the year golf match at Wentworth?" Ken turned round and gave Rob one of his famous 'froth and spit' jobs: "For Christ's sake Rob, could you pick a better time?"

The last race of the year is always the best one to win. As they say in so many sports, and particularly in Formula One, "you're only as good as your last result", so winning the last race keeps you going until the first one next year.

Though we didn't win the season's opening race in 1973 we finished second and third to Emerson Fittipaldi's Lotus 72 in Argentina. We always had a very friendly and healthy rivalry with the Lotus team, on and off the circuits – our water battles at the Autodromo restaurant were legendary. The waiters used to provide us with ammunition in the form of soda siphons under the table. I loved going to Buenos Aires, the people were great, the women were the best in the world, and combined with the food and the tango music it soon become the circus's favourite Grand Prix.

The second race was at Interlagos in São Paulo and Emerson and Lotus were on a roll, but I have to say that I didn't mind coming second, as watching Emerson starting his last lap was one of the greatest shows of patriotism that I've ever seen or will ever see again. The Brazilian fans were standing on their seats throwing paper streamers and yelling, forming the biggest human wave you've ever seen, almost as if it had been rehearsed beforehand. It was a joy to watch.

Lotus and Tyrrell were always close to one another in the paddock or on the race track, and I remember a time when I was working on the gearbox and Colin Chapman came to me and said, "Jo, come in and have a coffee with us." Colin was England's Enzo Ferrari and when he said jump, you jumped! He asked me how we prevented the big nuts on the pinion and layshaft in the gearbox from undoing themselves: the Lotus guys had tried split-pins, which always broke – and when that happens the nuts get loose, the gears move, and you're history! Perhaps I should have said, "Well, Colin, that's for us to know and for you to guess..." But being a puritan 'racer' and not wishing to alienate Colin Chapman in the small world of F1 racing, I told him to tell his crew to forget the split-pins, but to clean the nuts with acetone and spread 'Loctite' on the threads. Can you imagine this episode happening now, between Ron Dennis and a Ferrari mechanic?

In later years, Colin Chapman asked me to come to the Team Lotus HQ in Norfolk, as he had an interesting proposition for me. He showed me the factory and offered me a job, but what he needed was someone to look after the factory-based team and I wasn't interested. Once a racing man, always a racing man. But it was great to be asked, remembering my earlier days when I knocked on the Lotus door begging for a job; now I was 'big enough' to say thanks, but no thanks.

Stewart won in South Africa, Belgium and Monaco, where he was a specialist, but this year – unlike 1972 – everything was going his way. Towards the end of the Monaco Grand Prix he'd built up a good lead on Emerson, who was trying everything he knew to catch the Scot. Jackie, for some reason unknown to us in the pits, had started to slow down towards the end. Emerson was coming up behind him fast and furious, and as there were no radios in the cockpit in those days Ken was getting more and more nervous until, finally, the flag dropped with Emerson just a second behind, to the great relief of the whole team. It wasn't until Jackie came back from the podium that he explained to us that, knowing Emerson had the 'record' for damaged wheels in practice for the race, he'd been allowing him to mount a challenge in the hope that perhaps he'd touch a guardrail and damage another wheel, to make it Fittipaldi *nul points*.

After the 1973 French Grand Prix at Paul Ricard, we had one of the greatest team parties that I remember from my long career in the sport. We were sponsored by Elf, the mighty French fuel and oil company, whose sporting director was François Guiter, who helped the sport enormously in addition to being a great character. Formula One needs a lot more people like him. On this occasion he organised a dinner party at the smart hotel where only the top drivers and sponsors stayed, the Île Rousse, in the coastal village of Bandol. The night was hot and beautiful, the setting around the pool and the music were idyllic, but just as we were finishing the dessert the mechanics felt that it was time to liven up the party. This was unfortunate for Graham Bell of Goodyear, as he was the closest to the pool and therefore became the first victim. From then on, one after the other went the way of Graham, but when we got to François Guiter – a big man, in a Giorgio Armani suit – he dived into the pool like a mermaid. It was really the only thing he could do, having been one of the biggest instigators of the 'livening-up'. Somehow I managed to stay dry.

But it was the week where we had back-to-back races in Holland and Germany which truly stood out in my memory that year. We were 1–2 at Zandvoort and then again the following Sunday at the Nürburgring. At Zandvoort I witnessed the tremendous bond that existed between Stewart and François Cevert. François practically worshipped Jackie, and was very happy to finish second, learning from the master and patiently waiting for his turn.

Jackie missed a gear coming out of the big hairpin at Tarzan, and François had to brake hard in order to avoid hitting him, and then tucked himself behind again. As soon as the race finished, Jackie leapt out of his car and, coming over to François as he came to a halt in the *parc fermé*, put his head over the cockpit and said: "You stupid idiot, why didn't you pass me? I made a mistake! It was your race." François simply replied that it wasn't the way he wanted to win, he wanted to beat Jackie fair and square, not because he'd made a mistake but because he himself had been quicker.

There was also another incident that would have made me remember the Grand Prix at Zandvoort that year: during practice we heard that François Cevert had lost a wheel, so I took a wheel spanner and went to race control and sat in one of the pace cars waiting for the end of practice so that I could be taken to where

François's car was. I was hoping to be able to fix it to be driven back to the pits, but suddenly, five minutes before the end of practice, the red flag appeared: an accident had occurred on the circuit. Practice stopped, and off we went in the pace car...

I had no idea what was happening, I just sat on the car and was driven to the site of the accident. To my astonishment it was Emerson Fittipaldi's Lotus, trapped on the fastest corner of the circuit in the middle of a tangle of catchfencing poles and wire. When I got out of the pace car I was even more horrified to see that Emerson was still in the car, unable to get out as his feet were squashed between the pedals and the front bulkhead of the Lotus. I couldn't believe that all around him people were just looking, without making the least attempt to free him, and as I got closer I realised that he was in agony and was worried that the car would ignite, as all the fluids were dripping into the hot parts of the engine. I was just so glad to have the wheel spanner with me, and proceeded to lever up the various pieces of metal in order to get him out. This I managed to do, and Emerson was free and out of the wreckage; I didn't do anything more than any other man in my situation would have done, but Emerson was forever grateful.

Next day in the race came the terrible accident of Roger Williams, where his car turned over on fire and hundreds of thousands of TV viewers saw David Purley, in desperation, frantically trying to turn the car over on his own, with no help from the hundreds of spectators in that area. I wasn't surprised, as I'd seen the same thing happen the day before, when no one had helped Emerson. I just prayed that I never had an accident in Holland!

Jackie finished second to Ronnie Peterson in the other Lotus on the Osterreichring in Austria, and then came the Italian Grand Prix at Monza, where he was in a position to secure his third World Championship. He qualified fifth, but his engine dropped a valve during the race morning warm-up. Ken Tyrrell, who seldom took chances – especially on a race that could settle the championship – decided to go for a used and proven engine which we were carrying in the transporter. It had been Cevert's engine in the Austrian GP, but still had enough miles left to complete a race.

When François learned about Ken's decision to install his used engine he completely lost his cool. He went straight up to Ken, shouting, "You cannot do this, you cannot fit that engine, it was a complete dog. This is a very important race for Jackie and you're going to ruin it for him!" But Ken was adamant that we should fit a proven engine, since Cosworth had had a batch of suspect valves, so that was the engine we fitted, even though François wasn't at all happy.

In the race, Jackie kept his qualifying position until the seventh lap, when he came into the pits with a left rear puncture and more or less caught us with our pants down. We made a complete balls-up of the pitstop, and Jackie restarted in 18th place. From then on he drove like the champion he was, breaking the lap record several times and gradually eating his way through the pack. He needed to be fourth to clinch the championship, and on lap 49 – six laps before the end – he caught and passed François into fourth. It was then, within sight of Peter Revson in third place, that he made his last lap record of the race, almost a second faster than his own qualifying time.

After the race, I was asked by Franco Lini – then the leading Italian motorsport correspondent – to go to the press room to assist with translations. François was also present, looking very reserved and introverted and uncharacteristically silent. He was pleased for Jackie, but I could guess what was going on in his mind: he had a good car, a strong engine, he drove as fast as he could, he'd seen Jackie slowed down by a lazy tyre change, but still saw him get bigger in his mirrors and then pass him for his third World Championship. All this with an engine that he knew to be well underpowered, on a power-dominated circuit. He had enough reasons to be feeling down. As we said goodbye, I told him to cheer up and put it all down to experience. Jackie had at least half-a-dozen years on him and François had all the time in the world to learn from the Master. Sadly I was wrong. He didn't live long enough to cash in on all he had learned from Jackie.

The 1973 Italian GP and the 1968 Nürburgring, where he won by over four minutes, were perhaps Jackie's greatest races. To be able to catch the leaders on a circuit like Monza, before the introduction of chicanes where perhaps you could gain on other drivers, was nothing short of remarkable.

Then came the last two races of the year. We'd excelled in the United States and Canada last year and we were looking forward to returning. Mosport Park wasn't the ideal circuit and this year the race had the most bizarre ending I've ever seen, with three drivers – Emerson Fittipaldi, Peter Revson and Jackie Oliver – all standing on the podium claiming to be the winner!

The race started on a wet track, and everyone started on rain or intermediate tyres. But by the time the race was quarter-way through the pit lane had become very busy, with everyone rushing in for tyre changes. We even had the two Tyrrells in the pit for service on the same lap. Oops! This was an occurrence dreaded by every team. Soon after, Cevert collided with Scheckter's McLaren and this immediately brought out the pace car, but in front of Howden Ganley's Iso-Marlboro (the first Formula One car built by Frank Williams) instead of the real leader, as the officials were clearly confused. Howden must have had a smile from ear to ear and could hardly keep the car on the road after the pace car pulled off, as he was pushing like a real winner!

At the end of the race, Colin Chapman threw the traditional cap in the air as Emerson went by, thinking he'd won. But the flag man didn't wave the flag for Fittipaldi, but waved it at the next bunch of cars together, thinking for sure that one of these most be the winner! Clearly neither he nor the officials had any idea. McLaren were convinced that Revson had won, while Shadow's lap chart showed Oliver as the winner.

As you can imagine, the rest of us, without a stake in the outcome (as Jackie wasn't in the leading bunch), and even Howden Ganley's Williams crew, thought this was hilarious, and everyone was making jokes about it. A few hours later, after the officials had gathered all the information to hand, including the contesting teams' lap charts, they came up with the following order: Revson, Fittipaldi, Oliver. This, of course, would never happen (sadly!) in these days of fully computerised, idiot-proof systems.

'My' Tyrrell car was badly damaged in François's collision with Jody, and ended up hitting the guardrail head on at a hundred miles an hour. I was amazed that he managed to walk out of it with only strained tendons in his legs, as the top of the spaceframe aluminium monocoque was well over a foot below the bottom of

77

the chassis, and the steering wheel was bent 45 degrees from where he'd held on during the impact. He was taken to hospital for checks and dressings on his legs, and when I visited him that evening he showed me the two wide bruises indented in his chest and shoulders by the webbing of his safety harness.

Over the following days, Ken, Norah Tyrrell, Jackie, François and all the team went on a mini holiday to Niagara Falls on the way down to Watkins Glen for the last Grand Prix of the year, and Jackie, myself and the rest of the team took turns at carrying François around in order to hasten the mending of his legs ready for the next weekend!

When we arrived in Watkins Glen a new chassis had arrived via New York and was waiting for us to build up. Sadly it wasn't built up for long, as on the Saturday morning practice, when he was fourth fastest, François lost control at the fast esses before the straight. The car brushed the guardrail on the right and then slammed across the circuit into the left guardrail, where the chassis smashed into two parts. It finished on top of the guardrail, and the impact was so severe that François died instantly of massive injuries.

When the accident happened, I remember the place went very silent. The other cars started to come back slowly to the pits, and it was then I realised that someone had crashed – and François wasn't back. I panicked and ran to jump on a service vehicle that was just leaving the pit-lane for the scene of the crash, but Jody Scheckter leapt forward and grabbed me, saying, "Don't go, there's nothing you can do." He'd stopped to try to help but had come back with tears in his eyes.

After the accident Ken reluctantly asked us to go and see the remains of the car, which was at a garage in the village, to see if we could establish whether anything had broken which could have caused the accident. Roger Hill, Roland Law and I went down to see the car and I got sick when we saw bits of François all over it. But perhaps the worst thing was having to go to his room and gather all his clothes, case, agenda wallet, passport, return ticket and so on.

His death was a terrible shock. François was a man to whom it was difficult not to be close and attached. He was so full of life, loved by women. He looked more like a film star or rich playboy than a racing driver, but he was indeed a very serious racing driver. A man of many talents, beside his looks, natural charm and driving skills he was an accomplished pianist. Only the night before he'd played the piano at the Seneca Lodge, the popular place to stay, a hotel *cum* motel *cum* pub *cum* restaurant where everybody used to meet after rebuilding days, or practice days, for food and drink and *camaraderie*. François had played the Mexican Hat Dance, which I danced with Colin Chapman's secretary.

He had a very personal way of explaining situations. I remember talking to him at Monza, about which he'd say, "Taking the Curva Grande flat-out is not a question of bravery, it's a question of decision. Once you'd made the decision and taken it flat, your balls – which were up around your neck at the time – returned to their original position and you'd always take it flat again!" He taught me how to make a hand-brake turn in tight places without hitting anything.

There was something very spooky about François's accident. It happened on October 6, his race car number was 6, the chassis was 006, and the engine number was 066. But I've never been superstitious and I don't think that François was. However, when we returned to the UK and Ken sent the engine to Cosworths to be checked for any abnormalities, the engine men disassembled it and placed the engine block onto the workbench. Suddenly they saw this large, heavy lump of aluminium moving from the bench through the air and then smashing onto the floor. The mechanics called Keith Duckworth immediately and Keith related the story to Ken, adding that he wasn't about to believe the tale. He did say, however, that from the faces of the two astonished mechanics he had to believe that something had happened, almost as if François was trying to say something!

François had been more than ready to step into Jackie's shoes, to take over as the Tyrrell number one. Unfortunately he never knew that Jackie was going to retire that weekend. This was a very close-kept secret between Jackie and Ken. However, Jackie unwittingly gave me a hint as I was doing up his belts on the Friday. Knowing that I collected steering wheels, he said, "Is this the steering wheel that I've been using all this year?" I confirmed that it was the one. "OK, well I'd like to keep it if you don't mind…" "Well," I replied, "I think that could be arranged – at a price, of course."

Hearing this, and seeing the way that Jody Scheckter showed such concern towards me and towards Tyrrell over the weekend, it was easy to put two and two together and guess that Jackie was retiring and that Jody was to come in as number two to François. This would have been nothing less than a super team. As it was, the Tyrrell Team naturally withdrew from the race meeting, and Jackie stood by his decision to retire. The 1973 USA Grand Prix would have been his hundredth Grand Prix.

Now Ken had to replace François as well as Jackie, and in addition to Jody we got Patrick Depailler, who'd already made sporadic appearances with Tyrrell, starting at Clermont-Ferrand (his native town) in 1972, where he didn't arrive until five minutes after practice had started! The local boy had been caught up in a traffic jam – not the best way to start your F1 career. He was a very likeable young chap who was, unfortunately, his own worst enemy, as he was constantly breaking some part of his body in stupid hang-gliding accidents, or flying solo without wings! He was just a crazy man, always looking for danger, where he was at his best.

1974 wasn't a good season for Tyrrell. Jackie and François had left such an enormous gap that was very difficult to fill. The continuity had been lost, as Jody and Patrick just didn't have the experience to carry the team. Jody was proud of winning the accolade from the press of being the least co-operative driver in Formula One, but I sometimes felt that he was not particularly co-operative with his own team either, purely because of his introverted character.

At the start of the season we were nowhere, but slowly we gathered momentum. Patrick was fourth at Kyalami in South Africa, Jody was fifth in Spain, third in Belgium, and second at Monaco; and then for some reason we swept the board with a 1–2 in Sweden, with Jody crossing the line just ahead of Patrick. Jody soon fitted into the Tyrrell family and became a great member, winning the British GP and coming second in Germany and third in Italy. I remember that, as we were picking up the trophy from

Signore Tavoni, manager of the Autodromo de Monza who'd helped me early in my life, he said to Ken, as he shook my hand, "Ken, you have a wonderful team."

As we walked back to the garage, Ken said, "Ha! A wonderful team... and you're leaving." He knew already that I'd decided to go to Fittipaldi as team manager at the end of the season, but he was my number one supporter. When I left, he gathered all the team together, made a very moving speech, and gave me the trophy that François Cevert had won in Holland, second to Stewart; in his opinion it had been François's finest race. He also told me not to hesitate to go to him if I ever needed help, advice or guidance in my role as manager with a new team. I took him at his word and often conferred with him on important issues, and I always sat next to him during the frequent FOCA meetings.

I was particularly honoured to be asked the following year to be the mystery Father Christmas at the Tyrrell Christmas party in a Ripley restaurant, a task normally performed by the incoming race driver. I had a complete suit and beard and bought an electronic 'Ho! Ho! Ho!' box which I kept switching on and off – otherwise, if I spoke, it would have given the game away instantly.

Ken was a wonderful boss. I've never stopped patting my own back for having decided to approach him for a job. It was the most fantastic experience I'd ever had and I now felt more than ever prepared to handle a team manager's job. I knew now how to get the best from people, how to motivate them, how to make them feel wanted, how to create a happy atmosphere, how to approach problems in the most practical way – and how not to lose touch with reality.

Ken always joked with his drivers by saying that the easiest thing to change on a racing car was – the driver! He had a wonderful way of easing pressure when things were going wrong and of remotivating people. I remember him telling Jackie once, when he came into the pits in practice complaining bitterly about the car, "Ha! You think you have problems? England is 119 for 6 at Lords!" He was an avid cricket fan all his life.

But as Martin Brundle, one of his drivers, said with great affection, "Ken didn't only teach us about racing, he taught us about life. He was a wonderful tutor, he saw life in a deeper colour than the rest of us, and when he spoke those around him listened." His nickname changed from 'Chopper' to 'Uncle Ken' and he was admired by everyone in the racing world.

Perhaps the single thing that says buckets about the man was the presentation of his six-wheeler Tyrrell car, Project 34. It's a well-known fact that nothing is ever kept secret in Grand Prix racing, yet never a word got out about a car that took months to complete, with 40–50 people involved in it as well as outside contractors making the wheels, tyres, dampers, springs, brakes etc that had to be specially produced. So on 22 September 1975 the motor racing world was shocked by the sudden appearance of the new car. That's how much loyalty Ken inspired in his workers: they didn't even tell their own wives what they were building.

I was happy to attend the last Tyrrell Reunion Party to which Ken was able to go, on 24 March 2001, and was lucky enough to be at his table. He was a bit fragile but still well enough to give me a 'froth' lecture on what we (McLaren) should have done to beat the Ferraris at the previous two races, in Australia and Malaysia. I said to him that if he was going to come to any races this year he should choose Indianapolis, for my retirement party, and he replied that if he was well enough he'd certainly be there. Sadly, as I was driving to the Silverstone Historic Festival on 25 August I heard on the radio that he'd finally lost his fight with cancer and had left us. The BRDC Club House at Silverstone was a very subdued place, where once Ken had dominated the conversation.

On 15 November 2001 a memorial service took place at Guildford Cathedral to celebrate the life of Ken Tyrrell, and I'll never forgive myself for arriving late and not being able to sit in our reserved seats. It was the most moving event, a gathering of the great and the good of the motor racing world, organised by Jackie Stewart and the BRDC, with a Royal Air Force band and Dame Kiri Te Kanawa, who sang Richard Strauss's 'Morgen' as only she could, and the Chris Barber Jazz Band playing two more of Ken's favourites, the 'Panama Rag' and, at the end 'When The Saints Go Marching In'. A truly remarkable occasion.

I feel extremely privileged to have worked for such a man, and, along with everyone else fortunate enough to have been associated with Uncle Ken, I'll treasure those years forever.

As well as everything I learned from Ken, the added bonus of being involved with one of the greatest motor racing drivers of all time was immeasurable. Jackie Stewart was one of the most inspirational men I ever had the pleasure of working with, a man that I could only describe as the greatest ambassador the sport has ever seen.

People often talk about who has been the greatest racing driver of all time, something that is almost impossible to pinpoint, and one can only go by decades or eras. But I've seen Stewart crash at 150mph at Woodcote Corner at Silverstone while he was fastest in practice, and then get into his teammate's 11th-placed car and put it on pole! Now that takes some doing. Winning at the Nürburgring in 1968 by more than four minutes, on a day when visibility was scarcely 70m, he reached 170mph on the straight. With the intensity of the rain and the treacherousness of the circuit, this was just a crazy business, a race that today would never even have been started. I just wonder if the Sennas and Schumachers of this world would have been able to do that.

As a man, his life speaks for itself. He's a very wise businessman, extremely generous, and always willing to help. We always had a Christmas present from him – once a Rolex watch, another time premium bonds – and if you were out with him, he'd never let you put your hand in your pocket. He formed the Grand Prix Mechanics Trust in the days when no proper insurances existed within the teams to look after them in case of racing accidents or poverty later in life, and he's helped countless racing mechanics in need. I was honoured in 2001 to be asked by him to become one of the trustees of the organisation.

I've always envied his uncanny memory. He could meet someone one day then see them again 20 years later and still remember his face, name, and where and when they met. The fact that he was never lost for words must have proved an invaluable attribute too, that has no doubt served him well during all the ambassadorial appointments he's had since he hung up his helmet, for Ford, Jaguar, Rolex, Elf, Goodyear and the Royal Bank of Scotland to mention but a few. I remember him once saying, "I don't understand drivers these days. They're offered £10,000 to go and do a 30-minute talk somewhere, and they won't do it ... Well,

I'm happy to go and do it and I laugh all the way to the bank." But I think that the real reason the average driver won't do it is that he doesn't have the gift of the gab that Jackie has.

He's always said that he was handicapped by the fact that he's dyslexic, but he has hundreds of other attributes that make up for it. Probably his biggest achievement as a racing businessman was the creation of Team Stewart Grand Prix with his son Paul in 1997. The backing was mainly from the Ford Motor Company, and by 1999, when he decided to sell, the team had achieved one pole and one win, with a fourth place in the Constructors' Championship. Ford bought the outfit for a rumoured $60 million. When I congratulated Jackie on the deal he whispered in my ear that the media often got things wrong, but that it was a very good deal indeed. A year later the team changed its name to Jaguar, and Jackie remained as a consultant and figurehead.

CHAPTER 7

THE BOYS FROM BRAZIL

In 1974, after the disastrous rain-affected Brazilian Grand Prix, 12 cars were invited to the new circuit in Brasilia for a non-championship GP, and Ken Tyrrell decided to take Jody Scheckter and four mechanics including myself.

As we arrived in the city, I was driving the rent-a-car with Ken and Jody Scheckter on board, and it was one of those rainy Brazilian days. As we passed the circuit, Ken said, "Let's see if it's open. We might as well go for a lap to see how it looks." I can't remember what kind of car I was driving, but it was a big American job and I didn't have to be told twice to go for a lap, although Ken said to take it easy. Yeah, right...

I remembered the wet-weather driving lessons I'd had back home in Mexico all those years before, in Ricardo Rodriguez's gold Oldsmobile. "You're talking to a frustrated racing driver," I said, just as Jody in the back seat shouted, "Yeah, go for it Jo."

I don't know what it was, maybe the car was good or the tyres were great, but I certainly had a ball. I went for two laps with my foot on the floorboards, correcting, scraping and losing speed with the steering wheel without ever putting a wheel off the road, and feeling very proud of myself. Ken was holding on to anything he could find and 'braking hard' in the passenger seat, while Jody was moving from side to side in the back shouting, "I love it, I love it, faster, faster!" As we finished the inspection and Ken recovered his breath, he said in that inimitable way of his that I was in the wrong job. But Jody promptly added, "No, no, he'd better stay as a mechanic!"

Although the Brasilia circuit wasn't quite finished it was raceable, but I just didn't like the place at all and couldn't wait to get out of it. I'm pleased that this was the only race here, because, much as I love Brazil, I didn't like this place at all. They tried to make a new city in the middle of nowhere, and it didn't work. It may have been Nelson Piquet's kind of town, but it certainly wasn't mine. After the race, in which Jody finished second to Emerson, we returned to São Paulo and all went to the beach in Guaruja for couple of days off while the cars were travelling back home.

I'd often spoken with Emerson Fittipaldi about his ambition to make and race a Brazilian Formula One car, together with his brother Wilson, but this time they invited me to dinner and it was then, over *caipirinhas* (the local 40 per cent proof *pinga* drink) and *feijoda* (a local dish of pork, beans, rice and orange), that they disclosed their plans. The car was being made in Brazil and was well on the way to being completed: the team would be based in São Paulo but would eventually move to a British base for the European season. The president and managing director of Fittipaldi Emprendimentos (the company) was Wilson Fittipaldi. The designer was Richard Divila, a guy born in Brazil from a British mother and a Czechoslovakian father, and a long-time friend, mechanic and guru of the Fittipaldis. Chief mechanic was a Japanese, Yoshiatsu Itoh, who'd been Emerson's mechanic with JPS Lotus. The team would run only one car at first with Wilson driving, and Emerson would be staying on at McLaren.

They thought that I'd fit in well with the team because of my experience, my languages, and the fact that, being of Latin origin, I'd understand the way in which they wanted to work, as the rest of the team would be Brazilian. I was offered the job of team manager. Happy as I was at Tyrrell, this was an opportunity that had to be considered carefully, as it was a step up the ladder, and whether the team was successful or not, the experience that I'd gain in management would be invaluable – and I could always go back to the spanners if need be!

A couple of weeks later, when we got back to Europe, I told them that I'd take the job and would join them after the last race of the season, as was agreed beforehand. My one regret was that I should've asked for more money than I was offered, but, as ever, I didn't want to appear greedy. By God did I earn every little penny

I got! They must have felt proud of their best deal! A few years later I remember making comparisons and converting the money I used to make then in *cruzeiros* into the new *reis*, and then into pounds sterling: a month's wages wouldn't buy a pint of milk! Brazil was a lovely country, but I always wonder how the people still managed to smile and *samba* after so many political upheavals and economic crises.

The Fittipaldi team and car were presented towards the end of October 1974 in Brasilia, in the presence of the Brazilian President, all the big cats from the government and, of course, our sponsors – Copersucar, the Brazilian sugar co-operative, who controlled the marketing for all the independent sugar producers in the country. Together with coffee these are Brazil's two major exports. Without a doubt, this was the golden era of the Fittipaldi heritage: Emerson had just won his second World Championship in a McLaren and the brothers had just announced their ambitious plans. Their future was rosy and their spirits at their highest.

This was also my introduction to the team and the first time that I saw the car, naturally prettied up in show form. I was pleasantly surprised by the car – except for the body, as the glassfibre work left a lot to be desired. It was an incredibly revolutionary design for a newcomer to such a competitive business. Richard Divila didn't copy the Formula One cars available from the family collection in São Paulo, that would have been too easy. Instead he just took some layout tips on suspension and monocoque construction and cleverly incorporated extra suspension points in case they were needed. However, as far as the aerodynamics were concerned he had his own ideas, for which he largely drew on the help of the Brazilian aircraft company Embraer, which always gave the Fittipaldis great support. The car had fully enclosed bodywork (it didn't have an airbox like all the other F1 cars, but one which was placed under the rollover bar); the water and oil radiators were mounted at the far end; and the driver was lying in a much more reclined position than normal. It was the forerunner of the later 'Coca Cola bottle' shaped cars that were later to become ubiquitous.

Richard was a very clever and practical man with a brilliant brain and a wide knowledge of every subject, in addition to being fluent in six languages. His drawings weren't wonderful, but his ideas were. He lacked organisation, but given good and solid guidance he'd have gone on to much greater things. Nowadays he's the chief engineer of the Sports Competition Department of Nissan in Japan and has won numerous championships in the All-Japan GT and Super Touring track racing classes; but without a doubt he remained far too long under the Fittipaldi umbrella, and in my view he wasn't recognised sufficiently for his efforts.

He was assisted by Odilon da Costa, a very young and extremely gifted Brazilian. Odilon did all the drawings and every one of them was a work of art; he also made very detailed three-dimensional views, which were great for the construction and assembly of the car. In later years I tried to find him to take him to England, as he would be a great asset to any team, but unfortunately I heard that he'd taken a different route and become a laid-back hippie! A great loss to the motor racing world.

The rest of the team were all young locals, hard workers and extremely enthusiastic: Tommy, a brother of Suzy Fittipaldi, Wilson's wife, was the administrator; the mechanics, led by Itoh, were Darci, Joel, Gilberto and Luis Enrique. Together with Wilson, Richard and myself, we spent endless days and nights at our base just outside the Interlagos race circuit. Wilson was a great motivator and always full of fun; as friends we got on fine, although at work we had great fights. He had a typical Latin volatile character, often losing his cool. Emerson was always the mediator.

The problems were endless. From the start we had enormous battles with the customs and government officials, because all the materials that came from abroad – like engines, gearboxes, fuel tanks, brakes and so on – were detained by customs for weeks without a real reason. I felt frustrated. Here we were trying to push a project which would bring enormous exposure to Brazil throughout the whole world, and yet we received no consideration whatsoever. Even with big names like Copersucar and Fittipaldi involved the authorities remained blind and oblivious towards the project. But then again, bureaucrats have always been short-sighted. This made me so angry that often I exploded and spoke to the press, who were naturally following all our moves, but this also created some problems between Wilson and me.

We started testing in December 1974 with very little co-operation from the weather, but our worst enemy was the car's fuel system, which took ages to correct, and together with the erratic cooling system created a lot of animosity between the overworked and overtired members of the team. At one point I closed my desk, presented my resignation and disappeared for a couple of days, but, being near Christmas, the season of goodwill, we got together again thanks to Richard and Emerson, who always managed to calm Wilson after the storms.

During the critical points of our crises, Emerson and I used to suggest different solutions as we'd have done at McLaren or Tyrrell, but Wilson used to jump up angrily, shouting, "This isn't McLaren or Tyrrell, those are other teams, this is Fittipaldi and things here are not the same!" The family nicknames were *Rato* (mouse) for Emerson and *Tigrao* (tiger) for Wilson! Such conflicts normally lasted for a day, followed by laughs the next, when the mouse had finally managed to tame the tiger.

Then came the delivery of the team car transporter, which was proudly built by a local Brazilian firm and was going to take the car to Argentina for its first race. I swear to God, that, when I saw it, I didn't know whether to laugh or cry! It was definitely not a Formula One race car transporter, it was a tractor. Where they could have used a one-eighth of an inch plate, they used an inch. It was grotesque, it was horrible, but I had to be polite – they'd spent a lot of money and they were proud of it. We were going to Buenos Aires and therefore we were going to be the only team with a truck, as the European teams came by plane with everything packed in boxes, so every eye would be on it and I was going to be very ashamed of it.

Thankfully, with a lot of diplomacy and treading carefully, I managed to convince them that the 'truck' should stay in São Paulo and never come with us to England. Perhaps it helped that the very first time the tail lift was used, the cable snapped due to the weight of the tailgate and the whole thing fell down! Luckily nobody was standing under it at the time. Richard and I have had a lifelong aversion to standing under tail lifts after that.

Argentina did cry for us! The race in Buenos Aires was an horrendous start of the season, as if we hadn't already had enough punishment during building, planning and testing. Due to a suspension failure (so he swore), Wilson lost control on the 12th lap, crashed, and the car burst into flames, but he was OK. We returned to São Paulo with a half-demolished, half-burnt car and the longest job list ever created in the history of motor racing. Luckily, by then the Formula One bug had hit the whole team, the adrenaline was high and we were more ready and determined to face the challenge ahead.

The 1975 Brazilian Grand Prix at Interlagos was the second race of the season and, needless to say, the most important for our new team, and naturally we'd have preferred it if it could've been the last, as we'd be highly scrutinised by everyone. However, we managed to come in 13th, which was at least a finish.

To say that my years at Fittipaldi were happy ones would be a slight departure from the truth, but I'd made the choice, and I was going to make it work and see it through for as long as I could. I knew that things would improve when we moved to England – and they needed to, as even my health was suffering; I developed an ulcer and I started losing my hair!

The first job in England was to find a workshop, and even though the Fittipaldis wanted a state-of-the-art factory it wasn't possible to drink champagne on a beer income. I managed to find a small warehouse in Caversham near Reading owned by a friend of mine, Richie Bray, who ran a waste-disposal business and was a racing enthusiast.

There were lot of different chores to complete, like finding more personnel, a proper racing car transporter, companies to make our bodywork, machinists, and even a house to rent for the Fittipaldi family, in addition to being ready to go to South Africa for the third race in the calendar. Despite all the arduous work and testing at Interlagos and having improved the speed of the car by more than a second, we failed to qualify in Kyalami.

In the ever-increasing quest to save money, my wife Bea became my secretary in the mornings, and we found that we got on like a house on fire, as no one knew me better than her; I only had to say I needed to write to so and so for this and that, and she'd compose the perfect letter that always got results. Later on she used to come to races, and got quite good at timing all the cars with a single watch, and on race day she'd do the lap chart. In between practices she made the sandwiches for the mechanics. These were chores that she also did in later years, while I was at Shadow, ATS and Theodore – until electronic Longines timekeeping and plush motorhomes arrived, and then she felt like a spare part with no participation in the team. She hated that, and never came with me to a race again.

Our first race in Europe was the unfortunate Spanish GP at Montjuich Park in Barcelona, where the safety standards were very poor. Emerson, still racing with McLaren, decided to withdraw as a protest. Wilson, of course, followed his brother's lead, and we watched the race from our pits, which were the closest to the horrendous accident involving the Hill of Rolf Stommelen, who was leading the race for Graham Hill's team. Just as it passed the pits its rear wing support failed and the wing flew off, sending the car into the air and over the guardrail into the crowd.

Wilson and I were the first ones to arrive on the scene, which was horrendous – blood and bodies everywhere, with panic, tears and shouting. We immediately went to help the man we knew, Rolf, who'd broken his legs. Wilson was absolutely brilliant, helping Rolf and restoring order amongst the people and calming them. I was shocked by the whole accident. I tried to help an injured fire marshal and make him comfortable, but soon realised that he had no pulse and I was useless from then on until the ambulance arrived and got the injured aboard. Four other people also died.

The rest of the year was as expected: if and when we qualified it was at the very back, and we occasionally finished at the back too. But we moved to better premises in the Slough Trading Estate and generally improved our act and our image. The new car was a more conventional one, in which Richard had incorporated the lessons learned by a year at the deep end, and it did look very good. Our sponsors were patient and they even insisted on a second car, so we tested a young Brazilian, Ingo Hoffman, who was a champion saloon car driver and runner-up in the Super Vee Championship, and was racing in Europe in Formula 3. He surprised everyone by running almost a second quicker than Wilson, and Ingo was promoted to Formula One.

As Ingo returned to Brazil, Emerson was visiting our new headquarters and was very impressed with what he saw of the new car. When Emerson returned to Brazil he hadn't yet signed his new contract with Marlboro Texaco McLaren, and he was invited by Copersucar to test our new car in case McLaren wanted to negotiate for less money than previously agreed. Copersucar agreed to pay the extra that we needed to develop a car for a World Champion, and in November 1975 Emerson Fittipaldi shook the motor racing world by dropping a bombshell and signing with his own team. While the rest of the team managers were saying, "Well, at least we won't have to worry about Emerson in 1976," I suddenly found myself the manager of a double World Champion,

I couldn't for my life begin to imagine what this would mean – besides doubling the work, as we were entering two cars. I didn't know if we'd be able to give Emerson the means and organisational level that he'd been accustomed to, let alone provide him with a competitive car. Work has never frightened me, and the opportunity to have a proper racing driver on board was an unbelievable boost for the whole team. Wilson would now concentrate on the administration of the team and the bringing in of new sponsors.

The new car was taken to Brazil to be presented to the national press. The Argentinean Grand Prix was cancelled, so the race on our home track at the Interlagos circuit would be the first of the year, in January. In the first open tests with the new car Emerson managed to shut a few mouths and make those other managers worry about him again by turning the best ever lap at Interlagos. Our faces had never looked so good: there were smiles all round as, finally, the long hard effort was starting to pay off.

Emerson was a bit of a keep-fit fanatic, as most of the drivers were starting to be, and went mad with training and exercising – to the point where he damaged an arm, so that by the time official practice arrived he was in constant pain and was only able to do a few laps. This wasn't too much of a concern, as we'd done dozens of laps previously without the slightest problem, but obviously we wanted to put the car on pole. The first day we were third and the second day fifth and this was the high spot of the team's weekend. During the race, although Emerson was fourth on the first lap, an electrical misfire started and the car began to sound like a Brazilian coffee pot. He lost places every lap and finished 13th, with Hoffman 11th in the old car.

The next race was the South African, at the Kyalami circuit, and then I saw the real Fittipaldi, as a team owner rather than just a driver. He tried to be a car designer himself, and to dictate the design specifications needed for the race. "Kyalami is a different type of circuit. You need a car with a longer wheelbase and a wider track...", and he made us modify the whole car, when as far as Richard and I were concerned a car that handled well at Interlagos would handle well on 99 per cent of circuits.

So we arrived with a car completely different from that in which we'd competed in Brazil, and it was embarrassing that, having been so quick in practice in Brazil, we were so slow in testing prior to the South African Grand Prix. But no matter how hard we tried we couldn't convince Emerson to return to the Interlagos settings. It was only on the very last day, when Wilson practically had to threaten Emerson with a knife, that he agreed to change the car to a setting that at least allowed us to qualify, although unfortunately a strange engine problem prevented us from running in the last practice.

We were always struggling with money; we could hardly afford to do what we did, and I never knew exactly how much we received from Copersucar. Perhaps the sponsorship wasn't as generous as I'd been led to believe. What did upset me was that the Fittipaldis demanded so much with the little we got. They even sent a Brazilian economics expert to try to organise the bookkeeping and he was amazed to see how much we did with so little.

Overseas races were a real killer, as we didn't yet belong to FOCA (the Formula One Constructors' Association). Only the first ten teams (20 cars) were accepted, and one could only get into the club by merit, earned with championship points. Once you got there your freight and travel allocation was paid for, and there was more participation in prize money and a few other perks. But for the time being we were still a member of the wankers club!

One small milestone in my racing life was being able to pull a 'fast one' on Bernie Ecclestone – and not many people can say that. We were going to California for the USA (West) Grand Prix at Long Beach, and I was looking for deals with shipping companies to take our cars and spares when Bernie called me to offer us a place in the FOCA charter flight at $22,000. I knew that they only had room left for two cars with few spares and were keen to fill it. I said, "No Bernie, impossible, we can't afford that sort of money – I'm going to send them with Cazaly Mills" (a company that Bernie also used). "And how much are they going to charge you?" he asked. "$10,000," I said. "Impossible," said Bernie. "No," I said, "it'll go in consolidated freight, and although I have to allow two extra days it'll be worth it."

Bernie didn't believe me. So as soon as I put the phone down, I immediately dialled the boss at Cazaly Mills, a lovely big lady with a heart as big as she was, who'd always helped me with my freight, though this time I'd invented the whole thing. I said, "Miss Smythe, you'll get a phone call from Bernie and he'll ask you how much you'll be charging me to take our team to the USA, and as far as you know you'll be charging me $10,000." "OK," she said, "I'll do it." Late that afternoon I got a call back from Bernie saying he'd take our team for $10,000. I certainly owed more than a dinner to Miss Smythe, but I'd have to look after my kneecaps from then on!

By the time we got to California Bernie had discovered the plot and took it in good part. When he saw me, he pulled me to one side and said, "OK, Ramirez one, Ecclestone zero. We'll meet again in the second half!" In fact he never held it against me, but on the contrary has always helped me in my long and lonely road with small teams. A small man with a big brain who's done so much for the sport.

Maybe those $5,000 per car were a good investment, as we ended up gaining our first World Championship point when Emerson finished sixth in the race. Ingo Hoffman failed to qualify his car at Long Beach or in Spain, and we decided to concentrate on one car for the time being in an effort to improve our act and have a half-good single car rather than two bad ones.

But the result wasn't to be as planned. At Zolder in Belgium it was Emerson's turn to fail to make the grid. Needless to say, this was particularly hurtful for the team: the 1972 and 1974 World Champion had failed to qualify, a fact that pointed to the car being at fault. But as always, it was very difficult to be strong with Emerson. Richard would have loved to be able to say, "I'm the engineer here and I call the shots." But Emerson insisted on using 900lb/in springs, like Carlos Pace was using on his Brabham, instead of 400lb/in, and it was impossible to convince him that due to the pullrod suspension arrangement in the Brabham BT44, the spring-rate on our car was the same as on Pace's. So we had one car set up with stiff springs and one with standard springs.

Emerson went round and round in a car that was quite easy to drive, but had no grip due to its hard springs. It just slid around and didn't qualify. Towards the end of the session, I asked Emerson to change cars as it sounded as if an inner valve spring on the engine was broken, which was normally identified by a typical high speed flutter. Cosworth engines were prone to valve spring failure in those days. Emerson refused categorically, saying that he was driving the car and he knew what was going on, so he left the pits and never came back: the engine dropped a valve on the back straight. Then he went out in the spare car, with old tyres, and was quicker than he'd been all day, but he ran out of time with a best lap speed that was 0.026sec too slow.

There was no time to cry over spilt milk. We sent the team straight to the Paul Ricard test track, while Richard and I returned to the UK to prepare new 'go fast goodies'. Richard had designed a new suspension geometry and we managed to make it in record time. We flew down to the south of France to join the team at Ricard, and after a couple of days of back-to-back testing were happy to confirm that the new mods had improved the car dramatically. The power transferred to the road was a lot better and therefore the mechanical grip was much improved.

We drove to Monaco in a much better state of mind, hoping that our improvements would allow us to race in such an important Grand Prix; and the weekend couldn't have started better, as our guest for the race was the legendary Hollywood actor David Niven, a neighbour of Emerson and Jackie Stewart in Switzerland. Having dinner with David had to be one of the top perks associated with involvement in Grand Prix racing. He was the funniest after-dinner storyteller that I've ever come across, and his witty, dry sense of humour was a joy to share.

He told us about a time when he and Jackie were driving in the Swiss Alps on a cold and icy winter morning, and when approaching a petrol station Jackie had misjudged the turning and ended up skating into a stationary Porsche which was waiting to get out. The Porsche driver couldn't believe his eyes when he identified the two people emerging from the offending Ford Granada, and as Jackie, fresh from his second World Championship, was humbly apologising and telling the driver he'd make sure his beloved Porsche was restored to its original shape the man replied, "Please don't worry, Mr Stewart, I won't fix it. It'll make a great party conversation piece." He then took out a marker pen and wrote over the bumper: "OUCHES by Jackie Stewart".

This reminds me of another story concerning Jackie, when he was asked to make a demonstration run in Macao and promptly overturned the car in practice. The mechanics fixed the car for the next day and drew big arrows all over it with signs saying, "This way up".

The closing minutes of the final qualifying session at Monaco were a nail-biting affair, but got us into the race – just! We were running the car on the barest minimum of fuel, and I was debating whether or not we had enough to run the last few minutes or should bring Emerson in for a couple of litres and waste a lap, when Emerson came into the pits, mad as a hopper. Lifting his visor, he shouted to me, "You've fucked up a good lap, I've run out of petrol." I said, "OK, that's bound to happen sometimes, just don't shut the engine off," while we slammed in a gallon or so of fuel. Emerson took off sideways from the pits and sideways into the circuit, while Wilson, with both his hands in his hair, shouted, "Oh Christ, he's going to kill himself!" I said, "No way, he's far too good for that. He may even put in a good lap!"

And a lap was all he was able to do before the chequered flag came down, but it was a staggering lap, over 1.5 seconds better than his previous fastest, a time that brought him up from 20th fastest to seventh! He was all smiles when he heard his grid position, while the team was very disillusioned. I was livid, and said to him, "If you don't want to do it any more just say so. It's no good all of us working our asses off for you if you're not racing. From now on all we need to do is to upset you at the last moment and put in five litres of fuel to make the car 1.5 seconds faster!"

I was disgusted and thinking of ways to make Emerson regain the will to win, as there was no doubt that the talent was there, but unless he applied himself he'd demoralise the team and it would be impossible for me to motivate them again. We finished sixth in the race for our second championship point, and got another point at the British Grand Prix thanks to the disqualification of James Hunt's McLaren. The season ended on a low note when Emerson withdrew from the very wet Japanese Grand Prix at Mount Fuji, the famous race in which Niki Lauda also stopped his Ferrari and Hunt clinched the title.

Richard Divila got to an even lower point and was totally demoralised. He asked Wilson to start looking for another designer to take charge, as he could no longer cope with Emerson dictating design issues at the expense of his performance behind the wheel. Dave Baldwin joined the team from 1977.

At the beginning of the 1977 season Emerson seemed to have found a little more spark than he had in the previous year, and although we didn't qualify too well in Argentina and Brazil, we managed to collect two fourth places.

I think this was the year that Bob Dance, the Team Lotus chief mechanic – one of the greatest mechanics Formula One has ever seen, a completely unflappable man with the greatest sense of humour in the paddock – engineered the demolishing of the Interlagos race track toilets (if you could call them toilets). We'd asked the organisation to improve the standard of (or preferably rebuild) the 'bogs' year after year, but we were repeatedly ignored. This particular year Bob decided that enough was enough. After the race, while all the teams were doing the tedious packing up, Bob planted a series of mass destruction acetylene bombs which today Tony Blair would have been proud to find, and when we were ready to leave – BANG! The toilets self-destructed in less than 45 seconds, and the next year we had new ones.

Bob was always the one for practical jokes, the bright spark who'd initiate the clean and simple entertainment that always set the party on fire – sometimes literally! Formula One people will always remember Bob orchestrating the 'Kenny & Clive' show in the 1970s, when two of the Lotus mechanics dressed up in drag and entertained the Grand Prix circus, as well as any passers-by, at the Tip Top bar on the Sunday night after the Monaco Grand Prix.

The Tip Top bar, situated on the short straight between Casino Square and the Mirabeau corner, was always the place to be on any evening of the race weekend, and one of Bob's favourite tricks was to put cars on stools. I remember once an old lady arriving outside the Tip Top and parking her car right in front, despite the warnings of all the beer drinkers around the pavement. With a typically stubborn French attitude, she left her old Simca right there, only to find it two hours later across the road standing on four chairs, compliments of Bob and his band of helpers. Naturally it was all in good fun, and we lifted the car down once she'd deposited the 'parking fine' behind the bar!

The last time I saw Bob, a year ago at the Goodwood Festival of Speed, he said to me, "Hi, Jo. Do you remember the times when sex was safe and motor racing was dangerous?"

Meanwhile, back with the boys from Brazil, for a time we were at least qualifying in the middle of the grid, and collected another fifth place at Long Beach. It wasn't until the British Grand Prix at Silverstone in July that I once again had my doubts that Emerson was really trying to race. We nearly didn't make the grid, as a rear damper mounting broke, and without spares we had to make a last minute botch-up repair. But that did the trick, and we were 20th for the start.

But it was during the race itself that I was thoroughly disillusioned. When Emerson was lapped by the leaders (Hunt's McLaren and Lauda's Ferrari), he tucked in behind them and his times suddenly decreased by two seconds a lap. I couldn't believe what I was seeing, and after the race — which we failed to finish because of an engine problem — I showed him his lap times, and said to him, "How come you're able to do that?" His reply was: "I was only trying to see if I could keep up with them." "Right," I said, "so why didn't you try from the beginning of the race?" "Ah," he said, "but I was trying very hard indeed to do that," and he made a Brazilian sign with his thumb to his chin that meant he was driving to his limit. "Right," I said, "you were trying very hard and they were just out for a Sunday drive!"

Once again I felt, perhaps wrongly, that he wasn't trying his hardest, which was very demoralising for the team, having one of the greatest drivers in the world who seemed not to be giving of his best. He'd done the same the year before at Watkins Glen, when Lauda passed him and he tucked in behind, keeping up with him until the rear wing mounting broke. The team was working hard, but without that extra incentive of knowing that if you put in 110 per cent, the driver would at least do the same. In other words, our belief in Emerson was gone, and by the German Grand Prix at Hockenheim we'd hit rock bottom again and the team didn't qualify. By some miracle we finished fourth in Holland, only to fail to qualify again in Italy. We raced in the USA and Canada, but decided that it wasn't worthwhile to make the long trip to Japan.

By then our relations weren't perhaps the best. I was tired of pushing shit up the hill with a pointed stick, and the Fittipaldis wanted a more office-like team manager, someone who'd come to work in a suit and tie, not someone who was likely to join in and get his hands dirty. They enlisted the services of Peter McIntosh, who at the time was secretary of the Formula One Constructors' Association, and we parted on good terms at the end of the 1977 season.

Although the Fittipaldi team raced for four more seasons, they never re-invented the wheel, and except for a second place in 1978 at Jacarepagua near Rio de Janeiro, they were among the also-rans. Emerson retired from F1 in 1980 and later on changed his whole life. With his new wife, Teresa, he went to live in Miami, got his adrenaline and motivation back, and raced very successfully in the American CART Champ Car series, winning the championship. He also won the Indianapolis 500 twice, which for him was almost like winning the F1 title. We often see each other at various events and reminisce with affection about our old days of hardship.

CHAPTER 8

IN THE SHADOWS

When I left Fittipaldi I didn't have a clear idea of which direction to take, but I wasn't concerned about it, just relieved to be rid of the great burden I'd been carrying. I had a few tentative offers, but I wanted some time off to clear my head before approaching the next challenge. When I did finally commit myself it looked as if I'd gone from the frying pan into the fire, as the offer I took was probably the one that provided the biggest challenge. In addition to giving me the chance to remain in Formula One, it was also a very interesting proposal.

I received a phone call from Don Nichols, the enigmatic American entrepreneur-owner of the Shadow Formula One team, telling me that some of his management staff had 'done a runner' with all the drawings and personnel to form a team of their own, but that he wasn't going to give up and would I like to take over? We met in London as Christmas approached, and like a true masochist I took the job.

This was about four weeks before the 1978 Argentinean Grand Prix, and when I arrived at the Shadow base in Northampton there were only three employees left, but they were wonderfully loyal and hard-working: they were Ray Kent, the lady who looked after the accounts and anything else that would help the team, a real agony aunt, one of those characters who don't exist any more; Jim Eccles, the works manager and jack-of-all-trades; and Barry Evans, the chief mechanic. Barry was a young Australian for whom the longer the job-list, the happier he was, a real asset to the team. There were three DN8 chassis, some gearbox parts and a few other bits and bobs.

Jackie Oliver, Alan Rees, Tony Southgate, Dave Wass and all the rest of the 1977 staff had gone to Milton Keynes to form the new Arrows team, and in order to comply with FOCA regulations they would have to attend the Brazilian GP, having just missed the Argentinean. They must, therefore, build their car in practically two months, and this could only be achieved by using the same drawings that Southgate and Wass had already prepared for the Shadow DN9, which was in the process of being built at Northampton when they left.

It looked to me as if the previous Shadow management had had to leave in a hurry, as I found some very incriminating letters and documents in the offices, and this was the start of a very long and painful lawsuit. Don Nichols was determined that they should pay for their treachery and that the whole world should know about it. Fortunately for us, the Shadow team's main sponsor, Villiger (a German cigar manufacturer), remained loyal, which was a big vote of confidence; the *deutschmarks* were also very welcome.

With only ten days to go, I had to find mechanics, welders, fabricators, buy some engines and, of course, get some race drivers. I was busier than a dog digging a hole in a marble floor. Jim and Barry were priceless and we found a good group of people to form the team, among them Gene Lentz, a tall American looking for something different to do while he was young and footloose. Gene drove the truck, looked after the spares and kept everyone laughing with his stories. We engaged Clay Regazzoni and Hans Stuck to drive the cars, but I wasn't able to relax or have a good night's sleep until I was finally on the plane to Buenos Aires. We might not stand much chance of being competitive, but with the people we had we were at least going to have a lot of fun!

Not surprisingly, we didn't set the Formula One world alight in Buenos Aires, but at least both cars finished. However, two weeks later Regazzoni finished fifth at Interlagos, and it was time for *samba* and *caipirinhas*. Clay was a great fun guy, a team player, and a very good friend.

Once we arrived in South Africa the party was over. We didn't have the means to attend the previous week's testing at Kyalami, and we paid the price by not qualifying either of the DN8 cars for the race. I remember that we were practically eaten alive by the press, who said it was a very poor show for a team of Shadow's standing, but they forgot that really it was a brand new team on its third race. We finished the first of the DN9 cars in time for Long Beach, and the second before Monaco.

By the middle of the year the court hearing against the previous Shadow management was due, and the guilty parties wanted to settle out of court by offering us $150,000. As a racing man, I said to Don, "Take the money, we need it," but he wanted to go all the way and make them feel ashamed. Without a 'Shadow' of a doubt we won the case, and the Arrows FA1 was banned from racing. But they'd clearly guessed that this was going to be the outcome, and had made contingency plans by producing another car in record time. Consequently they didn't miss a race.

Don Nichols was really mad, and I guess he'd every right to be, calling them robbers and criminals. I'd worked very closely with Jackie Oliver when he raced GT40s and Porsches with JW Automotive, and with Tony Southgate in our days at AAR in California, and I always felt they were driven to do what they did by ambition and naivety rather than by intent to harm. Tony, particularly, was just a damn good engineer, who worked endless hours without ever looking over the edge of his drawing board.

We plodded along throughout the year with lots of DNFs, some DNQs, and occasionally a fifth place, for Regazzoni at Anderstorp and for Hans Stuck at Brands Hatch, which raised our spirits.

In the good old Brands Hatch days, the organisers would occasionally schedule some fun into the programme, and that year there was a Ford Escort race for the team managers. I managed to qualify in midfield, of which I was quite proud as there were some accomplished drivers there, including Frank Williams, Jackie Oliver, Gérard Larrousse, Guy Ligier, John Surtees and Stirling Moss (representing Tyrrell). However, on race day the grid was established by drawing a number from a hat and I was looking good on the second row, but seconds before the start McLaren's Alastair Caldwell passed me on the grass, and I then realised that everyone had jumped the start. On arrival at the Druids hairpin I found a big traffic jam, with cars facing in every direction, but I managed to avoid this and by the time I was in Bottom Bend I found myself in second place. I was so chuffed about this that I got overconfident, and soon after that I spun off and rejoined the race in last place but one. Then the Latin temper got the better of me and I carved my way up to seventh and fought for sixth, banging doors with 'Big John' Surtees on the last lap – a battle that I lost.

At the Italian Grand Prix in Monza we witnessed some of the most bizarre happenings in Formula One: at the start of the race there was an horrendous crash, probably triggered by the ill-conceived chicane which was introduced after the start, but at the time it was blamed on Riccardo Patrese, the young Arrows driver, for 'widening' the circuit. Whatever, the end result was a *carambola* of ten cars, and the race was stopped so that they could clear away the debris and rescue Ronnie Peterson, whose Lotus had had its front end completely torn away, leaving his legs exposed and badly injured.

My two drivers, Clay and Hans, were two of the many involved in the crash. I legged it to the circuit hospital and was relieved to find Clay with a few little lacerations but otherwise fine (in fact it was he and James Hunt who extracted Ronnie from the debris of his Lotus). Hans had a bump on his head from a flying tyre, but was also otherwise well. While we were there we checked on Ronnie, who was sitting on a stretcher waiting to be transported to the main hospital in Milan, and he seemed perfectly OK, talking normally even though his feet were pretty painful. As always, when there's a big accident the race loses its shine, but at least we left the circuit thinking that Ronnie would be racing again in a few months time!

Next morning we were shocked to hear that he had died during the night in hospital. He had suffered multiple compound fractures and as a result bone marrow got into his bloodstream, causing a massive embolism that took his life. That was one of the most tragic and unnecessary deaths the sport had ever seen – to die after surviving a crash like that. The conjecture was that his injured legs weren't attended properly: maybe they took too long to take him to the main hospital, maybe he should have had surgery there and then.

Nowadays I ask myself how come, ten years after the death of Ayrton Senna, the Italian police are still trying to reopen that case and find somebody to blame, whereas in 1978 they weren't interested in finding out why Ronnie wasn't given the right drugs to prevent his blood clotting?

As George Harrison said in the song that he dedicated to Ronnie, "He was faster than the bullet from a gun, he was faster than going faster..." But he was also the most unassuming, natural and humble person you could ever wish to meet. He used to live close to me in Maidenhead, with his wife Barbro and little daughter Nina, and we used to share a car to the airport every Grand Prix, but sadly I returned alone that weekend.

Throughout my two years at Shadow, which were character-building to say the least, I was very lucky to recruit some great people. John Baldwin engineered the car and I got hold of some new people from saloon car racing, who hadn't been 'spoiled' by Formula One and turned out to be excellent elements in the team. They included Brian Lambert, who went on to become test team manager for Williams, and Nigel Stepney, now a race team director at Ferrari. I remember that once we had barely half-an-hour left before the race and we needed to change the clutch, and Brian and Nigel replaced it and still had time for a cuppa...

These were tough years, and I had to learn to be tough, but in a small team there's no place for time-wasters. I always allowed everyone a day off after a race, but when we came home from Monaco with two crashed cars I got everyone together and said, "Sorry guys, there's a lot of work for the next race, so no day off tomorrow." The next day only Brian and Nigel came in. I was furious, and after conferring with Brian and Nigel, when the rest of the boys came to work the following day their toolboxes were by the door. I said to them, "What are you doing here? You had a job here yesterday, there's no work for you today!" That was a hard thing to do, but I didn't care if I had to do the job myself – we had to have discipline, and if we had to create a precedent to establish it, that's what I did.

Later on I was also lucky enough to recruit Alan Challis, ex-chief mechanic at BRM, who went on to become chief mechanic for the Williams Engineering F1 team when Keke Rosberg became World Champion in 1982. He's now the Williams factory manager.

For 1979, we had two young lions driving the cars and, once again, if we didn't win any races we'd certainly continue to have fun. Elio de Angelis, an Italian from Rome who was running away from a fruitless Ferrari contract, had raced a March F2 and had almost signed a contract with Tyrrell, but changed his mind at the last hour due to Tyrrell's lack of commitment. Instead he signed a deal with us, bringing $100,000 from the family construction business and sponsorship from Staroup Jeans. Elio was a classic Italian gentleman, good looking, well dressed, well spoken, well mannered and well educated. He was also very down-to-earth, and on the day that he signed our contract we went out to celebrate the occasion at Cagney's, the local hamburger joint in downtown Northampton!

He loved wristwatches, and I remember that he fell in love with a particular Rolex model but thought it was too much money for a watch, and couldn't justify it. I said to him, "For Christ's sake, you're a Formula One driver now, surely you must be able to afford it?" In Formula One circles, as in many others, it's who you know rather than what you know that gets you anywhere, and I got Elio a deal through Jackie Stewart, long-time Rolex front man. Elio was so delighted with his Rolex that he gave me his old watch, a lovely small gold Baume & Mercier, a real classic, which I proudly keep and only wear on a very special occasion. Ironically enough, I was wearing it on the tragic day in 1986 when Elio lost his life testing at Paul Ricard in the Brabham BT55 BMW.

Jan Lammers, the little flying Dutchman, took the other 1979 Shadow seat, with sponsorship from Samson tobacco. Jan, who started his career as an instructor at the skid school in Zandvoort, had just won the FIA European Formula 3 Championship. He was the most likeable young man, always ready for fun and taking life as it came, enjoying every minute.

The three of us hit it off immediately, and although there were many ups and downs throughout the years our friendship was always the same. Later on Jan and I worked together again in other teams and our friendship continues to this day. On testing days they would always stay at my home, and we were entertained by Elio's piano-playing and Jan's endless funny stories and jokes.

Elio had a little bit more experience in race cars than Jan, and I guess he had the edge between them, but occasionally Jan would outperform him, especially on twisty tracks where car control was important, in which Jan excelled.

Naturally, our American boss Don Nichols always toyed with the idea of having an American driving one of his cars, and he invited Hawaiian-born Danny Ongais to test our car at Paul Ricard. Backed by millionaire entrepreneur Ted Fields and his Interscope organisation, Danny had already done a couple of races or so with Penske in 1977 and Ensign at the start of 1978. He'd failed to prequalify when we'd run him in a third Shadow later that season at Long Beach and Zandvoort, but Don wanted to give him another try.

Danny was a great star of the dragster scene in the States, the fastest guy in a straight line, but always got a bit confused when he had to turn right or left. He was getting nowhere in the testing at Paul Ricard, lapping about three seconds slower than Elio, and I asked Elio to go around the circuit to see what he was doing wrong, as he seemed to be losing a lot of time at Signes, the fastest corner. Elio came back and reported his findings: Danny was complaining of heavy understeer at Signes, and Elio said, "Of course, because you're lifting. Keep the throttle down and it'll be OK." Danny was unsure, but Elio reassured him, saying, "Of course, that's what that pedal's for." Danny went out to put Elio's advice into practice and was one-and-a-half seconds faster on his first flying lap, but never came round again! No, Danny wasn't the answer to our problems.

The highlight of the year was undoubtedly the last Grand Prix, the USA at Watkins Glen. By then I'd already agreed to leave the team, as boss Don Nichols didn't have any concrete plans for the following year, nor did we have any sponsorship. I'd therefore accepted an offer from Günther Schmid to join his one-car ATS team for 1980, and Elio was in talks with other teams and was almost certain to be joining Lotus. Jan had nothing planned and therefore we'd probably be working together again.

The race started with Elio in 20th place, while Jan failed to qualify. At the time Elio wasn't at all a well man, being very much under the weather, and the last thing that he wanted to do was to drive a race car. The weather was awful, windy, dark and very cold, and 30 minutes before the start it decided to rain. Everyone went on to wet tyres except for Nelson Piquet's Brabham and Mario Andretti's Lotus. There were all kinds of accidents and people spinning off, as the conditions were very slippery. Then just before halfway through the race it stopped raining and people started coming in for dry-weather tyres.

Elio was one of the last to come in for tyres, and when he did so, from ninth place, he complained bitterly about understeering. The temperature was still very low, and after a split-second conference Bert Baldwin – the former Goodyear technician and now Don's right-hand man – suggested to me that we might use the front qualifying tyres. There was a 50–50 chance that they wouldn't survive, but if they did this was our last chance of scoring points! I yelled to the boys to put race rubbers on the back and qualifiers on the front. They thought I'd gone mad, but did what I asked. Elio went past on the next lap with his thumb up, and we all crossed our fingers and prayed that the front tyres would last the distance.

Elio had a good battle with John Watson's McLaren, which he won. "Wow!" I thought, "Whatever you're doing wrong, boy, keep doing it." Jody Scheckter's Ferrari and Derek Daly's Tyrrell had gone off, and then Elio beat Hans Stuck's ATS for fourth place, and that was how it finished. We celebrated at the Seneca Lodge that evening as if we'd won the race, and Elio played some of his best tunes on the old piano.

It was then that I realised that I'd shot myself in the foot. Ironically, when Elio had beaten Hans Stuck he'd also put Shadow ahead of ATS – my employer for the upcoming 1980 season – to take the last place in the Formula One Constructors' Association package, which would be worth as much as a quarter of a million dollars in freight travel and concessions for the coming year!

ATS team boss Günther Schmid was very pissed off, but I *think* he appreciated that as long as I was working for a team, I had to do what was best for it.

CHAPTER 9

CHARACTER BUILDING

Soon after the end of the 1979 season, I was asked by my new boss, Günther Schmid, to present myself at the ATS team's factory on the Bicester Trading Estate on a Monday morning to meet the German team secretary, Reh Kuster. I arrived at about 9:30, but for some reason Reh wasn't there, so I walked upstairs to the office only to find that the previous team manager, Vic Elford, was still there and had absolutely no idea that I was replacing him! What an embarrassment! I was mortified and Vic must have felt even worse. It wouldn't have been so bad if Vic had been a complete stranger, but Vic and I were friends, and worst of all Günther had assured me that Vic was aware that he was going to be replaced. All Günther had done was to instruct Reh to tell him, but she hadn't got there in time to do it.

So already, on my very first day, I had the feeling that I was about as welcome at ATS as a pork pie in a synagogue, and this was by no means the best introduction to my new team.

The set-up at the ATS factory was modest and just about good enough to run a one-car team, but Günther wanted to upgrade to two cars: although he had the right idea, this also proved that – a bit like the Fittipaldis – he had a champagne taste on a beer income. However, we were ready to give it a go. Gustav Brunner and Tim Wardrop were our designers, but I had to clear a bit of deadwood in the camp and fire a couple of mechanics who didn't have the right attitude. On the other hand there was a young Swiss guy who'd just started – Bruno Flückiger – who turned out to be a great pillar of the team. He had a reputable car maintenance business in Switzerland but couldn't resist working with racing cars. Up to this day we have kept up a good friendship and we often get together.

Within a short space of time we'd built up quite a good little team with excellent personnel. I managed to recruit my old friend from Tyrrell days, Roy Topp, as chief mechanic, plus Simon Hadfield, a very young, enthusiastic and hardworking guy who wasn't afraid to tackle any job. He now runs one of the best car restoration businesses in the country. In addition I hired Geoff Wyatt, Graham Humphrys, Peter Levitt and Bernie Marcus, with Mick Avery as parts manager and truck driver. As a kind of factory manager we had Ian Deacon, doing the buying and general organising. Ian was a very down-to-earth man who didn't take any nonsense and very often confronted and argued with Günther. Obviously a very brave man too!

The 1980 ATS drivers were to be Marc Surer, a fearless Swiss driver in the same mould as Patrick Depailler – both were quiet and reserved men, only happy when they were doing something dangerous – and Jan Lammers, who we rescued from the Shadows. We could barely afford to run the two cars, as we didn't have quite enough good parts for both. Marc Surer was the number one driver, as he was signed first and was the choice of Günther, so therefore he had the first pick.

We started the season driving D3s. Jan failed to qualify in the first two races, at Buenos Aires and Interlagos, but Marc picked up a seventh place in Brazil, which was quite a success for our small team and we had a small celebration. Jan Lammers, though, wasn't happy: his sponsorship was drying up and his future in the team was very unsure.

By the third race we'd decided that it was better to enter one complete race car rather than two halves, and we went to South Africa with just one new D4 for Marc, although we took the old D3 as a spare. Unfortunately, during practice Marc slipped his foot between the brake pedal and the accelerator and in a split second slammed into the concrete wall at Clubhouse bend (although on any other corner it would have probably been worse), trapping him in the car with his fractured ankles stuck between the pedals. The officials allowed us to go to his rescue and we were thankful that there were no leaks or fire danger, as it took several minutes for us to get him out. We then got him helicoptered to the local hospital.

As we still had the old D3 car, and Jan Lammers was there as a spectator, we decided we might as well have a go at qualifying since there were two places empty on the grid as a result of Surer and Alain Prost (who'd broken his wrist in an accident with his McLaren) being out of the running. However, Keke Rosberg's Fittipaldi and Geoff Lees's Shadow got the last two places.

But this wasn't the only drama that year in South Africa. As our British Airways Jumbo Jet was about to fly back home with the entire Formula One circus on board, it decided to blow up one of its engines in spectacular fashion just as we were taking off, and the pilot only just managed to stop the big aircraft sideways at the end of the runway. I remember Carlos Reutemann saying to me on the plane that if this mother had fallen out of the sky it would've been months before another Grand Prix could be run. As a reward (!) we all had a day's 'holiday' in Nairobi on the way home.

With Marc still convalescing, we decided to enter just one car, for Jan, for the fourth GP of the year at Long Beach, and set about finishing the second of the new D4s. The car was finished in a hurry, and we shipped it to California knowing that it wasn't 100 per cent good and therefore arranged for a quick shakedown test at Willow Springs to cure the teething problems. By Friday we were more or less in good shape for official practice and when this came we were pleasantly surprised with an eighth fastest overall, and this wonderful position, according to the rules in those days as set by the Goodyear Tyre Co, automatically allowed your car four sets of qualifying tyres for the last session on Saturday. Four sets! We didn't even have four sets of rims to fit them!

Goodyear boss Leo Mehl, who I knew very well from my AAR days, was delighted to offer us the sticky rubber and all the assistance we needed, as long as I promised not to tell him the old joke that Dan Gurney always cracked: "Leo, we only have four problems on our car. One on each corner!" The qualifier tyres for this race in the Californian sun were only good for one lap before they lost performance, but they could improve your time by up to 1.5 seconds.

Jan Lammers was perhaps not the fastest racing driver in the world but on slow circuits like Long Beach where precision and car control were required, he had a bundle of both, and he loved the circuit.

We'd also won third prize in the traditional car beauty contest in downtown Long Beach, so suddenly we got this up-rush feeling that we were no longer an also-ran but we were among the top racing teams of the world! And we felt we had to make the most of the opportunity. At most racetracks most of the time, the end of practice is when the circuit is at its best, when all the cars have left enough rubber to make the track faster. Sometimes, however, a car might blow its engine or simply spill oil, making the circuit slippery towards the end. We therefore decided to run two sets at the beginning and two at the end. This strategy worked, as the circuit slowed down at the end, and the teams who'd saved their tyres for it ended up with egg on their faces.

The end result was a magnificent fourth fastest, with only Nelson Piquet's Brabham, René Arnoux's Renault and Patrick Depailler's Alfa Romeo in front of us. As we got back to the enclosed 'paddock' in the Long Beach Exhibition Center, where all the teams were staged for preparations, we were sandwiched between the mighty Ferrari and the Marlboro teams of McLaren and Alfa Romeo. Only a short tubular fence separated the teams and we could see that really we didn't quite belong there. We had just one car, a spare engine, a few wheels and boxes, and a workforce of six men including Jan and boss Schmid, compared to these rich teams with all their equipment, spares and personnel. Still, we felt mighty proud of our performance as we acknowledged the congratulations from everyone around. Unless you've been there, you'd never understand that unbelievable buzz of having just beaten some of the top people in your field. If I'd not been swamped with work, I'd probably have gone out and got paralytic!

That afternoon a FOCA meeting was scheduled and I was up to my elbows in work trying to fix a leaking water header tank, as we didn't have enough personnel. Günther came and shouted at me that I was going to miss the meeting. Damn, I'd forgotten about it. I quickly brushed my uniform washed my hands and ran to the meeting room. As I arrived, about 15 minutes late and humbly apologising to everyone, Ron Dennis got out of his seat and moved a chair to the head of the table, saying, "After your performance today we've reserved this place for you." At the same time Bernie Ecclestone, Colin Chapman, Frank Williams, Marco

Piccinini, Ken Tyrrell, Peter Warr, Gérard Larrousse, Morris Nunn and Jackie Oliver all got up and applauded. I have to say I felt two feet taller as I sat down.

We continued our frantic work till late that evening, checking and re-checking every single component of the car, as we didn't have many new parts to exchange for the used ones. But sadly our glory only lasted 24 hours. After a fine start, our ATS rolled to a halt with a broken driveshaft universal joint, so we didn't even experience what it was like to run with the top guys for at least some of the race. Disappointment hardly described my feelings.

The race at Long Beach in 1980 was also marred by the horrendous accident to the Ensign of Clay Regazzoni, when the brake pedal broke at the end of Shoreline Drive straight and he went over the parked Brabham of Ricardo Zunino and into the concrete wall. Our great friend Clay has been confined to a wheelchair ever since, paralysed from the waist down.

For the next race back in Europe at Zolder, we again qualified reasonably well in the middle of the pack but scored a DNF with an engine problem only eight laps from the finish line. So the next one to look forward to was Monaco. We didn't reach the same level as at Long Beach, but we were in 13th place, which was again around the middle of the 20 starters. Unfortunately there was a massive *carambola* at the start in which Jan was hit by Riccardo Patrese's Arrows, which broke the ATS's front suspension. Jan managed to get back to the pits and had a very lengthy stop for repairs, but nevertheless produced an inspired drive for tenth place.

The following Grand Prix in Spain was one of the many races in the 1980s blighted by political problems, when the egos of the top men that govern our sport came head to head with each other, without either side giving way. It was always a very sad state of affairs, because when you examine the reasons for the disputes it really makes you laugh, as most of them were very childish. However, in this race the Ferraris, Renaults and Alfa Romeos decided not to compete, as they didn't want to get on the wrong side of FISA (then the separate motorsport division of the FIA) over a dispute with FOCA about drivers' fines.

It was the first year full of the politics which affected Grand Prix racing for almost a decade, as the newly formed FISA

(Federation International Sport Automobile) and its elected president, dictator and megalomaniac, Jean-Marie Balestre, flexed their muscles. Balestre's single-minded intention was to break the power of FOCA in sporting matters and, in the long run, to control the finances of Grand Prix racing, which continued to be inflated purely by the strong and hard negotiations of Bernie Ecclestone of FOCA. Their differences were such that, at some point, a split between the two sides was almost inevitable. FOCA had the majority of the cars and the television rights, but FISA could control the majority of the circuits. We should feel extremely relieved that it never came to that.

In spite of all this, the Spanish Grand Prix was a very good race in which Jan fought with the eventual winner, Alan Jones in the Williams, for fifth place, until his brakes gave up. Eventually, however, the results were declared null and void because of the absence of the manufacturers' teams.

The next race, at Paul Ricard a month later, nearly didn't happen at all, as this time the FOCA teams threatened withdrawal, but at the last minute FISA and FOCA temporarily patched up their differences and it was business as usual. By this time Marc Surer was almost walking and was good enough to drive again, and he replaced Jan Lammers, who went to drive for the rival struggling team Ensign. Surprisingly, Marc qualified in a very respectable 11th place but was out of the race by halfway while running eighth.

The rest of the year we seemed to just plod along. The car was basically good, but without any research budget to test and develop it we were falling backwards in a hurry. Jan, at the beginning of the year, and then Marc had done the best they could, but it was painful for everyone. Marc failed to qualify at Montreal, and finished eighth in the last race of the season, at Watkins Glen – our best result. However, with a budget of under £500,000 (less than McLaren's wind tunnel budget alone) I thought we did well, and I was very proud to have done so much with so little.

But the year had also seen the departure of another good friend. Patrick Depailler left the circuit at Hockenheim's very fast Ostkurve corner while testing prior to the German Grand Prix, and no reason for the accident was ever given. Patrick, who'd suffered so many accidents and had his feet and legs reconstructed so many times after painful falls with his hang-glider toys, this time didn't suffer at all.

For the 1981 season our boss Günther Schmid promised that he was going to behave in a more sensible and professional manner. He'd no longer interfere with the running of the team, and we should concentrate on running one car. Frenchman Herve Guilpin joined us to design a new car, and there'd be a lot more money coming in to allow for testing and development. Sure. It was too good to be true, but half of me wanted to believe it, as I really thought that we had the makings of a good little team that would be a consistent middle qualifier and occasionally finish in a decent position. Marc Surer decided to part company and join Mo Nunn's Ensign Team, and we snatched back Jan Lammers, so they literally exchanged teams.

Long Beach unfortunately wasn't a repeat of the previous year. In fact, Marc Surer blew us out in qualifying, and in the race Jan and Bruno Giacomelli's Alfa Romeo collided and that was that. It was an accident that really put us back in our schedule because with only two weeks before the next race in Brazil we literally had to just patch-up and make-do, so not surprisingly we didn't qualify. On the plus side we were at least back in Rio de Janeiro, one of my favourite cities in the world, but with only two weeks to the next race in Argentina it wasn't going to be easy.

In Buenos Aires, another of my favourite cities, things didn't improve but instead went downhill and another big row with our beloved boss took place. This time the autocratic and unpredictable Günther Schmid went completely crazy over an argument when we wanted to fit a smaller front wing and he was adamant that we shouldn't try it. He behaved like a spoiled child throwing all his toys out of the pram, and jumped on the front wing until it was destroyed! Lammers scraped into the last row in qualifying and finished 12th, a lap down.

After the race, despite having already made up my mind to leave ATS, along with some of the crew, we still had a chance to celebrate, and joined the race winner Nelson Piquet and the Brabham team at the popular Estancia restaurant. It was there that Silvia Piquet began a food fight with the Williams team, who'd finished second with local hero Carlos Reutemann. Bread, tomatoes and ice-cream were flying across the room. A TV crew managed to get in and were filming as the party degenerated into a free-for-all, which spread to the whole of the restaurant. It was all in good spirits by Formula One standards, but the owners got nervous and decided to call the police. Nelson, as the race winner, had to foot the damages bill to avoid joining the many Argentinean *desaparecidos*!

Günther having broken his promise, on our return to base in the UK I cleared my desk and left ATS together with some of the team's key mechanics, as we were all disgusted by Schmid's tantrum in the Buenos Aires pits. Reh Kuster, the team secretary, was very disappointed to see me going as she thought that I'd finally control her irascible boss, but I'm afraid I was yet another failed manager on that score. I was, after all, manager number six in the space of four years, after Peter Reinhardt, Ali Strasser, Dieter Basche, Fred Opert and Vic Elford. Unfortunately in those days we were the only 'German' team in F1 and the German fans followed us closely. The media always maintained that ATS was like East Germany with it's own *Führer* in Günther Schmid! Following our departure the headline in the newspaper *Blick* read: "Everyone leaves the sinking ATS ship".

For the San Marino Grand Prix, ATS briefly had the services of Roger Heavens as team manager, and a two-car team, with Slim Borgudd arriving with sponsorship from the pop group Abba. Later on Alastair Caldwell, a long-time McLaren team manager, joined ATS on the rebound from a short spell at Brabham.

As the season continued with the now familiar political bickering of the powers that be, I felt uneasy at the fact that it was the first time I'd left a team in the middle of a season and that this perhaps wouldn't look very good on my *curriculum vitae*. However, everyone within the sport knew that it was the only dignified step to take, knowing the reputation of Günther Schmid, and I sat at home once again thinking of my next move and waiting for the telephone to ring. During the writing of this book, I have learned that sadly Günther is no longer with us, have lost a long battle with a brain tumour.

Thankfully the phone didn't take too long to ring. Sid Taylor, Teddy Yip's man in the UK, called and asked me to take charge of the Theodore Team, which at the time was being led by ex-Lotus and Jimmy Clark mechanic Dave Simms, who wasn't getting on too well with the owners. Patrick Tambay was driving the one-car team and had already collected a point in the USA Grand Prix. The team was based in Birmingham, and with the job came the use of a flat above the factory.

This was a chance to be reunited with Tony Southgate, who'd designed the car and was operating as a self-employed engineer who came to the factory once a week and attended the race meetings. The car wasn't bad considering that it had had no testing outside what you get at races, and we had a good team of mechanics led by Terry Gibbons, while Julian Randles, another of those jacks-of-all-trades, helped with engineering and the cultivation of sponsors. We proudly qualified in Monaco and finished strongly just outside the points.

But of course, it was difficult to maintain the momentum, as Patrick Tambay was approached by a big team, Talbot-Ligier, and not wanting to stand in the way of his future we had to release him by the French Grand Prix. I was then reunited with Marc Surer yet again, who did well under the circumstances, because as one of the small teams we had to make do with the less than efficient Avon tyres. We were qualifying from middle to back of the grid and finishing about the same, except at Monza when we failed to make the grid at all. Along with Marc came my old friend Bruno Flückiger, and I was delighted to welcome him back. We also took on Ian Patton, Ken Wilcox, Gerry Burns and a newcomer to F1, Irishman John Walton, fresh from the Jordan F3 team. For years afterwards 'Johnboy' was always reminding me that I'd been guilty of getting him into Formula One! Sadly, John died on the eve of the 2004 British Grand Prix while he was commercial director of the Minardi team, and his absence is greatly felt in the paddock.

The 1981 season held a brief hope that Mexico would again have a top racing driver, in the shape of Hector Rebaque. Hector had come to Formula One back in 1977 and now, driving for a top team like Brabham, he was showing good form, especially in Argentina, where he qualified in sixth place and ran a strong second to team leader Nelson Piquet until his car gave up. Hector had the makings of a good driver, but in my opinion he never applied himself fully to the role of being in Formula One; he always rushed home to Mexico between races and was frequently suffering from jet lag at Grands Prix. He didn't do enough testing and his heart didn't pump enough fuel and oil through his veins.

And whilst I mention Hector, I must mention another Mexican driver who had the talent and the will to succeed, but unfortunately never got the breaks and the financial help to step up to Formula One. This was Adrian Fernandez, who I met in the 1980s, when he came from Mexico without two coins to rub together. I tried to help him, but apart from introducing him to some people there was little I could do. His perseverance opened some doors and he did some racing in Formula Ford, and later more opportunities came his way in Mexico and the United States, where he raced very successfully in Indy Lights and the CART championship, winning several races. He still drives competitively in the Indy Racing League series, winning three races in 2004, and owns his own Fernandez Racing Team.

For 1982 Theodore had a new car, the TY02, which, although it looked the part, never had quite enough spark – like other small teams, we lacked the luxury of sufficient track-test time. This year we had the services of Irishman Derek Daly, who, like all Irishmen, was great fun to be with. With a small team you need a driver with a reasonable understanding of mechanics, proven patience, and above all a good sense of humour. Life at the back of the grid is a lot different from that at the sharp end.

Even at the first race of the season we hit political problems: this time the drivers were rebelling against some clauses in the 'superlicences' imposed by FISA, and they hid in a big room of the Sunnyside Park Hotel in Johannesburg for a day and a night while negotiations took place. This solidarity among the drivers, led by Niki Lauda – who'd been tempted back to Formula One by McLaren after two years away – was something totally unprecedented. In the end they and FISA agreed to disagree, and the drivers were conned into a false settlement with FISA. So they all came to Kyalami for practice and the race, only to hear afterwards that during the race the stewards had issued an undated statement saying that a temporary agreement had been reached with the drivers only for the purpose of running the Grand Prix, and that as soon as the race was over the situation reverted to the way it had stood before and all the drivers' licences were suspended.

We'd had to take the old car to Kyalami, as the new one wasn't yet ready, and we qualified towards the back and finished 14th. Although not very healthy, we had a TY02 ready for Rio de Janeiro and we qualified much better, but it didn't survive long in the race due to a punctured tyre. The American Grand Prix at Long Beach was no different, and once we got to Europe there were political problems once again.

Although the 'superlicences' crisis was now over, most of the FOCA teams withdrew from the San Marino Grand Prix in protest at the introduction of a new rule to stop them from topping up the water tanks in their brake cooling systems after races to bring their cars back up to the minimum weight. Instead of merely implementing the new rule, FISA had retrospectively disqualified Nelson Piquet's Brabham and Keke Rosberg's Williams from the results of the Brazilian Grand Prix, in which they'd finished first and second. Only 14 cars therefore took part at San Marino, and ours wasn't one of them.

Shortly before Imola, Williams took our driver Derek Daly to replace Carlos Reutemann, who'd suddenly decided to stop racing. Once again we didn't stand in the way of a young driver's career, but at least we were recompensed for his release. The Theodore team seemed to be a trampoline to stardom, from which Keke Rosberg had jumped to Williams, Patrick Tambay to Talbot-Ligier, and now Derek Daly to Williams. So we called once more on the faithful Jan Lammers.

Unfortunately Jan wasn't able to qualify for the Belgian GP at Zolder, where practice was marred by the fatal accident of Gilles Villeneuve. Gilles was already in a bad frame of mind as a result of the race at San Marino, where he should have won the race, but teammate Didier Pironi had passed him on the last lap after both had been told to slow down and hold their positions! He was absolutely mad with Pironi, and with himself for letting him overtake, and he swore never to speak to him again. At Zolder, therefore, the atmosphere at Ferrari was rather tense and it got even worse when Pironi was slightly quicker than Villeneuve. As Gilles set out for his last qualifying run he misinterpreted a move by back-marker Jochen Mass, who was on a slowdown lap, and their cars touched, sending Gilles's Ferrari in the air, across a fence, and finally down the track in so many parts that it would have been a miracle if anyone had survived that impact.

One of the best racing drivers of the last six years, if not the best, had been killed, and yet there was no acknowledgement of it on race day – no minute of silence, no space on the grid, no mention of his name. Only Ferrari had, naturally, withdrawn its other car and left the circuit. It was really sad, as if the world hadn't noticed his absence, and I felt it was dreadfully wrong.

I thought Gilles deserved better than that. He was a real purist racer who loved his job more than anyone else on the grid. I had a recollection of getting a lift with Gilles once, from the Intercontinental Hotel on the outskirts of Rio to the circuit in Jacarepagua. I thought that I was a good driver in traffic, having once beaten Lorenzo Bandini from Monza to Milano in my Fiat 500 back in 1962, but Gilles was absolutely crazy. He used to judge the reaction of the people in front and dive on the opposite side, getting away with it every time! I don't know whether or not I enjoyed the experience, but I learned never to get a lift from Gilles again. Having been in a car with him I knew that he always took far too many chances and this was on normal roads! Somehow I didn't think that he'd ever make old bones.

Needless to say, we didn't make the grid in Monaco, which turned out to be one of the most exciting GPs in history, which no one seemed to want to win after a light shower in the closing laps converted the circuit into a skid pad and the leaders started to go off, including Alain Prost, Didier Pironi, Andrea de Cesaris, Riccardo Patrese and Derek Daly. Eventually Patrese recovered and took the chequered flag.

In a pre-race test at the USA Grand Prix in Detroit, Jan understeered into a wall and broke his thumb. We came up with the idea of offering the drive to Mario Andretti who was around, but not surprisingly he very politely declined. Geoff Lees replaced Lammers for the Canadian Grand Prix and qualified the Theodore, but was involved in the horrendous accident at the start in which newcomer Ricardo Paletti lost his life after crashing his Osella heavily into Pironi's stalled Ferrari. There was a huge fire and the race was stopped, but unfortunately we didn't have a spare car for the restart and Geoff had to sit with the rest of us to watch the race.

Thankfully Lammers qualified in his home town of Zandvoort, but he failed to finish because of engine problems. From then on we had a couple of DNQs, and at the request of Irishman Sid Taylor we sat his compatriot Tommy Byrne in the car starting with the German Grand Prix, but he hardly improved the *status quo*.

The last race of the year was also the second and last time that we raced at Las Vegas in Nevada, in the car park of the Caesar's Palace Hotel. Yes, you read it right, in a hotel car park; but then, everything is big in America. This was a really bizarre venue for a Grand Prix, but a US West Coast race was so important for Formula One that Bernie Ecclestone had to consider anything that was offered to him.

It wasn't only a strange venue, but strange things happened there. I remember that just before qualifying, Teddy Yip handed me a quite sizeable brown paper envelope, saying. "Here Jo, you'd better have this as the team are always in need." We were just taking the cars out for qualifying so I wedged the envelope behind my trouser-belt, as it was too large to go in my pocket. After qualifying (last) I had a chance to look at what was inside: it was a stack of $100 notes! I had to go into the toilet to count them with mounting disbelief – there was $30,000 cash in the envelope, and I'd been treating it like a bag of sandwiches! One could only assume that the money had been acquired during a few lucky placements at the casino tables...

The after-race prizegiving party also had to be seen to be believed. It was a Roman theme party, with gladiators built like brick shit-houses walking around with tame lions and tigers like pets on leads. I remember sitting at the same large table as Paul Newman, and when 'blue eyes' had gone a stream of American girls came by to rub their bottoms on the same chair where Paul had had his! But the highlight of the evening, without a doubt, was the grin on the face of my old boss Ken Tyrrell. The race was Michele Alboreto's first win in the under-sponsored Tyrrell 011.

Morris ('Mo') Nunn's Ensign team was very short of cash and had only just been able to finish the 1982 season. We at Theodore weren't exactly swimming in cash but at least we didn't have any debts, while Ensign had better cars, so we decided to join forces under the Theodore name for 1983, using the Ensign chassis numbers. The drivers were Roberto Guerrero from Colombia and Johnny Cecotto from Venezuela, with the main sponsorship from Café de Colombia. We weren't going to conquer the world, but we seemed a lot better prepared to face it with the engineering experience of Mo Nunn and his designer Nigel Bennett, ex-Firestone and ex-Lotus, one of the nicest and most pragmatic pencil men that I ever had the pleasure to work with. Nigel shared an office in the team's HQ (a converted Victorian house in Lichfield) with Graham Humphrys, who later went on to design the Spice Group C racing cars and has more recently been responsible for the Aston Martin DBR9.

The rest of the personnel were chosen from both teams, with Terry Gibbons remaining as our chief mechanic, and off we went to the first flyaway races of the year. The top teams – graded by performance – were included in the FOCA freight package, which included allowance for two cars, 3,000kg of spares and 14 passenger seats. But those of us who weren't members of the elite club had to make a deal beforehand, and paid a hefty charge for the privilege of sending our cars in the same planes, which naturally was the safest way of doing it.

Alan Woollard was, and still is, in charge of this operation for Bernie Ecclestone. Having agreed terms with him to send our cars and freight down to Brazil and then on to Long Beach, I spotted a loophole in the FOCA packing rules and used it in my favour, as they didn't specify a maximum weight for the cars. So I made some enormous plywood panels that were bolted to the sides of the bodywork and protruded up to the height of the roll-over bar for the whole length of the cars, forming two massive boxes in which we packed all the large and heavy items, thereby minimising the weight of our spares.

When Alan saw our cars arriving at the airport, he went ballistic! Not just because I was taking advantage of the extra 'free' weight that we were going to carry, but also because it was difficult to push the cars and move the steering wheel when loading them. From then on he made a new rule with a limit of 600kg per car.

But really the joke was on me: I was going to pay dearly for over-packing the cars. Roberto Guerrero qualified in a magnificent eighth place for the American Grand Prix at Long Beach, but the scrutineering officials found that the Theodore's bodywork was in fact 10mm too wide. This bodywork was the worst feature of the ex-Ensign cars; while the chassis were beautiful, made half in aluminium and half in carbonfibre, the bodywork was a mixture of glassfibre and 'Kevlar' – far too flimsy, as we couldn't get the right consistency without being too heavy. A combination of this, the Californian heat and the overpacked sidepods had made the bodywork bulge like a pregnant woman.

Although everyone agreed that there was no advantage whatsoever in being 10mm too wide, the cars weren't passed, and Roberto's Saturday time was disallowed. He had to qualify with his Friday time, which moved him to 18th place next to Johnny Cecotto, who was 17th. However, I was told that if I collected the signatures of all the team managers accepting that there was no performance gain to be had from the distorted bodywork, the stewards would be happy to reinstate Roberto's Saturday time.

This was a very reasonable solution, and quite realistic. There was much more *camaraderie* in those days, although this sort of help would probably never happen in the 'piranha pond' atmosphere that exists in modern Formula One.

So I prepared a convincing letter and set off in pursuit of all the signatures, which I managed to obtain – except from Roger Silman of the Toleman team, who wouldn't sign, in spite of the fact that every other team from one end of the pit-lane to the other had co-operated. I thought it was a very short-sighted attitude for a relatively new team that more often than not failed to qualify, and I also believed that the newer and smaller teams should stick together. I was, therefore, pleased to return the compliment later in the year when Toleman needed some help.

But not all was lost for Theodore at Long Beach, as Cecotto managed a very satisfying sixth place and the only point in a year that saw us sometimes qualifying in the middle of the grid but seldom finishing strongly. Towards the end of the season our money started to dry up and the future became unclear. Mo Nunn resigned from the team and in the last race but one, at Brands Hatch, we only entered one car, and withdrew completely before the last race at Kyalami.

The 1983 motor racing season wasn't yet over for Teddy Yip, however. One of my most precious recollections from my time with Teddy at Theodore Racing was our yearly trip to the 'Grand Prix' meeting in Macao, the Portuguese territory on a narrow peninsula close to Hong Kong. It was great at least once a year to come from the sophisticated and highly competitive world of F1 racing, where we were always the underdogs and also-rans, into the small world of Formula Atlantic, where we were the top cats. But of all these years, the most memorable was 1983, the year where the status of the race changed from Formula Atlantic to Formula 3; and if Formula 3 had always been the stepping stone to Formula One, the Guia circuit in Macao certainly confirmed when an F3 driver was ready to take the step. If a driver won in Macao, you could always be assured of seeing him shortly afterwards in an F1 car.

Theodore Racing used to contract the best British top teams and run the cars under the Marlboro Theodore Racing banner. That year we had three cars from Dick Bennett's West Surrey Racing and from Eddie Jordan Racing for Ayrton Senna, Martin Brundle and Roberto Guerrero. Ayrton and Martin had just been fighting the whole year for the F3 British Championship, which Senna won with a record 12 wins. Martin was having his first overseas race, while Roberto was our regular F1 driver and it was three years since he'd driven an F3 car. Dick and Eddie ran the cars, while Julian Randles and myself provided knowledge about the circuit and helped with the proceedings.

Teddy Yip was big in Hong Kong, of course, but in Macao he was even bigger. Among the many assets that he and his partner Stanley Ho had were the Jetfoil boats that provided the transportation between Macao and Hong Kong, and the Hotel Lisboa, one of the biggest and busiest hotels, with 24-hour gambling rooms which were always full. Even so, it was always impossible to get enough rooms, and Eddie Jordan and I ended up sharing for this event, which was no problem as we got along fine. At my farewell party in Indianapolis in 2001, Eddie shook my hand and, in his inimitable fashion said: "If I ever have to share a room with a f*****g man again in my life, I wouldn't mind sharing with you."

But other than sharing a room we were greeted everywhere

with the red carpet, and the night before the first practice there was a cocktail reception at Teddy's house, where we used to prepare the cars in the garage. This was followed by the traditional 13-course Chinese dinner party at the Lisboa, the only time that I could eat one of my all-time favourite delicacies, shark's fin soup, which is very expensive.

I'd met Ayrton Senna a couple of years earlier when he was racing Formula Ford at an F1 test session in Silverstone, where I was chatting in a motorhome with Emerson Fittipaldi. Ayrton came to say hello to his famous compatriot. We were introduced, and when he left the motorhome Emerson said to me, "You must keep an eye on this young man. He will become one of the greatest drivers the sport has ever seen."

Emerson had never spoken truer words in his life. From then on I naturally looked out for Ayrton and visited him whenever he was running at the same circuit at a Grand Prix weekend, but this was going to be the first time we were going to work together and I was very much looking forward to the occasion.

Needless to say, the three Ralt-Toyotas of Marlboro Theodore Racing were the quickest in practice with Senna on pole (having put wall marks on all four of his tyres), followed by Guerrero and Brundle. The race was run in two parts of 15 laps each, simply because the F3 cars didn't hold enough fuel for more than that and a 15-lap race could hardly be called a 'Grand Prix'.

For the first half, Ayrton didn't look right. He appeared to have had a stomach upset and to be suffering from lack of sleep. He was very quiet and preoccupied, and in fact when the flag dropped he didn't seem to be with it at all. Guerrero got the better of him, getting to Yacht Club Corner in the lead. But perhaps this was what was needed to wake up young Ayrton who, with more recent experience of F3 cars and the fiercest determination ever in a race driver, got out of Guerrero's gearbox in the short straight leading to Statue Corner and made a gap on the inside in which to squeeze by! Roberto was totally dumbfounded. Up to this day he has never known how on earth Senna was able to do that.

This was, in fact, what used to motivate Ayrton. He often said that anyone could go quickly in a racing car, but overtaking like this on a split second decision was what made the difference.

From then on he was on top of the world and felt, and indeed was, unbeatable. However, at the end of the first race, despite having won, he still looked no better than before and told me no way could he stay at the track: he had to go back to the hotel for some rest. He gave me a spare room key and asked me to wake him later, insisting that I must not only go and shake him awake but stay there until he was actually out of bed. He was very insistent about this, knowing his habit of waking up in response to a call and immediately going back to sleep again. I sometimes called him a professional sleeper! It was then he confessed to me that he'd been at a party the night before and had stayed a little too late and had consumed perhaps a little too much Vodka.

Perhaps it was the same party where Pierluigi Martini had been, and he almost missed the first race altogether. At the start he was definitely in another world and he should have stayed in bed all day, as he hit poor young Martin Brundle and sent him into the barriers at the start. Macao was the last Formula 3 race of the year after all the different championships of each country were run, and it was a very light-hearted event with everyone in a party mood, but when the flag dropped it was business as usual. The racing was hard because every driver was very conscious of what a Macao win would do to his CV.

When Ayrton woke up he looked a lot better and he even managed a smile. He won the second race in the same convincing style and Macao had its most distinguished podium of its 40-year history, with Roberto Guerrero and Gerhard Berger in second and third places.

For me, that weekend was an eye-opener into the career and life of this ambitious young man who was more focused than anyone I've ever seen on fulfilling his dream of becoming the world's greatest racing driver. There was nothing else in life for Ayrton: he was going to succeed or to die trying. His determination was second to none, and this weekend had made me realise the enormity of his potential and I'm just glad to have been part of it. From then on we kept in touch and I followed his steps even more closely than before.

This was my last race with Theodore Racing and these happy years couldn't have ended on a happier note than with a win on

Teddy's domain with the unforgettable Ayrton Senna. I joined McLaren that December.

Even so, Teddy was good enough to invite me to Macao for the following two years as a guest, together with my wife. There's no doubt that at the 'wrong' end of the Formula One grid you sometimes find a better class of people. Teddy died a couple of weeks after his 90th birthday in 2003. Beverly, his wife, had asked me for a quote for his birthday party and I wrote: "Wow, Teddy, if you'd known that you were going to live this long you'd either have taken better care of yourself or put more whiskey and less ice in your drinks!"

I was told he had a big laugh at that – he was a great character and people like him are very much missed in Formula One.

CHAPTER 10

THE POSTMAN
ALWAYS RINGS TWICE

One of the many perks of life in Formula One is the number of friends that you collect throughout the years. People of all nationalities, from every walk of life. One of these friends, a little younger than me, was Ron Dennis. Ron first worked in Formula One for Brabham and Cooper, and as well as being an excellent mechanic he was a very dynamic and entrepreneurial individual with a breadth of vision that I'd never seen in anyone before. Probably his greatest asset was that he could practically see into the future, and it wasn't difficult to guess that he was going to go far in motor racing. By 1971 he'd set up his own Formula 2 team, Rondel Racing, with his partner Neil Trundle.

In the late 1970s, Ron and I used to play squash at weekends when we weren't racing. One week we'd play in Maidenhead where I was living, and then come home for a bowl of spaghetti; another week at Woking, followed by lunch at his house with Sally Green, his girlfriend at that time. I really can't remember who used to win, but I think we were very equally matched – except that while I loved the game and the exercise, Ron just hated to lose.

One particular year he gathered too much sponsorship for his Formula 2 team, some of which he'd not be able to use as there were conflicting products. He therefore offered me the opportunity of starting a 'B' team with him, perhaps just running one car at the beginning. I was grateful to him for the offer, but I preferred Formula One – I was having fun running small teams, and furthermore I didn't think it would be long before Ron was in Formula One himself.

By 1980 Marlboro weren't happy with the recent lack of success of their main Formula One sponsorship team, McLaren. Ron saw the opportunity and approached Marlboro, who were quite ready to inject some young blood into the team. The amalgamation of Bruce McLaren Motor Racing and Ron Dennis's outfit, then called Project Four Racing, resulted in McLaren International in 1981. With Ron came John Barnard, who then designed the first carbonfibre composite Formula One monocoque.

Ron began the resurrection of McLaren by getting rid of some deadwood and restructuring the new workforce. It was then that he called and offered me a middle management job, which was very tempting, as McLaren had always been a top team and was bound to get better under its new management. However, I was still happier being a big fish in a small pond and the thought of getting into a big pond as a small fish was perhaps not so attractive at the time, so I declined the offer. In my defence, McLaren was then a bit top-heavy on the management side, and I felt that the time wasn't right.

By the middle of the 1983 season it was very clear that any Formula One team that lacked either a contract for a turbocharged engine for 1984, or, better still, an engine-manufacturing partner, didn't have much of a future. As ever, we were struggling at Theodore Racing and, without an engine in place for the coming year, we were planning to move to the USA to form a team for the CART Champ Car series. This didn't attract me a great deal and deep inside I was regretting not having taken Ron's offer, and hoping that perhaps he'd ring again. Happily for me he did, and I came to McLaren at the end of the year for an interview with Ron and John Barnard. By this time there was no one left from the old McLaren management and the set-up was a lot slimmer and more streamlined.

For the coming 'turbo' era, Ron had managed to convince Porsche to build a V6 engine for the exclusive use of McLaren, and what Porsche didn't know about turbocharged racing engines wasn't worth knowing. With this plan on the cards, he managed to obtain financial backing for the project from TAG (Techniques d'Avant Garde), the Arab-French company headed by Mansour Ojjeh, who later became co-owner of McLaren International. Mansour, his brothers Aziz and Karim, his wife Kathy and all the family, although very wealthy people, were always very unassuming, easy to please and fun-loving. It was always a pleasure to do anything for them. By the time I came for my interview, McLaren MP4s equipped with the TAG PO1 turbo engine had already run the last four races of 1983, and a serious attack on the World Championship was scheduled for 1984.

The job which was offered to me involved taking over a lot of the day-to-day arrangements for the racing and testing activities, leaving Ron to deal with more important issues. I was also to oversee the nuts and bolts relationship between Porsche and McLaren, from the buying of the engines and organising of rebuilds to organising and scheduling their movements to and from Stuttgart. I was also responsible for all the race and test team movements, personnel, drivers, cars, engines, spares, fuel and tyres – nowadays called logistics – plus relations between the team and the Formula One Constructors' Association. The job title was 'Team Co-ordinator'.

My official start was at the 1983 team Christmas party at the 'Good Earth', a Chinese restaurant in Esher – I was the 64th employee, and we could all fit into a normal restaurant. I arrived in a suit and tie, as I didn't know what to expect; the jacket and tie didn't last one minute. That was how long it took me to realise that at McLaren you work hard and you play hard, and Ron Dennis set the best example of this.

On my first day at the office I was pleasantly relieved to find that my colleague, who took care of a great deal of the work to do with bookings and travel, was Liz Wood, the former secretary of Peter Ward at Wolf Racing. Liz had started only a few weeks before me but she had a world of experience. Liz and I got on very well and we established a friendly atmosphere in our small but vastly busy department. Another friendly face was that of financial director Bob Illman, also formerly with Wolf/Fittipaldi. Besides being a great pillar of the team in the background, 'Folder', as he was known, was also a great friend, who always had time to listen and lend a helping hand where needed.

My first trip with McLaren was to the Rio test in January 1984, with both of the drivers – Niki Lauda and the newcomer to the team, Alain Prost, who'd had a fight with Renault and was returning to the team that had given him his break into Formula One. One had to feel sorry for John Watson, the McLaren driver he replaced, who hadn't done anything wrong, but Alain had more solid credentials. I'd met Alain for the first time in 1979 when, as a promising Formula 3 driver, he tested a McLaren Formula One car at Paul Ricard, with John setting the target times. I was there with the Shadow team. I'd asked the McLaren boys for the use of the lathe in their truck, and when Alain came in to change his overalls we'd started chatting. He was as happy as Larry, as all his dreams were starting to come true. When John came in to change his own overalls, he said to me: "No matter how quick I go that bastard still manages to take at least a half a second off my time!"

Alain had driven a Cosworth-powered McLaren in 1980 as John's number two before doing three seasons with the Renault turbos, during which he had established himself as a regular race winner. So team spirits were high as I, engineers Steve Nichols and Alan Jenkins, plus Hans Mezger and Ralph Hahn from Porsche and the rest of the team, set off to Rio de Janeiro. This was my first assignment and I was very apprehensive, as John Barnard had made a point of telling me before we left that whatever I did, *I must not fuck it up*!

It turned out to be a dreadful week in which we had nothing but problems. The Bosch 'Motronic' electronic engine management system refused to run properly and we barely accomplished 400 miles. I remember writing a painfully detailed, minute-by-minute account of the whole test in a report back to John Barnard, which he didn't even bother to read!

Nevertheless, I was starting to mingle at all levels in a team where there were very strong personalities – ego-busters as well as ego-trippers. Soon after I started, I was in the stores arranging space for the TAG engine parts when I was approached by chief mechanic Dave Ryan, a New Zealander, who perhaps saw me as a threat and wanted to test his case. "What are you doing here? They've created a wank job for you. We didn't need you last year and I don't think we need you this year." We exchanged a few 'pleasantries' and I told him that it was nothing to do with him – if he'd any problem, he should go and see Ron Dennis, who was the one that had appointed me.

I had a word with Ron and said that if my presence was going to unsettle the team then perhaps it was better if I left. Ron was very supportive and said that it was inevitable that the team would grow, and if there were some team members who were uneasy about it, it was tough shit. I never had a problem with David Ryan again, and he became team manager in the early 1990s.

After the horrendous Brazilian trip, Ron asked me what I'd done for fuel and oil on my little teams, and I said that I'd never had a hope in hell of getting a supply contract with a big company so I just bought it locally wherever we were racing. However, with ATS I'd built up a good relationship with Willi Förster, Shell's German distributor at Deutsche Shell in Hamburg, who was a great motor racing enthusiast and gave me free fuel at German events, and as much oil as we could fit in the truck! In typical Ron Dennis manner, he said to me, "Right, call him, send him a ticket and get him over here tomorrow." Not quite the next day, but in a couple of days we had him at Woking for a preliminary meeting and it wasn't difficult to persuade him to invest in McLaren, as he was a real fan. We also needed him to open the doors to the right people at Shell International, and this he did, so that in a couple of weeks we had all the top brass from Shell House in London down in Woking for a serious meeting.

It was then, for the first time, that I had the opportunity of seeing Ron Dennis at a top level discussion, selling our product to the top cats of an international company. I was totally overawed at the skill with which he could negotiate. He had the right answers for every question and he was never short of words – I was positive that he could have sold freezers to Eskimos. From that year on we had some cash from Shell and free fuel and oil at every race, and Ron told me to send a big present to Willi for his contribution, which was something Ron was always very good and punctilious about.

Ron cultivated the partnership throughout the season, and the following year we had an increased technical relationship with Shell, together with several million dollars, and the relationship continued and strengthened during the ten years of our long and happy association. One mustn't forget that fuel and lubrication were very important during the turbo era, because the Formula One fuel regulations then allowed the use of more sophisticated ingredients, which enhanced the performance of the engines. The Shell partnership was therefore one of the keys to McLaren's success, as it gave us access to the expertise, know-how and resources of one of the largest companies in the world.

In the late 1980s and early 1990s it wasn't unusual for me to cross the Atlantic to the United States for a day trip to get a couple of litres of some kind of aromatic or di-olefin, which I brought back in my briefcase. Back at the Shell laboratories in Thornton this would be mixed in to get 25 litres of 'rocket fuel' for qualifying, which could jack up the power output of the engine an unbelievable 10 per cent. We'd then transport this fuel by private jet or helicopter to the race truck.

This was typical of the level of commitment that McLaren had always had. For me, it was like a breath of fresh air after nine years of struggling to make ends meet. I no longer had to look after that side of it, but just had to be sensible of how the money was spent; but normally when I presented Ron with a list of forthcoming expenditure, his response was always, "If we need it, get it. I'll worry about the money."

It was very gratifying to see that after that first outing to Rio, the new car and upgraded electronics meant we never had to look in the rear-view mirror again! The drivers got alone fine too: Alain had already won nine Grands Prix and Niki was a double World Champion and one of the sport's recognised all-time stars. For Alain, it was hard to believe that he was teamed with his karting days' idol, a driver on whom he'd been modelling himself since his early days. For Niki, having done it all before, it was more difficult to pair up with a driver who'd still got almost everything to do. Alain was the quicker of the two for 90 per cent of the time, so Niki had to resort to other means of beating him. With his very strong personality this wasn't a difficult task, at least out of the car.

In the first race, back at Rio, Niki again had Bosch Motronic troubles and Alain won. This was, of course, a very important victory for McLaren and TAG history, and the whole team was ecstatic. Before Ron left for the airport he told me to make sure the team had a big celebration. Prost was also delighted, as he could look back at his old Renault team with his head up, happy that the future was looking brighter.

We were first and second in South Africa, despite Alain starting last from the pit-lane with the spare car after a fuel pump failure, which confirmed his speed and the superiority of the McLaren MP4/2. We had a weekend off-form at Zolder but returned to the top of the podium with Alain at Imola and again at Dijon with Niki.

At Monaco, Alain put the McLaren on pole more than a second quicker than Lauda, but Sunday was a very bleak and wet day that became wetter as it progressed. Prost led most of the time, except for a few laps led by Nigel Mansell's Lotus 95T until he went out after having an argument with a barrier – like many other drivers, including our own Niki Lauda. By lap 31 the rain was so bad, with visibility getting worse by the minute, that clerk of the course Jacky Ickx, a recognised rain master in his Grand Prix days, had no alternative but to stop the race. At the time Ayrton Senna in his Toleman-Hart was a close second and just about to pass Prost. In a typical no-win situation, Jacky Ickx was heavily criticised by a lot of people, some of whom even questioned his integrity, which affected Jacky for months after the event. The FIA even took away his licence, because he hadn't followed the correct procedure of consulting with the stewards before making his decision.

Senna had once again demonstrated both his virtuosity behind the wheel of a Formula One car and his unparalleled sensitivity in wet conditions, assuring the public that his time was coming. Although he'd always shown promise, this time, in a second-rate car, he'd battled convincingly against the best at a time when there were far more top drivers than there are now. Nevertheless, that weekend Alain deserved the win. Everyone got only half the usual points for their hard work, but in hindsight, of course, it would've been better for Alain to have finished second to Senna in a full race and have got six points instead of four-and-a-half, as he went on to lose the championship by a mere half a point!

The one and only US Grand Prix at Dallas almost didn't happen. In the high temperature of the Texan summer, the asphalt of the street circuit was virtually destroyed by the power of the Formula One engines, transferred to the road via the wide 'slick' tyres that we used in those days. The race was slightly delayed, as workers were busy laying extra coats of asphalt until just an hour before the start. Once the race started it was a case of survival of the fittest as the track began to break up. The drivers became exhausted, with temperatures in excess of 110° in the cockpit, and most of them started hitting the walls. I kept a picture from the *Dallas Post* of the eventual winner, Keke Rosberg, as he was driving the last lap, watched by Niki Lauda, Alain Prost, Thierry Boutsen, Eddie Cheever, Riccardo Patrese, Marc Surer and Michele Alboreto, all sitting on the wall with their overalls at half-mast, having all hit the wall. Typically, Keke is giving them the 'wanker' sign from the cockpit of his Williams...

The Dallas Grand Prix might not have been a successful race on the circuit, but it certainly was in the bank. Not that Formula One is driven by money (well, not in those days!) but money is often needed to 'oil the wheels', and for all of us in the Grand Prix brigade it was a very pleasant and different venue, where we had the chance to mingle at Southfork Ranch with JR, Sue Ellen and Bobby Ewing, the stars of *Dallas*, arguably the most successful soap opera ever.

From then on McLaren won every single Grand Prix. If Prost's car stayed in one piece he'd win with Lauda close behind and scoring in every race. But Alain retired on three occasions, and this gave Niki the edge in the race for the championship, so that when we arrived at Estoril for the last race Alain had to win, with Niki finishing third or less, to get the World Championship.

But as far as the team was concerned we'd won everything, and one of my priorities for the Portuguese weekend was therefore to find a venue for drinking and dining followed by a nightclub for more drinking and dancing: no matter what happened in the race this was going to be a great Sunday night. I'd booked all the team to return to base on the Tuesday, as I didn't think that anyone would be in a fit state to travel on Monday. We'd won 11 out of 15 races, and we were about to make it 12 out of 16, and at the time I thought that Grands Prix were so hard to win that I could live another hundred years and no one would ever beat this!

In the race Alain did what he needed to do and won. Niki managed to dial-in the perfect set-up on his car and ran the fastest lap in the morning warm-up. He'd also sent a plane to collect his wife, Marlene (the only time that we saw her at a race). He already had with him five TAG-Heuer watches as presents for his mechanics and engineers, so he seemed to have everything in place – but he was 11th on the first lap.

He began carving his way through the field, but when he reached third place behind Mansell he needed to make up half a minute, with half the race to go, to catch him. It looked as if it wasn't going to be possible and Alain was going to be the champion. But then, with 19 laps to go, Mansell spun and parked without brakes, and Lauda was second!

Hearing an account of those 19 laps from Niki, in full Technicolor, was an education: "When I got to third behind Mansell, I'd had trouble with some back-markers and I'd already used some extra boost pressure passing de Angelis, Johansson, Alboreto and others. So I didn't think it was possible and didn't want to risk the engine in case Mansell had problems. Suddenly I saw your board: 'Mansell out'! No, I thought, I didn't read it right. Well, next lap I'd watch more carefully. I saw a black car stopped on the circuit. Is it de Angelis? I missed the board this lap, and nearly went off the circuit trying to see which black car it was parked. The next lap I paid attention to the board. It had a big 'P2' on it. Wow! Is that true? I couldn't believe it. I looked at the parked Lotus and, yes, it was Mansell, and from then on those were the longest 16 or 17 laps in my life. I kept hearing strange noises from the back – the brake pedal was longer … oh no, fuck it, this mother is going to stop! I was a total wreck – everything was shaking inside me, but the car never missed a beat. I was second and World Champion."

Alain had lost by the smallest-ever margin of just half a point. I always thought that it was wrong, that there should be a closer link to race wins rather than just points: Alain had won seven races and Niki five, with Alain dominating all the time. Perhaps it would've been better for the team commercially if Alain had won, as we'd have had two World Champions for the following season, but Alain was the younger and had more time ahead of him. I always felt that Ron preferred Niki to win, but this could have been because Alain's contract was linked with performance – therefore it would have cost him a lot more money!

The party started from the moment the flag dropped. The Marlboro motorhome was a complete wreck – champagne, water, wine, cream, you name it, it was spread all over the place. We even had a women's fight as an afternoon show, between Sarah, James

Hunt's wife, and some Marlboro guests. Sarah was a great party animal: I remember James saying, "I finally found a woman more mad about sex than me – I had to marry her!" From the circuit motorhome we moved to the Biera Mar restaurant in Cascais for a team dinner, finishing up at the Penny Lane discotheque until nine the next morning. I remember singing Stevie Wonder's *I Just Called To Say I Love You* with Alain, Elio de Angelis and Princess Stephanie of Monaco, who was one of our guests.

What a great feeling! For a record-breaking year the hangover was worth every minute of it. Then came the celebrations with all the sponsors, with a great Christmas party at a nightclub in Paris where all the McLaren staff and partners were flown for a wonderful weekend.

It's always good to end the season as the team to beat because it keeps you feeling good all winter. Niki Lauda signed again with us for 1985, in spite of the fact that Ron really screwed him down on his package. It was important for Niki to race after winning the title, commercially and personally. Alain was also happy that Niki stayed, and all the team and sponsors, needless to say, were looking forward to another good year.

As the years went by, Formula One was becoming a very recognised means of worldwide advertising, thanks to the efforts of Bernie Ecclestone. Winning the championship made life easier for our marketing department under Ekrem Sami. We couldn't have had a better man for the job. Ekrem was every bit as good as Ron was, and getting even better, and it was always a great pleasure to work with him on different projects. I was pleased to be able to assist, especially in Italy with my contacts and language, and at that time we thought of approaching some old friends of mine at Segafredo, one of Italy's largest coffee companies. I'd had support from them in my old days and I'd maintained a good relationship with them thereafter, particularly with the boss and owner, Massimo Zanetti.

However, Philip Morris Inc, the big-name owners of the Marlboro brand, didn't think it appropriate to have Segafredo on the car when they were the owners of Maxwell House coffee! Ekrem did a wonderful job of convincing them otherwise, and we had Segafredo almost on board when we decided that if the mountain couldn't come to Mohammed, Mohammed must go to the mountain, and on a horrible wet, cold and foggy day we hired a plane and flew with Ron to Mestre in Italy for a meeting with Massimo. The plane couldn't land near Mestre because of fog and had to go to Milan, from where we hired a car. Ron said, "I'll drive and you navigate, because you speak the language," and no matter how many times I told him that he was no Niki Lauda, he continued to frighten me, as the fog was very bad. We then had to find a public phone to call Massimo and advise him that we were running late! Oh, for a mobile phone! How did we manage without them?

We had a great meeting with Massimo, even though he didn't speak a word of English. Ron presented him with Alain's helmet and we flew back from Italy on that miserable foggy winter evening with a $2 million contract in our hands. Ron had an unusual slip of the tongue as we were sipping a glass of champagne, and said, "You know, Jo, we should have a guy with contacts in marketing, speaking three or four languages. He'd be worth 30 to 40,000 a year." I couldn't help but laugh and say, "Yes, of course, Ron, I'll speak with Bob" [our financial director].

I felt so many times that I was grossly underpaid – I only started earning good money in the early 1990s. But then, I loved my job so much that I'd have done it for nothing.

The 1985 season was full of ups and downs, but the good thing was that the ups outnumbered the downs. Alain won at Rio. Ayrton Senna won his first Grand Prix with Lotus in a torrential rain storm at Estoril, confirming his virtuosity in the wet in a race that should have been stopped. Alain won at Imola, only to find that his MP4/2B was disqualified after the podium celebrations because it was almost 2kg under the minimum weight limit.

I was absolutely gutted at that, I felt that we'd robbed him of his win. But Alain took it so well by saying that he'd won a lot of races by being right on the weight limit, and he'd lost this one by being under it, and that was motor racing. I remain forever grateful, although I told him that if he lost this year's championship by nine points I wouldn't be able to look him in the eye ever again.

On Monday morning I had Peter Warr from Team Lotus on the phone claiming the trophies, as Elio de Angelis was now the winner. I called Elio first to ask him which of the two trophies he wanted and I sent Elio the silver plate and Lotus the gold cup.

We won the next race in Monaco with Alain again – and the post-race scales had the McLaren at only 800gm over the weight limit after they'd weighed the car several times. I remember complaining bitterly to Tim Wright, Prost's engineer, that if we carried on this way I was going to age quicker! But this had always been the McLaren way: never to break the rules, but always to run at the sharp end of what the regulations allowed you, and I guess it has proved to be the winning way.

Alain was third in Montreal, had a DNF in Detroit, and was third again at Paul Ricard before his next win at Silverstone. He had another second place on the Nürburgring before we arrived at the Osterreichring for Niki's home race. At this point, Alain had scored 41 points to Niki's five.

Niki felt that his motivation wasn't quite the same and that he was struggling more than before to stay behind Alain. He had three World Championships and he didn't need to prove anything more, nor did he have to risk his life now that his airline Lauda Air was starting to 'take off'. He'd decided to retire at the end of the year and he and Ron agreed between them that he should do it at the Austrian Grand Prix, once Ron had contracted Keke Rosberg for 1986.

Lauda called all the journalists into a hospitality tent and when he was starting to tell the world something that many were already expecting to hear, Ron took the microphone and made what can only be described as a really clumsy speech in which he didn't mention Niki at all, but just praised John Barnard for the design of the MP4. It was one of those typical famous 'Ron-talk' speeches in which he chose to use the most recherché and unnatural words, that even pedants seldom use, in an exaggerated attempt to hide his humble origins – and the English language is the one that most lends itself to this sort of waffle. The situation was so ridiculous that everyone looked at each other with incredulity. It was Niki's day, Niki's press conference, yet Ron just ignored him. Niki was visibly absolutely livid and has never forgiven Ron for that untimely intervention.

In his own book, *To Hell and Back*, Niki isn't very kind about

Ron, for this and for having screwed him down on his salary in the year in which he was supposedly defending his World Championship. However, Niki should have learned – as all of us have who've worked with Ron – that his flaws are sometimes as startling as his strengths.

I'm sure that in some ways we were all going to miss Niki, but I was never really a member of the Niki Lauda fan club. He was an excellent driver, but I wouldn't put him in the same league as Alain Prost. Perhaps some years earlier in his career he might have been, but at his peak with Ferrari he chose to withdraw from the 1976 Japanese Grand Prix because of dangerous track conditions when he had the World Championship almost won. He only needed to finish in front of James Hunt, but he decided to quit and lost the championship. In that moment he forgot the 70 people from Ferrari who were there supporting him, the thousands of Ferrari workers in Modena who had helped him to be there, the hundreds of thousands of people in the Italian industry that had contributed to the Ferrari success, and Ferrari's millions of fans all over the world. His selfishness was totally unacceptable to me and I could never understand his decision. If I'd been on his team I'd never have forgiven him. Mario Andretti, the eventual winner of the atrocious race, said in disgust, "For the World Championship I'd have driven to Mount Fuji!"

In 1979, in the middle of Friday practice at the Canadian GP, Niki decided that he'd had enough of "going round and round in circles" and quit racing, something that didn't go down too well with Bernie Ecclestone, his boss at the time, or the Brabham team, who had no warning at all. Even if anyone had understood that, they'd have been totally confused by the fact that in 1982 he was tempted back by Ron Dennis. Sadly, much of his fame came from his horrible crash at the Nürburgring in 1976, when he was scarred for life yet was back in the cockpit only a few weeks after.

Niki's book is a very good read, which I couldn't put down until I'd finished it. Somehow I wished that Niki could have written the book before he drove for us, and then I'd have known the man better. Of all the drivers with whom I've been associated in my life, Niki was perhaps the one to whom I've been the least close. But that was Niki. He was a very reserved and pragmatic individual to whom no one was really close, but nevertheless a fascinating personality, and now that I know what makes him tick I probably feel closer to him. He was the first arrival at my farewell party saying, "I don't believe you're quitting, so I had to be here."

Funnily enough, at the next race after announcing his retirement, at Zandvoort, Niki won his best victory in a McLaren, in a race where he and Alain drove wheel-to-wheel and finished first and second only two seconds apart. Niki said: "Not that Alain will need any help to win the championship, but if he does I'll help, but not just yet. There are still five races to go."

Niki crashed at Spa when the throttle jammed open and sprained his wrist, missing that race and the European Grand Prix at Brands Hatch. Being in Britain, Ron called in John Watson as a replacement, but poor John, having been out of racing for two years, was out of his depth. In testing he was three seconds slower than Alain, but with time running out we couldn't get another driver. We gave John another test session to improve, but he could only qualify on the 11th row of the grid. As the race progressed so did he, but he finished just outside the points.

To the relief of everyone in the team, Alain Prost won the World Championship by finishing fourth at Brands Hatch, in the same race that saw Nigel Mansell achieve his maiden Formula One win in a Williams-Honda, beating Senna in a Lotus-Renault.

After winning the title at Brands Hatch our luck changed, and we didn't do much in the remaining two races. The only thing that stuck in my memory from these events was the mesmerising lap by Ayrton Senna for pole position in Adelaide. He was more than half a second quicker than the next man, Nigel Mansell. I've never seen a lap like it, it seemed as if the car never had contact with the ground. He was handling a Formula One car as if it was a go-kart and I had to go to the Lotus pit and thank him for the pleasure he'd just given the onlookers. He was quite delighted with his lap saying, "I guess it was special, but it went so quickly that I really don't remember much about it!" Niki, who started 16th, led briefly, but the chances of him winning his last race went up in smoke together with his brakes, which sent him into the concrete wall and out of the race.

At the end of 1985 – in fact on the very last day of the year –

Ron Dennis married Lisa, his girlfriend of three years, and with his usual luck he couldn't have chosen a better partner. A Californian, Lisa was the perfect wife for him: full of class, great personality, good looks, very attractive and able to keep up with the rising star of her husband-to-be and bring him back down to earth when necessary. It was always a pleasure to see her at a race meeting, as Ron was always a better person with her at his side.

With Niki out of the team and Ayrton with a tight contract with Lotus for 1986, Ron had signed up Keke Rosberg, who was unhappy at Williams. There weren't many rule changes for the new season, except that – in a move to control power outputs – the fuel capacity had been restricted from 220 litres to 195. Thinking about this 20 years later, it seems absolutely crazy that the fastest cars in the world, in the lavish sport of Formula One, had to be careful about fuel consumption! It was hard to get the message across to the public, as already in 1985 we'd had to freeze the fuel before putting it into the cars in an effort to squeeze perhaps three per cent more in, and it wasn't unusual for a leading driver to run out of fuel on the last lap! 1986 would be even more critical, and Porsche worked very hard to make our TAG Turbo V6 a very fuel-efficient engine. So much so that, in the first race in Rio, both cars went out with piston failures! We were running the engines perhaps a bit *too* lean.

Keke Rosberg was a great guy to work with, both on the race track and off it. He was more Latin than Finnish and one of his best attributes was his honesty. If he went off at the circuit by making a mistake, he was the first to tell you, saving you from looking at the damaged car for clues as to what might have happened. During his first test in Rio, he had a major shunt in the fast corner at the end of the straight and destroyed our car. He himself was completely destroyed, as it wasn't a good way to start life with a new team. As I came back to the pits from collecting the wrecked car, I said to him, "Wow, Keke, you really made a good mess of this one," and he replied "Thanks, Jo, I really needed that," which made me feel pretty bad. Keke really didn't need to be reminded, he already felt bad enough.

The problem with Keke was that he used to hate an understeering car. He just couldn't drive them. He always excelled in car control and therefore preferred a car that oversteered, which he could control single-handed; but an understeering car was definitely a handful. He always had long arguments with John Barnard, when John would tell him that a race car is designed to go forward and if you go sideways you're scrapping speed and will go slower. During the first half of the year, Keke started to cope with his McLaren and JB perhaps allowed him a more neutral car. At Brands Hatch he was finally able to outqualify Prost, and he took pole at Hockenheim next time out. He announced his retirement at the end of the year, and also reiterated Watson's views on Prost: "No matter what time you do, that fucking little Frog will always go a bit quicker!"

To say that 1986 was a tight year would be the understatement of the century. When we got to the halfway point in the calendar, at Paul Ricard, Alain was leading Mansell by one point, but by the time we got to the last Grand Prix of the season, in Adelaide, the score was Mansell 70, Alain 64, Piquet 63. Therefore unless disaster struck, it was Mansell's year.

Alain, who was renowned for chewing his fingernails, was standing by his car before the race, biting his nails as usual and with his legs constantly on the move. I remember grabbing his legs to steady them and saying to him, "You'd better put your gloves on while you still have some fingers left."

Unluckily for Mansell, disaster did strike, and although it could have been avoided Williams didn't react quickly enough. Rosberg took off like lightning and was leading from lap 7; Prost followed him, and it was a McLaren 1–2 until lap 32, when Alain hit Berger's Benetton-BMW and damaged a front tyre. He came into the pits and we changed all four tyres and sent him away. Goodyear, who'd recommended changing tyres during the race, then changed their mind when they examined Alain's used tyres and decided that they could have lasted longer. However, disaster struck again when Keke – who was leading by miles – had a rear tyre delaminating so badly and causing so much vibration that he thought the engine had gone, so he switched it off and stopped.

Word of the tyre failure quickly reached the pits, but before Williams could make a decision Mansell had a massive rear tyre blow-out which sent him through the escape road at 180mph.

Williams then called Piquet in for a tyre change, which left Prost in the lead with his own purgatory, as for the last 15 laps his on-board computer was telling him that he had five litres of fuel! He was still pushing at the time but he never thought he was going to finish. When he finally saw 'P1 Lap 1 World Champion' on the board, he coasted the car to the chequered flag, parked just the other side, got out of the car and jumped three feet in the air.

This was one of just two occasions during his McLaren days that Alain had brought his wife Anne Marie to a race, and I grabbed her by the arm and we legged it to the podium, which Alain had reached seconds earlier. When they saw each other they hugged with tears in their eyes and neither of them could talk.

I'll never forget checking Alain's brakes after the race and comparing them with Keke's. While Alain's could easily have made another race, Keke's discs were almost paper-thin and there was no way that he could have finished the race with them. Alain had to be the smoothest-ever Grand Prix driver. Sometimes in qualifying we used to say to him, "Let us know if you're going to do a quick one – otherwise we might miss it."

I leave you to imagine what sort of a party we had. We not only had to celebrate Alain's back-to-back championship title, but we also wanted to send Keke Rosberg to his pension in the required manner. Traditionally we always threw a party at Guliana's, the nightclub of the Adelaide Hilton, which was pretty much the focal point of the weekend. Every Formula One team member was allowed in, as long as we could do so without it becoming uncomfortably crowded, and at times it did get a bit out of hand! But Bob McMurray always got it under control.

Ron Dennis had been courting Honda for an engine for some time and on one occasion that summer he took Alain Prost to Japan to convince Honda that McLaren was the team to back. However, for 1987 Honda retained both Williams and Lotus as their teams. Ron also made a concerted effort to take Ayrton Senna away from Lotus, but this didn't work either. Ron's consolation was, as he said, that "Lotus have spent so much money on keeping Ayrton Senna that I can't see them having enough in the kitty to develop a winning car!"

Ron also tried to get the services of Nelson Piquet, who he

brought to the factory after-hours to show him our headquarters and what we were planning for the next year. Throughout the tour, Nelson's only words were: "How much, how much?". He wasn't interested at all in the car development but only in his personal salary, which didn't go down very well with Ron. So McLaren finally signed Swedish driver Stefan Johansson, who was fresh from Ferrari and very apprehensive to be joining twice World Champion Prost, especially after hearing the remark made by Keke Rosberg that "Peter Warr did Ayrton Senna an enormous favour by keeping him at Lotus, because the myth around Ayrton would totally vanish next to Alain." Stefan was another great guy, a real team player, and he fitted in very well. He and Alain hit it off from the start and Stefan was delighted to be learning from Prost.

We started the 1987 season as champions with first and third in Brazil, which set the team off in a good mood; we had a team dinner party at a Copacabana restaurant, and four of us took a taxi with Alain from the hotel. As we'd already had the mandatory *caipirinhas*, I took the driver out of his cab and set Alain at the wheel. Wow, the taxi driver thought that Christmas had come early and he was ecstatic: "Wait till I tell my friends that Alain Prost has driven my taxi … My wife will never believe me!" He didn't even want to take any money, even though his taxi was a lot the worse for wear after Alain's demonstration drive!

We had an unexpected 1–2 at Spa-Francorchamps, but we weren't by any means the team to beat any more. We were totally engulfed by engine-related problems, mostly with the alternators and more specifically with rubber alternator belts, as we didn't seem to have any rubber belts that could last the distance. The final straw was at the German Grand Prix when, four laps from the end, another alternator belt split on Prost as he was leading. On Tuesday morning I was on the first flight to Atlanta and on my way to Elizabeth Town where, we'd heard, Gates Rubber Inc could produce belts that were practically indestructible. I flew back overnight with a case full of the magic belts, but unfortunately too late, as we were almost out of the championship fight.

That year, in practice at the Osterreichring, Stefan Johansson had an experience never before encountered in Formula One, when he suddenly found a deer crossing the track right in front of him. There was a massive impact, which sent Stefan out of control into the barriers at over 150mph. It was a horrific experience, both for Stefan and for our mechanics, who had to clean up the mess afterwards and fix the car. I don't think any of us will ever forget the smell!

We of the previous Formula One generation remember the true, original Osterreichring almost with awe. The 1987 Austrian Grand Prix was the last to be held there, after we actually saw not one, not two, but indeed three starts. A lot of cars were demolished, which no one likes to see, and the Osterreichring lost its yearly battle for survival and kissed goodbye to the F1 calendar for the following ten years.

We didn't suffer any more problems with alternator belts, but although Prost won in Portugal and finished second in Spain, he was only fourth in the championship.

Ron Dennis and Mansour Ojjeh hadn't given up on Honda engines, and once again they made a trip to Japan, this time taking Alain Prost – and Ayrton Senna. Ron had finally succeeded in prising him from Lotus, and they finally convinced the Honda hierarchy that we were the team to back. At Monza in September 1987 it was announced that we'd be Honda's premier team the following season: Williams had lost the engines despite the fact that Nelson Piquet had won the 1987 championship and that their contract still had one more year to run.

During 1986 we had lost John Barnard to Ferrari after a lot of fights between him and Ron. In the old factory, my office was next door to Ron's, and whenever JB came in for a meeting it was always a desk-hitting and wall-trembling affair. I always felt sorry, because undoubtedly at the time they were the best two in the business at their particular roles, but their egos were too big to fit under one roof. John Barnard used to say that, in Ron's eyes, there was only room for one genius per company and Ron automatically took that place.

Steve Nichols assumed the chief engineer's post, and we'd also just recruited Neil Oatley, who came with good credentials from Williams. We had more than enough talent within the team to design an F1 car, but to satisfy our big-name sponsors Ron felt he also needed a big name to accompany our design force. We also needed a project leader: John Barnard was a natural leader, but neither Steve nor Neil was regarded as being in the same mould. However, Gordon Murray, the Brabham designer, was no longer enchanted with his boss Bernie Ecclestone and Ron took the opportunity to grab him. Gordon had made winning cars and had won championships, so he had the know-how, and he was going to implement new systems at McLaren. Gordon, who hailed from South Africa, was eccentric and laid-back and fitted in very well with the team.

Although many people have credited Murray with the creation of the all-conquering MP4/4 of 1988, which won 15 out of 16 Grands Prix, make no mistake – this car was all the work of Steve Nichols, Neil Oatley and their design team.

With the immediate future in place, we had to wind down the TAG Turbo engine project and our relations with Porsche. We gathered all the engines and parts, together with drawings etc, and brought them back to England to be stored in a McLaren warehouse. With the passing of the turbo era, the engine became obsolete in Formula One, but for years we tried to sell this successful design, and it was almost used for a helicopter project. However, this never materialised.

When Ron Dennis and Mansour Ojjeh had signed the TAG engine deal in 1983, the Porsche executives had been adamant that the name of the engine should be at all times 'TAG', and that the word 'Porsche' wasn't to be mentioned. This was down to the fact that they were very concerned that if the whole project didn't succeed in the high-profile business of Formula One, their name would be associated with failure. But no sooner had we started to have success than we found ourselves reading and watching news articles, TV broadcasts and reports that talked about 'McLaren-Porsche' and even sometimes (in Germany) the 'Porsche-McLaren'! I continually fought against this, but it never affected our relationship with Porsche.

Some of the McLaren personnel involved with the project, together with Ron and myself with our wives, were invited to the Porsche headquarters in Weissach in January 1988 for a farewell dinner party, and we were each given a titanium TAG-Heuer watch with the inscription: "For the good times shared". My wife Bea has used it every day since.

CHAPTER 11

THE UNTOUCHABLES

Going into 1988, we'd had two drivers in the past couple of years – Keke Rosberg and Stefan Johansson – who were more than capable of winning Grands Prix, but neither of them had added a McLaren victory to their records. I was disappointed, and even wondered if it was McLaren that had failed to deliver. But now not only did we still have the number one driver in Alain Prost, but also the guy that we'd all wanted so much to join the team, Ayrton Senna. For Alain, it was no problem at all having Ayrton as his teammate, and he received him with open arms and open mind. We were going to have one of the best engines available, and all we needed was to produce a good enough chassis to face the opposition.

Traditionally McLaren had always been late getting new cars ready for the start of the season. The suggestion for the media was that we always used all of the time available in the design stages, only pressing the 'go' button right at the very end in order to make it right: if the car was good, the competition would have less time to copy us. This approach seemed to work in the 1980s, but it used to scare the shit out of me.

The new MP4/4 was due to be tested at the official FOCA test in Imola before the start of the season in Brazil. After many long days and couple of all-nighters, we finally finished the first car and rushed it to Luton. There it was loaded onto the charter flight to Bologna with yours truly in the jump seat, while Ron Dennis flew in his own Falcon and waited for me at Bologna airport. The part of the story that has gone down in 'truckies' history, and has given us great dinner party mileage, is that the truckies arrived in Bologna from Imola to collect the car without the truck! The truck eventually arrived as we completed the paperwork, and the car was transported to Imola. We finally completed all initial checks etc in the small hours of the morning and collapsed on our beds in a state of exhaustion!

The next day was the last of the six-day test and our final chance to test before the start of the new season. As we wheeled the car out of the garage, everyone was eager to see what the car to be driven by the two best drivers in the world looked like. Alain was the first to go out, and while the hotshots so far were doing high 1:28s, Alain was on low 1:28s immediately! He got out of the car and pulled me to one side, saying, "I can't believe this car. I promise you, I'm driving it with one hand – it's absolutely fantastic! I just hope that Ayrton takes it easy, we mustn't show the world what we have!"

Ron Dennis took Ayrton into the corner of the garage and explained what Alain had said, and asked Ayrton to cool it – we had a great car! After a day's testing during which all we changed was a rear anti-roll bar (and Ayrton couldn't resist doing a high 1:27) we came back home extremely tired but elated. We'd just produced probably the best ever Formula One Grand Prix car.

Back at the factory Ron did his usual pep talk to all his employees, and after thanking everyone for their efforts he went on to say that we had a package able to win all the races! They all thought he was dreaming, but it turned out to be true. The 'dream team' had just taken off, and slowly but surely we became 'The Untouchables'.

To Rio, then, and it was the first race and time to meet all of Ayrton's family, friends and great string of followers. Brazil has had great champions, but Ayrton had definitely something more to give to all these millions who in a short space of time grew to idolise him, and we were about to find out why. Ayrton just adored Brazil: he was unbelievably proud of his nationality and he cared enormously about his countrymen. One of his purposes in life was to help Brazil to make its mark on the world map, and he worked relentlessly to this end, both in and out of the race car.

Ayrton put his MP4/4 on pole in his beloved Rio but unfortunately this was of little use for him, as his gearlever stuck in first gear during the warm-up lap and he crawled the car to the pole spot and then put his arms up to delay the start, to give him time to change his car. This he did, and he started from the pit-lane with the spare car, but in doing so he had, in fact, technically broken the rules, as he'd changed his car after the green flag. But it was Brazil, he was charged up, and we had to do our best. Ron spent the rest of the race in the steward's office trying to stop them from black-flagging Ayrton, which they eventually did at the 30th lap, when he was already in sixth place. He was not a happy boy.

It seemed like a repeat performance of the Italian Grand Prix in 1986, when Prost had a similar episode when his alternator packed up on the grid and his car refused to start. We told him to jump out and run for the spare car, but sadly it was split seconds after the green flag. Alain started from the pit-lane and by lap 21 he was already in fifth place, only to be black-flagged on lap 26 almost at the same time that his engine exploded in a big way. Alain had been furious and exchanged a few harsh words with the FIA stewards for having let him race hard and take risks before finally stopping him. What he didn't realise was that the reason they took so long was because Ron and I were fighting with the race officials to let him continue. Alain's anger cost him and McLaren a $5,000 fine. But this time it was Alain who ended up winning the race, and he wasn't about to shed a tear for Ayrton.

At the next race, at Imola, we monopolised the front row and finished a very close 1–2 with Ayrton having his first win in a McLaren, lapping the entire field. We really hadn't bargained for this, but of course Ayrton and Alain were having their own battle and this was worrying us because of the fuel consumption at a hard circuit like Imola.

In Monaco both McLarens were again on the front row, with the pole specialist Ayrton Senna a staggering 1.5 seconds quicker than Prost! Alain himself couldn't quite believe how Ayrton could be so quick at a circuit where Alain had always been the benchmark, and even now Alain was a clear second quicker than third man Gerhard Berger, in the new John Barnard Ferrari. Ayrton was obsessed about Alain: Prost was the number one, the best driver in the world, and from the moment that he joined the team Ayrton was only interested in beating Alain. He always wanted to know what settings Alain was using, and now he wasn't only beating him but was completely clobbering the champion and this was a definite personal achievement.

Often when you were able to catch Ayrton on his own, especially when he'd just managed to not only beat his hero, but totally overshadow him with the same car, engine and tyres, he used to become very mystical, waxing very lyrically about the way in which he'd achieved this. It was as though even he couldn't believe that he'd actually beaten 'The Professor'. He would say that, when driving the car, he no longer felt as if he was on a race track, but in a tunnel where he was perhaps exceeding his own capabilities. As long as he was comfortable with it, he'd carry on, but if he felt the next level was unobtainable he'd stop. I couldn't really understand all this, or perhaps I didn't have time for all this nonsense. As far as I was concerned he was simply the fastest racing driver the world had ever seen and that was all there was to it.

In the race, both started neck-and-neck, getting to St Devote almost together, but Prost missed a gear which also cost him second place to Berger, and he remained in third place, unable to get past the Ferrari, for 54 laps. Meantime, Ayrton had got a lead of about 50 seconds, but once Alain disposed of Berger he started carving the seconds away. Ayrton saw the board with Prost second and gaining on him so he pulled out all the stops and started making fastest laps. With about 15 laps to go, Ron went on the radio, shouting to Ayrton, "Slow down, he'll never catch you up, slow down!" But Ayrton's obsession had also made him deaf and on lap 67 he touched the inside barrier at Portier corner, which sent him out of control into the guardrail and his race was over. Prost won a race that wasn't his.

This was, without a doubt, Ayrton Senna's biggest career mistake. He was completely gutted and so depressed that he just walked to his apartment – conveniently situated in Boulevard Princess Grace not far from Portier – to drown his sorrows on his own. For hours we tried to contact him without success: his telephone wasn't answered, and later it was always engaged or off the hook, until finally at about nine in the evening I managed to get an answer from Isabel, his Brazilian housekeeper. At first she insisted that 'Senhor Ayrton' wasn't there, but I pleaded with her in Portuguese, knowing that Ayrton *was* there, and asking her to tell him it was Jo. She finally handed the phone over to him and Ayrton was still crying. He spoke quietly in Portuguese: "I don't know how it happened. I must have just brushed the inside curve or barrier, the car jumped, the steering wheel came out of my hands, and in a split second I was crashing on the outside of the corner. I must be the biggest idiot in the world."

The thing with Ayrton was that he made so few mistakes that when he did make them, he used to punish himself so much that not even Ron could tell him off. He was a perfectionist. He couldn't tolerate mistakes by the team, and he tolerated his own even less.

The Mexican Grand Prix was on its third outing since it was reinstated in the World Championship in 1986. By now Ron had started to relax and accept the fact that the race, being in my hometown, always generated a lot of media interest around me, as I was the only Mexican in Formula One. I was now allowed to speak more with the local TV and press and it was partly because of me that McLaren was adopted almost as the national and favourite team, and certainly as the crowd's favourite. I'd always been given several tickets for the principal grandstand, which all my family and friends occupied wearing special 'Jo Ramirez' T-shirts made by my niece Patricia.

Although he was once again on pole Ayrton was feeling the pressure, with Alain leading the championship by 15 points. In the race Alain got the better of him from the start, but it was still another 1–2 for McLaren, and I was delighted to have given my own 'fan club' something to cheer about.

It was a great weekend except for an unpleasant episode when Placido Domingo, a good friend of Alain, came to the circuit on his way to the airport to say hello. Because of the typical Mexico City traffic Placido was delayed and by the time he arrived he literally only had a few minutes left before his flight. He asked me if he could say a quick hello to Alain, who was just about to jump in the car for a practice session, so I rushed him over. Alain was delighted to see him, but Ron shot across the pit-lane, pushing Placido aside and ordering Prost to get in the car. This was in front of a great many horrified onlookers, because besides being one of the most distinguished and important personalities in Mexico, Placido is the most loved. I could only think that Ron didn't know who the visitor was, so I whispered to him that this was Placido Domingo. He shouted at the top of his voice, "I don't give a shit who he is, I'm running a racing team not a social event!" Alain just shook his head, while Placido very apologetically said to me, "Yes, of course, he's right – and I'd better be going before I miss my plane."

Unfortunately Ron could often be unnecessarily abrupt in showing his authority. Obviously Placido didn't hold it against me personally, as he came to Indianapolis in 2001 for my last race, to say goodbye.

Montreal and Detroit were also double wins for the team, both headed by Ayrton. But when we got to the French Grand Prix at Paul Ricard circuit, a different and more determined Alain Prost appeared, ready to fight back at the dominating Brazilian. In practice, Alain found the perfect set-up for his car and grabbed the pole with half-an-hour of the session left. He got out of his car, changed into his jeans and T-shirt, and stood by the pit wall to watch the rest of the qualifying. When we asked him why he'd stopped running, because he still had another set of tyres and plenty more time, he replied, "That was a perfect lap. I certainly could do no better than that. If he [Ayrton] can go quicker and make a better time, he deserves the pole."

But the more Ayrton watched Prost in his jeans on the pit-wall, the harder he tried and the slower he went. Alain beat the 'pole master' by almost half a second.

The basic difference between the two men was that, while Alain was unbeatable in a perfectly set-up car, Ayrton was more able to improvise in a car that was far from perfect, and since more often than not the car wasn't absolutely perfect Ayrton was able to get the edge. In the race Alain led at first, but was overtaken by Ayrton at halftime when they both changed tyres. Alain then lost a bit more time and Ayrton excelled at passing back-markers, which gave him the lead. However, the revitalised Alain didn't give up, and started chasing his teammate until he was able to give him back some of his own medicine, boxing him in behind a back-marker after the fast corner, Signes. Alain had taken the corner flat-out, allowing him the speed to get past both Ayrton and the back-marker before the next corner, a move of which even Ayrton would have been extremely proud. Alain took a very rewarding win on his home ground.

Back in England we had an all-wet Grand Prix at Silverstone. The Ferraris booked the front row as the McLarens weren't quite sorted, but Ayrton the rain master won the race. Alain withdrew for safety reasons after 25 laps, a decision for which he was severely criticised by the press and public. Alain stood by his assertion that the lack of visibility was such that the race should not even have been started.

What many people don't know, or forgot, was that it was Alain who was hit in the back by Didier Pironi's Ferrari back in 1982 at the German Grand Prix in Hockenheim on a very wet afternoon. Didier simply didn't see Alain slowing down into the pits and ran into the back of his Renault. Pironi's legs suffered multiple fractures and he was never able to race again. Alain was very much affected by this accident, caused by lack of visibility rather than a driver error. Pironi died a few years later in a motorboat accident.

The next race, at Hockenheim, was also wet, so there's no need to say which of the two McLarens won, but after his criticisms at Silverstone Alain made a good show to finish a strong second, only 13 seconds behind the indisputable 'King of the Rain'.

The Hungaroring produced yet another 1–2 with Senna ahead, but it was at Spa-Francorchamps that Alain hoped to take his revenge because it was one of his favourite circuits. However, right from qualifying Alain realised that this wouldn't be an easy task: Ayrton took pole position half a second quicker. As always, before he changed into his civvies Ayrton sat on the floor of the truck unwinding from the 'trance' of concentration that he put himself into. In the meantime, Alain and myself were near the door of the truck looking at the timing sheets, with Alain commenting: "Half a second faster than me, *here*. I can't believe it, not here of all places! He's fucking quick."

As he said this I turned my head to look at Ayrton, who'd heard Alain's remark, and he winked at me with a greatly satisfied smile – another personal milestone achieved!

But this is exactly how great it was working for these two titans of the sport, because they had an unparalleled respect for each other's ability. In the race Alain had the best start, but Ayrton passed him halfway into the first lap, and they stayed like this the rest of the way for another 1–2 finish.

How could I ever forget the 1988 Italian Grand Prix at Monza, the only race that escaped us through Ayrton's impatience? Ayrton and Alain fought hard in the first half of the race until Prost's engine exploded, and then Gerhard Berger's Ferrari started to close the gap followed by Michele Alboreto in the other Ferrari. Ayrton had barely enough fuel to finish the race, let alone start a battle with Berger. Two laps from the end he was only four seconds ahead of Berger as he decided to overtake (for the second time) Jean-Louis Schlesser – who was sitting in for Nigel Mansell in the Williams-Judd – just before the chicane instead of after it. Schlesser, panicking, moved to the extreme right and lost control under braking, spinning out of the circuit and collecting Ayrton's McLaren on the other side of the chicane, ending the one and only chance for McLaren to win all the Grands Prix in one season. 'The Untouchables' were touched, and I was sure that the *Commendatore* had something to do with it!

Barely a month had passed since the death of Enzo Ferrari, and many believed that it was him 'up there' who put a jinx on Senna, in order to allow his beloved cars to win the Italian GP in a 1–2 formation, and, yes, the atmosphere was a bit spooky!

It was at Ferrari's death that the Automobile Club of Italy commissioned the Enzo Ferrari Trophy, a very strange and very heavy sculpture designed by Giò Pomodoro, a prominent Italian artist. This was going to be presented to the first team which won the Italian Grand Prix three times. We won it in 1989, and I was invited to their annual dinner at the end of the year to be presented with a very elaborate and elegant manuscript saying that we'd won one-third of the Enzo Ferrari Trophy – and believe me, we were very eager to have this sculpture in our trophy room. We won the Italian GP again in 1990, and once more I went through the rigmarole of the dinner and the second manuscript. When we won it again two years later, in 1992, the Automobile Club of Italy wasn't happy at all, as naturally they wanted Ferrari to have the trophy. I wasn't surprised when I didn't receive the usual invitation to their end-of-season party in Milan, but I was when they avoided any correspondence and declined to answer my faxes demanding our trophy. Finally, the week before the 1993 Grand Prix, I categorically stated to the hierarchy that the trophy was ours and that if we didn't receive it I'd have to go to the press and say that they were a lot of liars and thieves! They finally agreed to present it to Ron Dennis in a small ceremony just before the start of the race, and needless to say, Signore Pomodoro's sculpture now stands proudly in a prominent spot in the McLaren trophy room.

At Estoril, Alain once again felt that he'd made a magical lap and, with 15 minutes to go, while a red flag had temporarily stopped the session, he quickly changed from his driving suit and watched as Senna went out for the last few minutes on a track that looked like the M4 in rush hour. The trick worked again! It was another pole for Prost, who took the race but not without a fierce fight from Senna. There was a second start and Ayrton went out in front and led the first lap, but at the end of the lap Alain came out of the corner and entered the main straight carrying more speed that Ayrton and was able to slipstream alongside the pits. Ayrton decided he was having none of this and he pulled right across Alain, almost squeezing him against the pit-wall and the mechanics' boards.

The whole Grand Prix fraternity couldn't believe what they'd just seen: if the two cars had touched Alain's might well have flown directly into the pit-lane, with horrendous consequences. After the race Alain was mad, and rightly so. He shouted across to Ayrton, "If you want the championship so badly that you're prepared to kill or be killed, you can have it."

At Jerez, once again, the revitalised Alain Prost won from second on the grid, driving a perfect race. Senna, from pole, could only manage fourth place, running with some technical problems.

Then came the grand finale at Suzuka in Japan. Ayrton, on pole yet again, completely screwed up his start by stalling the engine, but he was lucky. As he let the car roll on the slight downhill of the start/finish straight, he dropped the clutch and to his immense relief heard the Honda V6 turbo engine restart, and he was off. I believe he lost 14 places, but completed the first lap in eighth place.

From then on the world witnessed his fiery determination and will to win, as he visualised the possibility of grabbing the World Championship. He drove lap after lap like a man inspired until he caught and passed his teammate, and he wasn't challenged again. Towards the end of the race a short shower made the track very slippery, and although Alain was very close behind, both of them slowed right down, and the championship was won. On the last lap Ayrton went completely berserk over the car intercom: he was so happy at having achieved his life's ambition that he was practically delirious. We exchanged a few impolite words in Portuguese by way of celebration!

That day in Japan, Ayrton was unbeatable and was very happy after the race. Alain was inconsolable. He wasn't the only one who thought it was unfair: after all, he had won the higher number of points. But 1988 was the first of three years in which the FIA decided (God knows why) that only the best 11 results from each driver would be counted towards the World Championship. There were 16 races and, after Alain had closed the season by leading another 1–2 (our tenth) in Adelaide two weeks after Suzuka, our cars had been so fast and so reliable that the drivers had finished 27 times in the points from their 32 starts. Senna had scored 13 times and had to drop four points, but Prost had scored 14 times and had to drop 18! Without this insane rule he'd have won the title 105–94!

Ironically, Alain was betrayed unwittingly by his own French compatriots from the FIA. Back in 1984, when Alain won seven Grand Prix and Niki Lauda won five, the championship went to Lauda by half a point and I really thought then that it was a great injustice. This time, at least the championship had gone to the man who'd won more races, albeit only one more. Certainly, the way in which Ayrton had won in Japan made him a worthy champion.

Up until now, relations between Prost and Senna were still fairly good. After the race they happily posed with Mr Honda for a celebration photo, and Ayrton took the whole team to the steak house at the Suzuka circuit hotel for a celebration dinner. It had been an unbelievably successful year but also a hard one.

After a few whiskies, *saki* and wine, Ayrton still couldn't believe that finally his lifelong ambition had been achieved, and he repeatedly asked me to pinch him to assure himself that he wasn't dreaming and he really was World Champion! I said to him, "Tomorrow morning when you're sober and the room maid brings you the papers, you'll be able to read it for yourself and then you'll believe it! Yes, Brazil has another World Champion."

It was a wonderful end to the year. I'd have never imagined in 1984, when we won 12 out of 16 races, that we could have beaten this record, but only four years later we'd made it 15! We rewrote the record books, but we did it racing and without cheating the public – no team orders, identical cars for both drivers, and the two best in the world fighting on equal terms. One driver won eight and the other won seven races. No one talked then about penalising us with extra ballast for the coming year, or of rewriting the rules to make the sport more even and create a better spectacle.

In fact for 1989 the major change was in the engine regulations: the FIA finally succeeded in implementing a ban on turbos. We therefore changed the faithful 1.5-litre Honda V6 Turbo for the not so faithful but very powerful Honda 3.5-litre normally aspirated V10 in preparation for the new season. Honda had already built this engine a year or so ago, and it had been fully developed on the test-bed before it was tested in the car. In those days our design department wasn't very big, and in order not to take any engineers away from the design of the new car, Gordon Murray used to send me to Japan several times during the winter months to supervise the on-car engine testing, which was conducted by Honda at Suzuka and Fuji race tracks, with Emanuele Pirro doing the driving.

The engine, which had been conceived with a belt-driven valve timing distribution, wasn't very satisfying because the accuracy wasn't as precise as it needed to be, but the more immediate problem was that the belts hardly lasted 200 or 300km. So it was decided to change the whole system for a gear drive, and as you can imagine, in addition to the design time there were castings and gears to produce, and it was a real eye-opener for all of us to witness the unbelievable speed with which a big manufacturer, with an equally big desire to succeed in Formula One, reacted to the urgency. The whole affair took about two weeks, where it would normally have taken months.

There was no doubt that part of the great success that we had was due to the great level of commitment that Honda had devoted to their Formula One project. We were, however, under no illusions that we'd have the same degree of superiority as in 1988. The new Ferrari 640 designed by John Barnard was out, and with Nigel

Mansell and Gerhard Berger in the driving seats they were going to be very difficult to beat. Nor, perhaps, were our two champions as enchanted with each other as they were at this time the year before. Alain, after being the recognised number one in the world, was facing another season with a teammate who had incredible speed together with a dedication and a level of commitment which had never been seen before, and the most uncanny determination and will to win. So Alain had mixed feelings as to whether or not he was looking forward to 1989. Ayrton, still delighted with his championship, was looking forward to defending it.

As he viewed his car for the Brazilian GP, he turned round and said, "You know what's the best looking thing about this car? The Number One on the nose!" Indeed, that number was very difficult to come by.

Ron Dennis made an unusual appearance at a test session in Brazil, the day before a big press conference where an announcement was due to be made regarding another big project upon which McLaren was embarking. It was a very well kept secret within McLaren, and the rumours included an Indycar project, a Land Speed Record programme, and a sports car. I wasn't too interested in finding out beforehand as I had my hands full with F1, and I was most certainly not going to be involved, but being a race-man I was faintly hoping that it was an Indy or Le Mans car.

I went to the airport to collect Ron and on the way back he was telling me with great enthusiasm about the new roadgoing 'supercar' project. I had to make the right noises and show a bit of interest but quite frankly I was tremendously disappointed. I couldn't give a stuff. Who needs a 'million dollar car'? I thought that the whole project was badly timed: by the time the car was ready for sale it would be seven or more years too late. The world economy was nowhere as good as it had been in the 1980s. But Ron and Mansour set out to build the best car ever, and they easily achieved that, though to me the best part was when it was converted for racing and they dominated the Le Mans 24 Hours. I believe they sold a total of 100 cars, and their price, believe it or not, has appreciated since then.

Ron Dennis's unstoppable ambition always kept him busy finding new adventures. He'd already founded TAG Electronics Systems with Udo Zücker, the main man behind Bosch Electronics at the time of our TAG Turbo engine. He'd impressed Ron, who set him up with the capital to start the company, which was going to design and build electronics management control systems for road and racing cars. Based just a few hundred metres from McLaren headquarters, it became a very successful venture. However, the main problem of all of such ventures was that every time Ron let himself be distracted by them his eye wasn't on the ball in Formula One, and the race team inevitably suffered. Perhaps, if you follow history, that's why the team appeared to lose its way in the years leading up to 2004, when Ron finally fulfilled his lifelong ambition to create the world's ultimate automotive technology centre.

In those days, the economic situation in Brazil was very unstable, so one always had to find a friendly taxi driver or hotel porter who would agree to exchange your dollars at a better rate. Knowing the language, I had some contacts right in the centre of Rio who would sell me *cruzeiros* at a handsome profit and I used to arrive in the hire car with substantial sums in cash in a brown bag in order to pay hotels and incidentals, saving $3,000 or $4,000; but in retrospect it was a pretty foolhardy thing to do, as sadly some people down there would kill you for a lot less than that, and I don't think that Ron appreciated that I was risking my life more than his drivers!

The Brazilian Grand Prix started as we'd started the year before, with Senna on pole, although soon after the start he collided with Berger's Ferrari and had to come in for a new nose. Berger retired soon after, and he was livid. He said to me: "I'm tired of Ayrton's attitude that whenever there are two cars in the circuit fighting for a spot, Ayrton always feels that he has the right to that spot, and the other driver has to lift to avoid a crash. I've had enough and won't be lifting again. If we have to crash, that's what we'll do."

Of course, for Ayrton in Brazil it was a terrible blow, but again this was one of his downfalls. He suffered from an acute lack of patience, just as when he lost the Italian GP the previous year: he could have waited and passed Schlesser after the chicane but he didn't, making Schlesser panic and lose control, with the inevitable result.

Nigel Mansell won the race in Rio on his debut with Ferrari, and Prost was second. The next race at Imola was to be a black Sunday in McLaren history even though we finished 1–2. We found ourselves back to the *status quo* of the previous year with both cars on the front row, well over a second in front of the third man. It would really have made no sense to battle at the start and risk banging wheels, and Ayrton suggested that they didn't race with each other until after the Tosa corner, to which both Alain and Ron Dennis agreed.

The race started and Ayrton pulled away. As they started braking into the Tosa, Ayrton was first followed by Prost, Patrese in the Williams-Renault and Mansell in the Ferrari. On the third lap Gerhard Berger went off at Tamburello in a big way. His Ferrari caught fire and the race was stopped to rescue Gerhard, who fortunately only had a broken rib and minor burns. Before the restart, Ayrton and Alain agreed again on their previous strategy.

This time Alain had the better start. He checked his mirrors after leaving Tamburello and saw Senna and Mansell behind so he saw no need to defend track position and placed himself on the right line for Tosa when Ayrton, who was slipstreaming behind him, passed him almost before starting to brake! Alain couldn't believe it. From that moment on his race was done, his anger being such that his driving was appalling, as he couldn't concentrate. He even spun couple of times, but still managed to finish second behind Ayrton. After the race he didn't want to talk to anyone: he was so upset that if he said something there and then he'd most probably have regretted it later and he therefore decided it was better to just leave, thereby missing the post-race press conference – which cost him a $5,000 fine.

The following week we were testing at Pembrey in Wales, and Ron Dennis summoned both drivers to attend, as he was determined to re-establish law and order. Ayrton was refusing to apologise, and I even heard that he'd apparently said that the deal had been to not overtake under braking for the Tosa hairpin, and that as he'd actually passed Prost by slipstreaming before that the move was allowable! But that was Ayrton: he seriously believed that version. He really only apologised because of the pressure under which Ron put him and for the good of the team, but he

ABOVE: *The earliest known picture of the wannabe racing driver...*

RIGHT: *At the Modena autodromo in 1962 with Sarita and Ricardo Rodriguez and Juan Manuel Bordeu.*

BELOW: *With Giancarlo Baghetti at Zandvoort in 1962, after he had given me a lift from Milan to my very first Formula One Grand Prix.*

LEFT: *At Le Mans in 1963 with Gian Paolo Dallara of Maserati, one of my first mentors.*

BELOW: *With Dan Gurney at Monza in 1962. I didn't know then how involved I would become with the great American driver.*

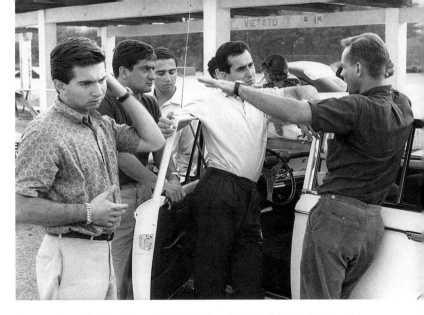

ABOVE: *Assembled for a Ferrari test at Modena in 1962: left to right, Ricardo Rodriguez, Juan Manuel Bordeu, me, Lorenzo Bandini and Phil Hill.*

BELOW: *Daytona 24 Hours, 1971: one of the most satisfying victories of my racing life.*

ABOVE: *A happy Eagle mechanic at Spa-Francorchamps in 1967: the first of 'my' 116 Grand Prix victories. Dan Gurney starts his last lap with a lead of over half a minute.* (Phipps/Sutton)

BELOW: *With my boyhood hero, Juan Manuel Fangio, and my current hero, Dan Gurney.* (Bernard Cahier)

ABOVE: *The 3-litre Weslake V12 engine certainly was a beautiful machine.*

BELOW: *This is the entire 1973 Tyrrell race and factory team: we had just won the World Championship.*

LEFT: *Our two-seater Tyrrell was much earlier than the McLaren! That's Patrick Depailler on the sidepod.*

BELOW LEFT: *With Emerson when he was the World Champion at Lotus.* (Phipps/Sutton)

RIGHT: *The Shadow team: at the front, me, Jan Lammers and Don Nichols; at the back, Gene Lentz, John McLoughlin, Brian Lambert and Nigel Stepney.* (Charles B. Knight/ Moto Foto)

BELOW: *During the team managers' race at Brands Hatch in 1978, in the 'fun' days of the sport.*

ABOVE: *An argument with ATS team owner Günther Schmid in the pit-lane –
not an unusual occurrence. Marc Surer is in the cockpit.* (Jutta Fausel)

BELOW: *For a small team, ATS were very competitive in 1980 with
Jan Lammers.*

ABOVE: *With Jean-Pierre Jarier and Teddy Yip in Macao – the one place each season where Theodore were the cat's whiskers.*

BELOW: *My first Grand Prix win with McLaren at Rio de Janeiro, in 1984.* (sutton-images.com)

LEFT: *With 'Le Patron' in Mexico: "Can we get more miles out of that engine?"* (Joan M. Palenski)

BELOW: *Testing in Rio with the two greatest.* (Jad Sherif/Pan Images)

ABOVE: *The most charming Princess I have ever met.* (Studio Colombo)

RIGHT: *With the wonderful Belgian Grand Prix trophy under my arm – I wanted to keep it!*

BELOW: *A Marlboro party at Monaco with Vanessa, my daughter, on my left and Caroline Sayers of McLaren on my right.*

TOP: *The McLaren team in 1991. It was one of my favourite seasons, for lots of reasons, not just because of our fourth consecutive World Championship.*

ABOVE: *Ayrton and me with Mario Andretti, one of the most versatile champions in all of motor racing.* (sutton-images.com)

LEFT: *Marlboro made a photographic collage of the six seasons that Ayrton had with us, and Agnes Carlier and I gave it to him at his last Grand Prix in a McLaren, in Australia in 1993.* (Jad Sherif/Pan Images)

ABOVE: *At Jerez, we finished the European season with a different kind of party – and sore backsides!* (Jad Sherif/Pan Images)

RIGHT: *David Coulthard's win in Melbourne in 1997 ended a 49-race drought for McLaren. I had desperately wanted to avoid reaching 50 races without a victory in the team's history.* (Daniele Amaduzzi)

BELOW: *Whoever said Mika Häkkinen didn't have a sense of humour?*

LEFT: *With the top, top boss, Mansour Ojjeh. It was always a pleasure to work for him.*

RIGHT: *With one of the all-time greats, Stirling Moss, and his wife, Susie.*

LEFT: *You never argue with Bernie Ecclestone. As he would say: "Jo, be reasonable – do it my way."*

ABOVE: *A family reunion in Acapulco for the Millennium with Vanessa and Bea.*

BELOW: *From Mika Häkkinen and David Coulthard, the ultimate leaving present: a Harley-Davidson. It made this one of the best days of my working life.*

ABOVE: *Carrera Panamericana is quite simply the greatest week of the year. With everything locked Beto and I wondered if we were to going to make it round the corner. We didn't...*

LEFT: *Passing through the traditional arch at the end of the Mexico City stage.*

wasn't happy about it. When Ron returned from Pembrey he told us that all was well, that peace had been made and there'd be no further mention of the incident.

A few days later Prost had a long interview in the French paper *L'Equipe* where he called Ayrton a dishonest man who couldn't keep his word. All through Alain's career his one failing was that he always used the press to let off steam, and as you can imagine, this wasn't always well received by those who were implicated. Ayrton was very upset and regretted his reluctant apology even more, and he decided to completely cut Prost from his life and never speak to him again.

From Monaco onwards they hardly spoke to each other, which of course made life very difficult for the team. Alain later tried to get back on speaking terms but Ayrton wouldn't hear of it. In Mexico a TV reporter ask me to arrange an interview with both of them, and I thought that this might be an opportunity to get them back together, but there was no way that Ayrton would do anything with Alain. By then, Alain was regretting having given that much talked-about interview in *L'Equipe*, and he felt that somehow he was losing his grip on the team which for years had been moulded around him.

In Monaco, Ayrton got pole position with another mesmerising qualifying lap, a second quicker than Prost, and beat him by almost a minute in another McLaren 1–2, a lap in front of the opposition.

In Mexico he was again on pole ahead of Alain, but more important was the fact that he chose the perfect combination of tyres for the configuration of the circuit and higher temperatures of race day. Alain went for the softer choice on the basis that he was, if anything, a smoother driver than Ayrton, but this decision backfired on him and he had to come into the pits for a tyre change after 20 laps. In the confusion, we fitted the wrong tyre combination – and as if this wasn't bad enough, we repeated the mistake a second time! Alain finished a distant fifth to Ayrton and felt really beaten psychologically by his teammate in a tactical game at which he'd always been a master, hence his nickname 'The Professor'. He was also much bothered about the fact that we were able to make the same mistake twice in the tyre change: being a little bit paranoid, he wondered if the team was starting to take sides.

Senna was on Pole in Phoenix but failed to finish due to an electronics glitch, and Prost won. In Montreal we qualified at the front again, with Alain on pole for a change, but there were no McLarens at the finish. Alain had a suspension failure on the first lap while leading and Ayrton suffered a rare engine blow-up three laps from the end, also while leading the wet race. Even so, we headed back to Europe with Prost and Senna leading the points table 29–27.

In spite of leading the World Championship, Alain was in two minds whether or not to stay with the team the following season, and Ron had asked him for an answer by the middle of the year. He had a few sleepless nights, but by the time we arrived at Paul Ricard for the French GP he'd made up his mind to go. At the Marlboro cocktail party I spent a long time with him, desperately trying to convince him to stay and not make a rash decision. I said, "If you leave now it will look as if Ayrton is kicking you out as well as beating you on the track and taking the team away from you. You've shown many times that you can beat him. Even last year you got more points than him, and if your mates from FISA hadn't changed the rules you'd have been champion now." But he was really depressed, and said, "I really don't think we can work together again. Unlike Ayrton I'm not obsessed with winning. I've won a lot and I still want to keep winning, but I don't want to die doing it. I love my profession and I want to keep driving for a long time, but I must have fun. If I'm not enjoying my work it's not worth doing it and I no longer enjoy working with Ayrton."

I had no answer to that, because I relate to the same principle: life is too short, and enjoying what you do has to be the most important thing.

Next morning at nine o'clock, Alain Prost announced in a press conference that he wouldn't be driving for McLaren in 1990. The 'dream team' was starting to break up, although we were still doing must of the winning, albeit with not as much fun.

Later that weekend, Prost won the French Grand Prix from pole position, after Senna had been stopped a hundred yards from the start line by transmission failure. Then at Silverstone the team had a big pep talk from Ron Dennis, and although I've no wish to inflate his ego, the two most important things that I've learned from Ron are "Never accept no for an answer" and "Never give up". The British Grand Prix was a good example.

That year's practice at Silverstone was the first time we ran a six-speed transverse gearbox which had the oil tank incorporated in the casting, and for some reason the oil system wasn't working correctly. Intermittent blue smoke was coming out of the exhaust and the engine was showing signs of oil starvation. We changed and modified dozens of different components, but we weren't able to completely separate the air from the oil and we were only running a lap at a time. There were many trips back and forth from the factory in Woking and we even ran another car at the Honda proving grounds in Newbury.

After a night of frantic work trying different oil tank tops, during Saturday morning Ayrton blew up his engine as a result of the problem, while Prost's car seemed to have a better oil tank top. Ayrton had a major bust-up with Ron at that, accusing him of favouritism and of giving Alain a better tank top, while in reality we were all in the dark just trying to find the best solution for both cars. By now the whole team was just about ready to throw in the towel and say – forget it!

Time was running out, and Ron got everyone together and went over the problems and changes in a systematic way, using his so-called lateral thinking process, keeping the good bits and discarding the bad ones. We also fitted an extra oil tank with a catch tank and a pump to recirculate the oil. We were still fitting bits and pieces up to the last minute, but the McLarens ran trouble free. Ayrton spun off and Alain won the race.

At Hockenheim a delay in Ayrton's tyre stop cost him the lead, allowing Prost to get ahead, although Alain lost sixth gear two laps from the end and Ayrton passed him to win. After the race Senna was furious, saying that the guy who was on the offending rear wheel normally worked on Prost's car, and that he'd deliberately slowed down the stop, and he demanded that this particular mechanic didn't work on his stops again. Such was the paranoia of Ayrton as the pressure mounted, with Alain 17 points in front.

At the Hungaroring Nigel Mansell beat Senna in a very clever overtaking manoeuvre, taking advantage of the sick Onyx of Stefan Johansson while Prost was delayed by a pitstop. Ayrton finished second and Alain fourth. The Belgian Grand Prix at beautiful Spa was wet from flag to flag and we saw another demonstration of the incredible talent and car control of Ayrton in these conditions, with Prost trailing second all the way, defending himself from the various attacks of Nigel Mansell's Ferrari.

The Thursday before the Italian Grand Prix at Monza, Ferrari announced that Alain Prost would be joining them to race with Nigel Mansell in 1990. This was almost the last nail in the coffin of the relationship between Alain and McLaren. Some weeks earlier it appeared as if he'd be joining Williams, which wouldn't have been seen as too bad by Ron Dennis, but for him to go to Ferrari of all the rival teams was almost like a personal insult. He couldn't bear it that Alain might be taking with him to Ferrari the Number One earned by McLaren.

In the race, Ayrton achieved one of the most incredible poles of his long list of poles, a second quicker than both Ferraris and a staggering 1.79 ahead Prost in fourth place. Alain, who would soon be the new kid on the block, was getting all the cheers of the crowd every time he left the pits, and it was clear that he was well received by the *tifosi* as their new hero; but he was very unhappy with the performance of his car, both engine and chassis, and suggested that he'd been unfairly treated, although his suspicions were completely unfounded.

Once the race started, Ayrton drove just as if he was in a different league, and disappeared from everyone, including Alain – something we'd never been seen before between the two. When Ayrton's engine blew up near the end of the race, Alain was able to pass the two Ferraris and won.

At the podium ceremony, a thousand *tifosi*, proud of their future driver, shouted to him, "*Copa, copa, copa!*" Alain was so overwhelmed by the reception of his new fans that he instinctively felt obliged to hand the cup to the crowd below, despite knowing that, under his McLaren contract, all trophies belonged to the team. Ron Dennis watched the cup fly from the podium with disbelief. I was watching all this from the short corridor between the podium and the control tower, and as Ron passed by I tried to speak with him, but he wasn't about to listen to anyone. I don't think I've ever seen him so upset in all my years with him. He turned back and waited for Prost, and as Alain came close Ron smashed the Constructors' cup at Alain's feet, and only Alain's quick reflexes saved him from some very black toes!

Alain was completely bewildered, not realising how his action had infuriated and hurt Ron. "But what was I supposed to do?" he asked. "I drive for Ferrari next year. Surely he must understand that?" "No," I said, "I think he feels that you've just showed the world that you don't care about a McLaren victory. But you go to the press conference and I'll try to speak to Ron and calm him down."

I finally managed to catch Ron on his own and tried to explain Alain's motives, but for all the qualities that Ron has as a businessman and a team owner, he found it difficult to understand Latin emotions. From that moment onwards the friendship between the two men faded further.

The cup itself was completely destroyed by the crowd: they broke it to pieces! I saw the top going to one person, the handles to someone else, then the base, etc. It was very flattering for Alain that I had several calls and faxes from Italian fans offering to pay for a replacement cup. I'd already arranged for a replica cup to be made, a cup that I kept in my office cupboard waiting for the right opportunity for Alain to give it to Ron once the air had cleared. Unfortunately we had to wait six years, and Alain finally presented it to Ron at the 1995 Christmas party in the Science Museum, after returning to the team as a consultant and drivers' guru.

The post-race conference at Monza had done little to improve matters, as once again Alain used the press to speak his mind and complain that he was given inferior equipment. This even prompted FISA supremo Jean-Marie Balestre to insinuate that perhaps Honda hadn't been giving both drivers equal chances, innuendos which naturally upset Honda, because their integrity was being put in doubt. This led to them refusing to give Alain engines for the rest of the year.

Ron had a big predicament on his hands and was unable to speak with Prost since none of his calls were returned. Ron called me into his office, saying that he'd have to put another driver in the car unless Alain apologised for his allegations, and would I try to contact him as all Ron's efforts had failed. I spent all that Friday evening trying to find him and when I did I begged him to urgently come to Woking for a meeting with Ron.

The following lunchtime Alain and his son Nicholas came to Gatwick in his private plane, from where I collected them, and while I showed young Prost his father's cars Ron and Alain wrote a letter of apology to Honda and a press statement. A 'dream team' it certainly was, but not without its tribulations...

At the next race, at Estoril, Senna collided with black-flagged Mansell's Ferrari and he went out while leading. Berger won with Prost second. Ayrton won at Jerez with Berger second and Prost third. The relationship between the two titans had been deteriorating race by race, and with two races to go and Alain leading by 16 points the atmosphere was very tense, especially on Ayrton's side. In addition to the existing tension, he was becoming obsessed with the idea that Alain was going to Ferrari and was going to take all of McLaren's and Honda's secrets with him.

But if there was one driver who could react positively to pressure, that driver was Ayrton Senna. In qualifying at Suzuka he put out one of the best laps of his racing carrier to establish his 41st pole and show his determination to win the race and keep his championship. That lap completely mesmerised Alain, who was under no illusion that he could contest such an almost incredible lap time, but would have been happy to start side by side with his teammate if he was to have a chance at winning back the title.

Alain did manage to put his car on the front row, although a clear 1.7 seconds slower than Ayrton's time. On race day, as you can imagine, the pressure on the team and on Honda was greater than ever before. We had to deliver two absolutely perfect cars. Prost made a better start and showed that he was ready for the battle by taking a lead of almost four seconds in the first five laps, and the gap between them more or less stayed the same until the pitstops.

After the stops Ayrton seemed to find more speed with his new rubber and cut the gap from five seconds to half a second in the next ten laps, breaking the lap record in the process. He was using every curve to its maximum, and as they got into the chicane on lap 47 Ayrton thought he saw his chance by getting on the inside. Alain, not being exactly an amateur, had covered the gap well – now, of all times, he wasn't prepared to give way to Ayrton's aggression any more. However, by this time Ayrton was committed to the manoeuvre, and rather than give up he put his two right-hand wheels off the circuit by the entrance of the pit road, and then on the grass. Alain couldn't believe Ayrton's determination and instinctively turned right earlier into the chicane, shutting the door and colliding with his teammate.

Both cars came to a pathetic stop in the middle of the chicane infield. Alain undid his belts and jumped out, thinking it was all over, but Senna being Senna stayed in his car and demanded that the marshals push him backwards and then forwards to restart. This they did, and he was able to get back on to the circuit, but his mistake was that he completely overshot the chicane: if only he'd gone backwards and re-entered the circuit without cutting the chicane perhaps he'd not have been subsequently penalised. Anyway, he was able to get back to the pits and change his front nose and carried on for the remaining few laps, long enough to catch and overtake Alessandro Nannini, who'd taken the lead in the meantime.

Though Ayrton had won on the track, the win was disallowed because he'd cut the chicane and didn't regain the track at the point at which he'd left it. The rest of the team felt totally gutted and cheated, as we'd dominated the entire weekend yet were going home empty-handed!

Next day as I sat with Alain at the airport having a post-mortem, I pointed out that he'd probably made two of the biggest mistakes of his racing life. Firstly, having seen Ayrton coming in like a missile on his inside before the chicane, he should have just moved out of the way, as there was no way that Ayrton would have been able to negotiate the corner. He wouldn't have had the grip to slow down on time and would have gone straight on. Secondly, I asked him, "Why did you get out of the car? If the marshals had pushed both of you, maybe the authorities wouldn't have penalised either of you! Your car was completely OK and in one piece, including the nose!"

The new World Champion turned to me and laughed. "It was a mighty old bang. My right wheel was on full lock to the right, and I thought the suspension was broken. I should have looked at the left wheel – that was probably on full lock to the right as well!"

This incident, which completely finished the personal relations between the two drivers – if there was any left – was to cause one of the biggest Formula One controversies of the decade. It was followed by weeks of appeals, threats, counter-threats, fines, press conferences and so on. Senna's exclusion was upheld and they added a $100,000 fine with a six months suspended ban! Clearly in anybody's eyes this was totally outrageous, as you can plainly see both from the trackside camera recording and from Alain's car camera that he instinctively closed the door on Ayrton by turning into the chicane far too early. In a reverse situation Ayrton would have done the same. He had to be fully aware that he was taking a risk by putting himself in a position where he was in Alain's hands, but he did it all the time and got away with it most of the time. Having said this, it was a racing accident for which exclusion from the race for having overshot the chicane was more than enough punishment.

With one race to go the 'dream team' had turned into a nightmare, and the Australian Grand Prix was a very subdued affair for McLaren. The weather was appalling and the fact that it was a street circuit without proper drainage meant there were puddles all over the place. The start was delayed, and once the race started Alain did just one lap and stopped, complaining of lack of visibility. Senna collided with Martin Brundle's Brabham, and there were many other incidents until only seven cars remained at the end. It was a miracle that no one was hurt.

At a small gathering we said goodbye to Alain, who had his third World Championship in a McLaren, and I presented him with the steering wheel of the car in which he won his last Grand Prix for us, with a plaque which read: "Alain Prost 1989 Italian Grand Prix 39/40 Grand Prix Wins – With best wishes from your team".

The story was that the 1989 Italian Grand Prix would have been his 40th Grand Prix win, but the team had lost the 1985 San Marino Grand Prix for him, which made it only 39 wins.

Later on, he thanked me for my part in his success at McLaren, and knowing that I collected steering wheels he told me that I should keep the wheel to remind me of the good times that we spent together. The wheel now hangs proudly on my study wall.

Six great years, 30 Grand Prix wins, three World Championships – we'd most certainly miss this great little man. As a person he was always very friendly and attentive, as a professional he was certainly the easiest champion we ever dealt with. He never had a manager at the circuit (he only appeared once a year for contract signing) and although he was a 'superstar' it was never obvious – he was very down-to-earth. As a driver he was undoubtedly one of the quickest and almost incapable of making mistakes. In six whole seasons he'd only damaged two cars and was always the smoothest driver on the circuit, winning races at the slowest possible speed.

For all the troubles and controversy over the last few months about whether or not Alain was being given inferior equipment, the McLaren cars were like two peas in a pod. Their mechanics and engineers simply wouldn't have allowed any differences between them. As far as Honda was concerned, people used to say that Alain was a McLaren driver with a Honda engine and that Ayrton was a Honda driver with a McLaren chassis. But the truth is that while in the days of turbo engine power Alain's smooth throttle application was certainly the way to go, with normally aspirated engines the revs needed to be up – and stay up. The way in which Ayrton used to operate the throttle while cornering, as if he had a spring attached to his foot functioning like a blipper, was a fantastic system for keeping the revs up. It was a real treat to see him and hear him doing it. Alain used to say that though he'd tried this method himself so many times he just wasn't able to do it as well.

On the other hand, especially in the later part of the year, Ayrton spent endless hours talking with the Honda engineers after practice and testing, controlling the telemetry and checking all the data every evening. For the life of me I never knew how they could spend so many hours talking about it. The McLaren debriefings were long enough already, and neither Prost nor Senna dared to leave before the other just in case they missed something!

Alain also agreed that in those two years without any strong competition, one of Ayrton's biggest advantages was his unbelievable speed on a qualifying lap, something that he frankly admitted he could normally never match. Starting from pole in equal cars was a very great help to Ayrton. Prost had to admit, though, that if Senna was able to do the fast laps he was entitled to have the advantage.

Thus ended the era of 'The Untouchables', during which all those of us who were lucky enough to have been part of this 'dream team' witnessed the ferocious fight between the two greatest drivers of the day, as Alan Henry, one of the most distinguished writers in the sport, put it his book *McLaren: The Epic Years*.

Ayrton Senna had achieved his ambition by crushing Prost's morale, undermining his confidence to the point where he felt there was no longer a future within the team he'd regarded as home for the past six years. However, Prost turned round and nipped him painfully in an almost symbolic last farewell, and looking back on the Senna/Prost partnership it now seems as though they fed each other's competitive instincts, each driving the other on to scale greater pinnacles of achievement. Only after Alain had stopped did Ayrton realise how much of his motivation had been generated by the desire to beat the little Frenchman with the crooked nose. The reality was that Senna and Prost had more in common than even they realised.

I always felt that had Alain been World Champion in 1988 it would have been much better for their relationship, and I said as much to Ayrton, which I think he understood. Many times I'd say to him, "Look you're the new guy, the young guy, you're going to race a lot longer than Alain, you've got time." Although Ayrton won the title, he was well aware that Alain had scored a lot more points (Alain used to remind him quite often...), and to some extent he felt he still had something to prove.

For 1990 the likeable Austrian Gerhard Berger was joining McLaren, in a straight swap for Prost. Meanwhile, back at the ranch, we'd been joined by a new member of the management team, Martin Whitmarsh, as our director of operations. Ron spent months looking for this special person, who in later years would become the man who'd eventually replace him. Ron's own ambitions were taking him into new territory, as the TAG-McLaren group was continuing to expand and was taking up more and more of his time.

Martin was chosen from the British aerospace industry, as Ron was adamant that he didn't want anyone from the motor racing world. He turned out to be a highly ambitious, clever and motivated man who in just weeks embraced the entire world of Formula One and everything that he needed to know about it. What impressed me most about him was that on his first week, even before he sat at his desk or picked up a pen and paper, he went round the factory spending a few minutes with every single member of the staff, hearing their views and taking on board their complaints. Later his office door was never closed, and although at times he didn't quite manage to fulfil his promise he was always very fair. He's now the top man but he still answers the telephone for a chat.

The winter of 1989–90 was a nailbiting time for me. One of our top engineers, Steve Nichols, had gone to Ferrari, and Alain Prost had just driven his last race for us and was southbound to Maranello; and then I too got a call from Ferrari. I don't care who you are in this business, driver, engineer, manager, mechanic, truckie or floor sweeper – when Ferrari calls you, you listen. The myth behind the name is far more tempting than anything you may have at the present, so I was flattered and overwhelmed. Twenty-eight years earlier I was their 'gofer', begging for a proper job that they couldn't offer me, and now I was being invited to fulfil a top role. I went down to Modena for secret meetings with Cesare Fiorio, who was then the team principal.

But somehow Ron Dennis – who rarely missed anything – got to hear about it and he immediately called me into his office. "What were you doing in Modena last week?" I was totally taken by surprise and a bit lost for words. I just said that when Ferrari calls, you answer. He agreed that I was right to look and see what was around the corner. I told him that I didn't expect him to match what they were offering me, as it would be beyond him. He then went on to deliver the best sales pitch I've ever been subjected to: "Look, if I take your arm and I cut a vein, the blood that would come out would be the red and white of a McLaren. You're McLaren, you couldn't join another team because McLaren is impregnated all through you!"

I was torn in half. It would be great to continue working with Alain, and being part of Scuderia Ferrari would be a great privilege and a personal milestone. On the other hand, I'd be leaving a team where I was very happy, and of course I was anxious for the opportunity to follow Ayrton Senna, who was the future's greatest star. In those days Ferrari wasn't by any means the team it is now: there were a lot of internal problems and the personnel were changing all the time. The management back then used to joke about it, saying, "We don't have many sitting-down jobs at Ferrari because people don't usually stay long enough to get a seat."

In the end I was very glad to have been convinced by Ron to stay put. My money was improved – not to match Ferrari's offer, but at least to a level more appropriate for the job – and I took it as a kind of backpayment for the past, when very often I felt underpaid. I was also asked to sign a contract, but by then I was happy to do that. Formula One racing is a very rich sport and drivers are renowned for getting obscene amounts of money, but the money the team principals and drivers get bears no resemblance to what is earned by the rest of the team. However, it's not really important because at the end of the day, it's still a team.

CHAPTER 12

THE LORD OF THE TRACKS

When Ayrton Senna returned to Brazil after the last race of the 1989 season in Adelaide, he held a press conference in which he accused FISA and its president of manipulating the end of the World Championship in favour of Alain Prost. Jean-Marie Balestre went berserk and summoned Senna to Paris to explain himself. The meeting was useless, as Ayrton refused to withdraw his comments, and his attitude irritated the World Motor Sport Council even more.

Senna went back to Brazil without commenting on the encounter, and the WMSC refused to grant his application for a 'superlicence' for 1990 unless he came up with an apology. It even threatened him with legal action. Senna hibernated as usual in Angra dos Reis and for the next two months we didn't know whether or not he was going to be allowed to drive our car in 1990. There was also the small matter of the $100,000 fine that Ayrton had chosen to ignore. I'm sure that Ron Dennis aged more during the Senna years than all the other years put together, and there were still more troubles to come!

FISA's deadline for driver nominations was 15 February 1990, and the telephone lines between Brazil and Woking were buzzing all the time. When the deadline arrived and McLaren had to submit the names of its drivers to FISA, Gerhard Berger and Jonathan Palmer were the names that were published. Finally, however, Ayrton agreed to make an apology in a press statement from Brazil, and FISA changed Palmer's name for Senna. McLaren paid the fine.

The whole affair had affected Ayrton more than he was able to admit. When we got to the first race in Phoenix for the US Grand

Prix, everybody wanted to talk to him about it – but he just wanted to be left alone to get on with his job. He had all kinds of problems in practice and only managed fifth, while the new boy, Gerhard Berger, put his MP4/5B on pole and was the happiest man in Arizona. We were all happy for him too, as he was starting a very difficult period of his career and the pole was just what he needed to give him a lift, if only for a short time. Then again, you couldn't possibly *dislike* Gerhard – he was a very good-humoured man, very open, always ready for a laugh and very honest. Being so tall, he was incredibly uncomfortable in our car: he was all legs, with a short body! Unfortunately, he didn't complain enough during testing, but when he started racing he found that he was losing time because the cockpit was very cramped, and as a result he had a small accident at Phoenix.

Ayrton won a nice battle with Jean Alesi's Tyrrell, with both of them passing each other back and forth during the course of the race. In fact, this race ended up being a great boost to Alesi's career, as top teams started looking at him with interest.

The Brazilian Grand Prix returned to São Paulo in 1990, with the Interlagos circuit shrunk from 7.96 to 4.35km. Both the McLarens were on the front row and Senna was the clear favourite to win in his homeland, where a great number of fans were wearing T-shirts with the words: 'Fuck Balestre'. Ayrton had with him his new girlfriend, Xuxa, a beautiful blonde girl who'd been promoted by Pele to become Brazil's most famous woman. Xuxa had a daily TV children's programme as well as a chain of shops retailing clothes bearing her name, and I must admit that I used to love watching her TV programme. She was so full of life, charisma and sex appeal that even though it was a children's programme you couldn't bear to change channels or stop watching her. So when Ayrton told me that he was bringing her to the circuit I was eager to meet her, though I was apprehensive about the inevitable upheaval there would be from having the country's most popular man and woman both in our pits.

I have to say that it was a great disappointment: all that personality and charm that she showed behind the cameras seemed to be non-existent in the flesh. Their affair was far too demonstrative – they were all over each other, almost as if they were trying to draw attention to themselves. She also came to

Monaco, and it crossed my mind that perhaps it was just a publicity stunt to increase each others' earning power in Brazil. Whatever it was it didn't last long.

The race, by all the normal rules, should have been Ayrton's first Brazilian win after six attempts in Rio. But it wasn't to be. Once again he was the victim of his own impatience. In the lead by 13 seconds from Prost's Ferrari, he tripped himself up when lapping Satoru Nakajima. To give Satoru his due, he moved his Tyrrell aside to let his former teammate through, but in doing so he spun against the McLaren. The McLaren's nose being the most affected, Ayrton charged like mad after the pitstop but only managed third behind Gerhard, with Alain Prost rubbing salt in the wound by winning Ayrton's home race for the sixth time.

After the race Ayrton wouldn't give in by assuming any responsibility for the accident, insisting that this was the way he drove and when he decided to pass somebody he committed himself 100 per cent. If people thought that he was taking too many risks, he said, then perhaps his limit was a little bit higher than the average. The race could arguably have been won by Gerhard, but he had to slow down with a very painful right foot impeding him from braking hard enough – another legacy of his cramped driving conditions which was corrected at last over the next two races.

Back in Europe, at Imola, Ayrton led from the start, but had a mysteriously broken wheel which left him stranded out on the circuit to watch the rest of the race, giving his driving gloves to the crowd and signing autographs. The Italians had Prost now, but they really wanted Senna: they absolutely worshipped him, and it doesn't bear thinking about how it would have been if Ayrton had lived long enough to drive for Ferrari! The 'Sennamania' would have surpassed anything Formula One had seen before and it was definitely on the cards, as there was no doubt that Ayrton would have eventually driven for Ferrari.

At the end of that year, Ayrton was invited to the yearly party of the popular magazine *AutoSprint* and the World Champion asked them for a $20,000 donation to a children's charity in Brazil. *AutoSprint* were taken aback, as no other champion had asked for that much money before, but they had to have him there. I was asked to come with him and I can only say that I've never witnessed such a scary, though friendly, mass demonstration by the fans, despite the very strong security arrangements. Everyone wanted to have a closer glimpse of their idol.

Once again in a class of his own, Senna won in Monte Carlo as if there were no other drivers around. Jean Alesi was second, with Gerhard finishing third in a now more comfortable race car. In Canada, a wet race, Gerhard led all the way but was sick as a parrot when he jumped the start and was penalised by a minute, which made him fourth at the finish. Ayrton won as the best of the rest and Gerhard didn't know whether he was more pissed off by his mistake or more pleased to have Ayrton thanking him for his win, as the only reward for his efforts.

The 1990 Mexican Grand Prix was the 100th Formula One Grand Prix for Ayrton, and I'd asked my sister Ana Elena to make a cake for Ayrton celebrating the occasion. Ayrton had cut half the cake and when I turned round that half ended up on my head! It was a great occasion, where Ayrton showed that was becoming a more relaxed person, perhaps through the influence of Gerhard in the team as they were becoming great friends. As fast a driver as Gerhard was, he was never really a threat to Ayrton. In Gerhard's own words. "He taught me to drive and I taught him to laugh."

In the race Gerhard took the pole but Senna led from the third lap for the next 60, until a rear tyre burst and he was out. His fury was compounded when his arch rival Prost won the race from 13th place! And as if this wasn't enough, Alain went on to win the next two races, at Paul Ricard and Silverstone, and passed him in the championship by two points.

Ayrton had won at the Hockenheimring in Germany for the last two years, and now he made it a hat-trick, but unfortunately he wasn't able to celebrate. His lifetime friend, manager and father figure Armando Botelho had died the night before in São Paulo, a victim of cancer. Ayrton was inconsolable, crying on his sister Viviane's shoulder, and he left the circuit early on a day that had seen both success and great sorrow. Armando was the most decent, level-headed and intelligent person that you could imagine. He was a great influence on Ayrton's life and business and he was always very welcome at races, because Ayrton was a much better person when Armando was around, more human and more reasonable. This was a loss that affected Ayrton for a long time. His father Milton was a good person to have around too, but he always kept out of the way, as he'd rather go for pasta at the Minardi motorhome than have lunch at McLaren, no matter how many times I said to him that he was a McLaren man and was more than welcome in our motorhome.

Senna won the three-start Belgian Grand Prix, beating Prost's Ferrari fair and square, and he loved that win after surviving the three starts. Berger was on the third step of the podium. At Monza in Italy it was the same again, Senna followed by Prost (just like the year before, but with different cars), with Berger third. A win in Italy is always wonderful, especially when a Ferrari is in the second place. Ayrton was delighted with both the win and the fact that he'd pulled out a 16-point lead on Prost in the championship.

After the press conference and before everyone left the room, an Italian journalist, Carlo Marincovich, shouted, "We are now in the country of love – why don't you two shake hands?" There was a very tense moment in which everyone held their breath, while the two men just looked at each other. Alain was the first to break the silence by saying that at the start of the racing season he'd offered his hand to Ayrton but that Ayrton had left it in the air. Ayrton retaliated by saying that he didn't think this had been a sincere gesture, but after a few words from both of them, remembering past experiences and taking into account their mutual great passion for the sport, they shook hands and patted each other's backs to the applause of all present. However, the feud was far from finished, as was proved a few weeks later in Japan.

We had a new floor to test for the next race, and we wanted Ayrton to test it, but it was never easy to get Ayrton to a test. First you had to go through the normal procedure of saying what you wanted to test and why, and he'd reply: "Why can't the test driver do it, why do you need me? I don't want to go and drive and drive around to check components. If you have something worth testing I'll go, otherwise Jonathan [Palmer] can do it."

We managed to convince him to go to Hungary, where the test team was working, and we finished the floor of the car at the eleventh hour. I rushed to Heathrow with the floor as my hand baggage! The British Airways personnel saw me coming and said, "You're having a laugh. Surely you don't imagine you can take that thing on our plane?" Although only a few millimetres deep, the carbonfibre floor was the length and width of the race car, so it was quite an impressive piece of kit. They positively refused to take it on board on the grounds that it wouldn't go into the aircraft hold door.

Having become familiar with all the doors and baggage holds of the various aircraft used in Europe, of which I had a comprehensive list in the office, I said that it would go in, and I gave them the measurements of the floor and of the doors. I begged the BA personnel to give me the benefit of the doubt and to let me go into the loading bay to try – something that under no circumstances would they ever have considered doing, as it's strictly forbidden for passengers to go airside. However, after my having shamelessly used the weight of the McLaren and Senna names, and seeing my anxiety, they gathered that the situation was urgent, and to satisfy their own curiosity they agreed to try it. To everyone's delight the floor went in and within minutes I was on my way to Budapest.

To make things worse for Ayrton, because it was the height of the Budapest tourist season we couldn't get a room in a top hotel for him. Actually Ayrton was never too bothered about luxury, and the hotel we got had a gym, so he was happy. That afternoon we asked him to just do a couple of laps before the end of the day, to see if he liked the gear ratios or whether he wanted to change the basic set-up before we fitted the floor overnight to save some time tomorrow.

The end of a day's testing will always remind me of our test team manager Indy Lall's funny remark whenever anyone that came to a test asked him, "What's a good time around here, Indy?" Indy would always answer, "Five-thirty," which is when the chequered flag drops at the end of the day and they can start the hard night's work to get the car ready for the next day! These days, with so many testing time restrictions, the test teams really have to work hard right around the clock to meet deadlines.

Anyway, Ayrton got in the car and did just what he was asked, a couple of laps, and he was two seconds quicker than the best time that Palmer had managed in two days' testing! Poor

Jonathan, I never saw a man so distressed. He turned round and said quietly, "I guess you don't need me here tomorrow. If I hurry I can get on tonight's flight back home."

This was something that Ayrton always did. It was part of his philosophy to demoralise the opposition, by intimidating other drivers into a feeling of inferiority, starting with his own teammates. He had to be fastest all the time, in testing, practising or qualifying. Once his name was on top of the list everyone knew that the competition started after Senna. He did the same in Japan once, when we were testing with Emanuele Pirro. Senna was invited by Honda to present their new sports car, the NSX, to the media, and while he was there we asked him just to check the latest engine development on the Formula One car. He jumped in the car and did a couple of laps and was a clear second quicker than Pirro. Emanuele, one of my best friends in racing, wasn't happy: "Dammit, why does he have to do that? There was no need at all!"

I never rated Senna as a good test driver. Prost was much better, and in fact more often than not when they were together with us at McLaren Senna just followed Prost's lead in the way the car was set up. On the occasions when he did make changes I often argued with him that they appeared to be ridiculous changes, but he reckoned that he could feel a half-pound of tyre pressure in just one tyre. I seriously doubted that, but it didn't matter at all because he was just so dammed quick anyway.

The 1990 Portuguese Grand Prix was a strange one. By the time Estoril came round it had been announced that Nigel Mansell was leaving Ferrari, and of course he wasn't bothering to help Alain Prost to win the championship. On the contrary, he was doing his own thing and perhaps helping Ayrton rather more than Alain. The race was shortened by ten laps because of an accident, just when Ayrton was lining his McLaren to regain the lead from Mansell. On the podium, Mansell also chose to ignore Prost and congratulated Ayrton, and once again Alain was mad and after the race made some disparaging remarks against Ferrari, saying that Ferrari didn't deserve the World Championship as they didn't know how to manage a team battling against McLaren.

On the Friday before the Spanish Grand Prix at Jerez, the Lotus of Martin Donnelly crashed heavily into the barriers just at the back of the pits. The noise of the impact was heard by all of us standing in the pits, and we turned our heads in time to witness the car bouncing from the barriers in a million parts, with Martin thrown out of the car still strapped to his seat. It was a horrendous accident that stuck in everyone's minds for a long time. Ayrton was very depressed by it and next day he felt that he had to make the pole and dedicate it to the speedy recovery of poor Donnelly. It was clear that the Ferraris were superior to our cars at the Jerez circuit but Ayrton once more drove an incredible lap to be half a second quicker than Prost. It was his 50th pole position. Unfortunately, during the race his radiator was punctured by a falling bracket from another car, and it was another win for Prost. This cut Senna's lead in the championship to nine points, with two races to go.

Suzuka was another circuit where Ferrari had the edge, which worried Senna very much, but in spite of it he got the pole again. This time it was to his disadvantage, however, as it was on the inside of the track and not on the racing line, and was thus on the 'dirty' side, with less traction for the standing start. Before the practice, he and Berger had already asked the stewards of the race to change the grid, with Prost's knowledge, as Prost was unconcerned with it. However, the stewards declined to comply. I don't recall hearing it, but it was rumoured that Senna had said that if Prost was ahead into the first corner, he wasn't going to be able to turn into it because Senna would be on the inside.

At the drivers' meeting before the race, the clerk of the course announced that if any driver wasn't able to negotiate the chicane they could use the escape road provided they didn't gain by it. Ayrton was so mad that he stood up and left the room, as this was precisely the reason why he was disqualified from the previous year's Japanese Grand Prix.

It was then I realised that he was capable of doing whatever was necessary to secure the title. Two hours later the championship was decided in 400m and just a few seconds: as expected, Prost made a better start from the outside line and was first to the corner, but Ayrton on the inside refused to lift and with almost two wheels on the grass, the nose of the McLaren hit the gearbox of the Ferrari and both cars ended in the gravel trap.

I couldn't believe my eyes – what a terrible way to finish the championship! We were all glued to the TV monitors, thinking that the two archrivals would come to blows, but they just walked to the pit without even meeting each other's eyes. I can imagine that Alain must have been kicking himself for having left some room and putting himself at the mercy of Ayrton.

When Senna got to the pits and saw us watching the TV monitors, he asked me: "They're not going to stop the race, are they?" I replied that I doubted it, but deep inside me I was praying for them to stop it and have a restart, because I really felt that Ayrton, on that day and in Suzuka, would have been able to get his championship in a straight fight. The millions of spectators worldwide had been cheated. The team was very subdued, and with Berger spinning out on the first lap we'd achieved *nul points*. Ron Dennis was the only one to congratulate Ayrton on clinching the championship.

What had happened, even though expected, left a sour taste. It was revenge for last year but something unworthy of a driver of Ayrton Senna's standing, to get his second title in this undignified manner. When Prost took Senna off the year before, he did it instinctively on the chicane at 60kph in the closing stages of the race, but this time Ayrton did it deliberately at 180kph on the first corner with 200 litres of fuel in the cars.

What Prost said about Senna then was unrepeatable, but as far as Senna was concerned this was a normal racing accident. He was unbothered by Prost's accusations and blamed him for closing the door, saying that the World Championship was the result of the whole season's racing and not just a single race. That Monza handshake seemed so very long ago! It took months before Ayrton Senna finally admitted that Suzuka 1990 was his revenge for Suzuka 1989.

The 1991 season was one of my favourites at McLaren. As usual, after the end of the 1990 season Ayrton hibernated in his Brazilian beach house for the winter. Gerhard Berger said to us, "Forget about him, leave him bronzing himself, I'll do all the testing this winter," and he really worked himself hard, both physically and mentally, with Joseph Leverer, our excellent physical trainer. He was quick in the car and tough and hard out of it and when the first race came in Phoenix, USA, he was more than ready to beat Ayrton, who'd just come from Brazil via a quick test at Silverstone. Ayrton then proceeded to rubbish the Honda engine, which he said hadn't improved, and put his McLaren MP4/6 on pole a second quicker than Prost's Ferrari and two seconds quicker than Berger. Gerhard was destroyed, so demoralised that he said to me, like someone on the verge of quitting, "What the hell does a man need to do in order to beat him?"

It took him weeks to get to grips with himself again and realise that beating Senna was impossible: the best he could do was to get closer to him. Yet the longer they worked together the greater their friendship grew.

Ayrton won the first four races of the 1991 season, but although he was looking strong in the championship the Williams-Renaults were getting stronger every race, and of course there was Prost in the Ferrari – always a danger, even though the Ferraris had fallen behind in performance. Senna finally won the Brazilian Grand Prix for the first time after a fantastically close race against Riccardo Patrese's Williams, which towards the end was closing fast. Ayrton's McLaren ran out of all gears except sixth, and Ayrton had to change his driving on a circuit that he knew so well. This tremendous effort caused him to have such terrible cramps and exhaustion that at the end of the race – which he won by two seconds from Patrese – he couldn't restart after he stopped on the slowing-down lap as usual to collect a Brazilian flag. As he was towed to the *parc fermé* he got soaked by the rain, which aggravated the cramps, and he wasn't able to get out of the car without help.

Being able to improvise was one of Ayrton's greatest assets; he was able to change his driving and nurse the car to the end. No other driver without the same gifts and determination could ever have won that race. Berger was third, making it a wonderful day for McLaren.

I remember celebrating that evening at one of São Paulo's top nightclubs with some of Ayrton's family, Emerson Fittipaldi and Edson Arantes do Nascimento, Brazil's other great hero, better known as 'Pele'. Ayrton was immensely happy to have won on his home ground in front of the public that idolised him so much. The whole place was shaking: it was a wonderful experience to share.

We had another good result at Imola, Ferrari's home circuit, where Senna and Berger did a 1–2. In Monaco, Senna won for the fourth time, but Mansell's Williams was second.

Then came a lean period. We didn't finish in Montreal, and in Mexico Senna suffered a massive accident in practice on the elevated fast corner of the circuit called La Peraltada, where he finished upside down. It's a very fast corner and he was a bit shaken after that, since for a few long seconds he was struggling to get out of his belts, release the steering wheel, and slide out of the cockpit with the ever-present danger of fire. He was taken to the circuit hospital for checks and later released. I drove him back to his hotel and sat for a few minutes with him in his room, where he was able to reflect on the incident. He said to me: "Today I saw it come close," but I quickly replied jokingly with an old Mexican proverb, "*Mala hierva nunca muere*," which means "A bad plant [a weed] never dies," trying to take his mind off what could have been a very serious accident.

In spite of his accident he finished third in the race behind the two Williams of Patrese and Mansell. The next three races, at Magny-Cours, Silverstone and Hockenheim, were all won by Nigel Mansell, which made a big hole in the lead that Senna had built up. But then Ayrton won at the Hungaroring and we had our revenge, although Mansell and Patrese were second and third. In the meantime, we enjoyed the win in Budapest, one of Ayrton's favourite cities. He loved the Hungarian people and saw a lot in common with his Brazilian countrymen. I normally took the following week off, so I caught a lift with Ayrton to Nice, where my wife and daughter were waiting, and then spent some days at our house in Cogolin.

We had another 1–2 at Spa-Francorchamps, although it was a lucky one because the Williams team had troubles. Ayrton chose this opportunity to avoid the celebrations after the race and in the race debrief started swearing and shouting, reminding us that this was a lucky win and that he'd been complaining all year about lack of power in the engine and other deficiencies in the car, and that we hadn't come up with any solutions. Although he was right, we were all rendered speechless by his aggressive approach. I had the audacity to suggest, on a lighter note, "Yes, yes, but the team has worked hard anyway and the cars ran until the end. Can't we just have a drink, say well done boys, and then slam the desk?" This seemed to make him even madder, but that was Senna, always very tough, and although his criticisms were always constructive his timing was sometimes very undiplomatic. On this particular occasion, I realised later, he was especially annoyed because he'd just discovered that Frank Williams had signed Mansell and Patrese again for 1992, and therefore he'd lost some of his negotiating power against Ron Dennis.

By now McLaren had one of the most impressive trophy collections in Formula One, except, of course, for Ferrari. One of the most wonderful trophies that we possessed was without a doubt the Coupe SM Leopold III, presented by the Royal Automobile Club of Belgium. The deal was that the team that won it kept it for a year and brought it back the following year for the next winner; but they also gave a cup commemorating the win for the team to keep. In 1991 we won it for the fourth consecutive year, but the organisers forgot the cup which the team would keep.

Ever since we'd had a trophy stolen from the German GP in the 1980s, right after the podium ceremonies, I'd made it my job to make sure that all the trophies found their way safely to the factory. As Ron Dennis said, the trophies were something tangible that reflected the achievements of the team. He cared so much about them that after he took over McLaren, it was always written into the drivers' contracts that the trophies belong to the team. The drivers normally asked me to get them a replica, which I always did. However, Ayrton Senna changed that from his second year in the team, wanting to keep the original, and then I got a copy for McLaren; but since Ron always insisted that we keep the original, and Senna insisted on keeping it too, I always told them both that they had the original!

It was as I was taking the trophies from the podium at Spa that I saw there was no cup for the team to keep, so I asked circuit boss Roberto Nosetto, a former Ferrari team manager and San Marino Grand Prix promoter, and a very good friend, "Hey, Roberto, what about our cup?" "Oh hell!" he said, "I forgot it. I'll send you one next week." "No, no thank you, I'm happy with this one. We'll keep it now as we've won it so many times."

But he was insistent that I had to bring it back again the following year. A couple of weeks later a cup duly arrived at the factory and I couldn't believe my eyes, it was such a crappy, cheap old tin cup, not even as good as any third place cup for a Mexican go-kart race in the 1950s. I was so disgusted that I sent it back and told them to stick it where the sun doesn't shine, and that we'd keep the SM Leopold III trophy. I followed it with a letter to Bernie Ecclestone, complaining about the quality of the trophies when you consider how difficult and costly it is to win a Grand Prix. Since the 1990s, the standard of the trophies has been specified within the FIA rules and they're now very expensive and attractive.

The Belgian Grand Prix trophy, which is a hexagonal silver cup mounted on an ebony base, had the names of all the previous winners before and after 1950, when the Formula One World Championship began. These included some of the most charismatic names in the history of our sport: Nuvolari, Brooks, Fangio, Ascari, Brabham, Clark, Surtees, Gurney, McLaren, Rodriguez, Fittipaldi, Stewart, Lauda, Andretti, Reutemann, Scheckter and Prost to mention but a few – and, of course, Senna, four times in a row. Ron was so delighted with the trophy that he commissioned his brother Michael, an accomplished silversmith, to produce the most fantastic replica. However, he gave it to the leading member of a foreign royal family in a business deal, which I think in later years he regretted very much.

The following year, Roberto Nosetto was no longer in charge of the Belgian Grand Prix, and the new management team weren't interested in the old trophy. I felt that I'd fought for the trophy almost as much as the drivers, and I became so attached to it that I almost asked Ron if I could keep it when I left. Somehow I don't think the answer would have been in the affirmative!

As regards Ayrton's harsh comments after the Belgian Grand Prix, the team wasn't falling asleep: we kept working as hard as ever. In Formula One the top teams can make major improvements very quickly, but things cannot always be changed from one race to the next, particularly engine issues, which take a little bit of time. Williams again won the next three races, with Mansell at Monza, Patrese at Estoril, and Mansell at the new Catalunya circuit near Barcelona. This is how right Ayrton had been!

But by the time we got to the last two races, Japan and Australia, we'd tested a range of new components at Silverstone that had improved our MP4/6 beyond recognition, and we were more than pleased with the results. For me this achievement was very special because it had been a real team effort. McLaren had produced a longer nose which dramatically improved the aerodynamics of the car by creating a much better balance; Honda produced a more powerful and lighter engine; and Shell came out with a fuel recipe which increased the V12's engine power. The end result was that we arrived at Suzuka so confident that we could plan our own race and dial out the destiny of our arch rival, Nigel Mansell – Senna's only remaining rival for the championship.

During Mansell's spell at Ferrari the Italians nicknamed him 'The Lion', because of his no-nonsense approach to racing. It was all or nothing, bless his heart – because that was how he drove, with his heart, all the time. The impression was that his head never took part! He was therefore so predictable that we felt we could foresee how he was going to react to any given situation. Mansell had to win in Japan if he was going to make a serious assault on the championship. So this was McLaren's strategy: Gerhard was going to be the 'hare' starting from pole, with Ayrton right behind, driving on his mirrors, stopping Mansell from passing and letting Gerhard take a commanding lead.

Sure enough, Mansell soon become desperate when he was stuck behind Senna and saw the signs from his pit putting Berger 12 seconds in front! It was now easy to induce him to make a mistake, which he did in the tenth lap, finishing his race in the sand when Ayrton left him some room on the first corner! Ayrton saw Nigel in a cloud of dust in his rear-view mirror, and although he didn't burst out laughing he wasn't exactly sorry. The plan had worked – Mansell *nul points*.

Senna then went on to do fastest lap after fastest lap, and by lap 18 he was in the lead. Towards the end of the race Ron reminded him by radio that the last part of the plan had Gerhard as the race winner, as a thank you for his help throughout the year in what was McLaren's fourth consecutive win of both the Drivers' and Constructors' World Championships. Ayrton at first radioed back saying that he hadn't heard, "Please repeat, please repeat!"

But clearly he was just teasing, and finally he replied, "Yes OK, OK," and with only 300m to go before the flag he moved out of line and braked hard to allow Gerhard to pass, letting the whole world know that it was his own present to Berger and showing that Ayrton Senna didn't give anything for nothing! Gerhard wasn't very happy, and rightly so; he said that this wasn't quite how it had been in the script, and furthermore it looked embarrassing for the team.

But Ayrton was happy, not only at winning his third World Championship but also with the recent change of supreme command at FISA following the nomination of Max Mosley as its new president. At the press conference after the race, Senna took the opportunity to accuse Jean-Marie Balestre again of manipulating the outcome of the 1989 championship in favour of Alain Prost. He then admitted that in 1990 he'd deliberately taken Alain's Ferrari out of the race at Suzuka in order to win his second title. I really thought it was all a bit silly and unnecessary, but if anyone could hold a grudge it was Ayrton, and this episode just gave Ron Dennis more headaches trying to patch things up once more with the FIA.

A lot has been said and written about the practical jokes exchanged between Ron Dennis, Ayrton Senna and Gerhard Berger during the years that the Austrian was driving with us. Ron had always been a man who enjoyed making bets, and often liked to settle a disagreement by the toss of a coin. Even during the negotiations of Ayrton's first contract, when they reached deadlock over the last half-million dollars and neither of them wanted to give in – even though Ayrton couldn't wait to drive for McLaren and Ron didn't want anyone but Ayrton to drive his cars – it was decided by the toss of a coin, something that Ayrton found quite bizarre, especially for that much money.

When Gerhard, who was a fun-loving character, joined the team, the practical joke season started in earnest, although it didn't last too long, as both Ron and Ayrton realised that they just couldn't compete against him. Gerhard was unreal: he didn't have limits – he just didn't care. While Ayrton's jokes were mild and funny, Ron's were more sophisticated, like having the fabrication shop build a bullet-proof armoured case into which Ayrton's briefcase was often put during his visits to the factory. In order to get the key from Ron, Ayrton would have to offer some kind of bribe – normally something like a guest appearance for a sponsor.

Part of Ron's Sunday morning ritual when he got to his motorhome at a circuit was to prepare the clothes that he was going to wear on his way home – usually a new set of Boss clothes, which were carefully folded and left in the cupboard. One day Gerhard sneaked in and took Ron's new clothes from the cupboard and, with the help of some kitchen scissors, he cut a leg off the trousers and a sleeve off the shirt. A not very happy Ron therefore had to go home in his red uniform, which he hated to do.

On another occasion, as Gerhard boarded Mansour Ojjeh's boat for lunch in Monaco, he had the notion to appropriate the wicker basket at the entrance holding all the Gucci, Ferragamo and Versace shoes of the beautiful people, and toss it into the sea! But probably his masterpiece was dropping Ayrton's briefcase out of the helicopter while approaching the runway at Monza. As they got out of the helicopter and Ayrton was looking frantically for his briefcase inside, an old boy came running up with the battered bag, calling, "*Signore, il suo maletin e caduto.*" Ayrton wasn't a happy man, and yelled at Gerhard, "This is too much, that was a $1,000 briefcase," to which Gerhard replied, "Oh well, it's your fault, you should have a fifty quid bag like mine. In any case, you're lucky, I tried to open it but I could only open one lock, you'd locked the other one!"

His jokes went to the extreme of pinching Ayrton's passport and, with Ron's help, removing Ayrton's photograph and replacing it with a same size picture of a man's genitals out of a porno magazine. It was very cleverly done, and you wouldn't notice it unless you looked closely at the picture. This caused Ayrton a lot of embarrassment at the first passport control where the officials had to check the passport, and there was a considerable delay until the offending picture was replaced.

Ron Dennis might have done Ayrton out of half-million dollars at the signing of his first contract by the toss of a coin – three times that amount, in fact, as it was a three-year contract – but ultimately Ayrton was able to beat Ron at his own game by winning a bet with him and getting away with his winning car of the 1990 Italian Grand Prix at Monza, the McLaren MP4/5B-6, complete with a working Honda V10 engine.

CHAPTER 13

CALM BEFORE THE STORM

The 1992 season was to mark the slow decline of our team. We fell from our own pedestal to become second to Williams, and although we won five races – which by any other team's standards would have been a reason to be proud – it wasn't up to the standard we'd set by winning so comprehensively the previous year. The Honda engine was a little late, as was our chassis together with our new active-ride suspension. Williams's 'Active' had been one of their main advantages in 1991, and, as always at McLaren, we were trying to do outdo our rivals and not just be level. Therefore we were late, as our system was very sophisticated.

Ayrton – who'd had a few race engineers at McLaren, from Steve Nichols to Steve Hallam (who joined us in 1991 from Lotus, where he'd looked after Ayrton's car) – had asked Ron to change his latest one, James Robinson, as for some reason he didn't get on with him. We'd just recruited a new engineer from Ferrari, Giorgio Ascanelli, who came highly recommended by Gerhard Berger, with whom he had worked. Ayrton soon grabbed him as his own engineer, and thus began the most wonderful love/hate relationship. Ascanelli was a man who always called a spade a spade and took a no-nonsense approach to his job. Both men respected each other's abilities and had tremendous mock fights, both in the pit-lane and in the office. Giorgio was a breath of fresh air at McLaren as he didn't mind going against the establishment, and he had the same relationship with Ron as he did with Ayrton; but he was very much respected by all. He developed the active suspension until it was banned, after which, sadly, family problems forced him to return to Italy, where he rejoined Ferrari.

So we started the 1992 season with a slightly improved version of our 1991 car, knowing that the best we could hope for was a third place; and that was exactly what we got in the first two races, at Kyalami and in Mexico City. Then panic struck: the next Grand Prix was in Brazil. In theory it's always the case that a new car should be much better than the previous one, but the new MP4/7 hadn't yet been properly tested. However, we had to make the effort to take it to Interlagos, if for no other reason than not to let our champion down on his home ground. So we airfreighted two MP4/7s to Brazil at great expense and had the two busiest practice sessions that I ever remember. At one point we had two cars broken down on the circuit, the drivers going round in two more, and the fifth car warming up its engine in the pits. I loved it! But the MP4/7 wasn't quite the answer we needed, although we qualified third and fourth. We had all kinds of problems with the car and even with the engine.

As well as these problems, I was surrounded by Brazilian bureaucracy that reminded me of my Fittipaldi days. Due to the country's continuing economic crisis, the customs authorities at the airport asked us for an extra $12,000 for 'fuel tax', as well as the amount that we normally paid through FOCA. I went ballistic. Although the local Shell agent was happy not to cause trouble and to pay the extra amount, I flatly refused purely on principle, even though the amount wasn't about to cripple the Shell empire, and I hoped that Ron Dennis and Ayrton Senna would back me up. I suggested to the officials that if they didn't release the fuel, I'd appear on national television and say that Ayrton Senna wouldn't be able to participate in the Brazilian Grand Prix as customs had created an extra fuel tax purely on his fuel. I was putting my head on the chopping block, but the trick worked and they released the fuel!

In the race, Ayrton started to lose places, and after a few laps he decided that it wasn't worthwhile to continue. He was very angry as he came into the pits, and revved the engine to full power in an attempt to blow it up, which he failed to do. He then jumped out of the car and disappeared from the circuit. We were stunned and totally in the dark about exactly what troubles he'd had, and quite upset by the way in which he'd stopped. In the heat of the moment, when a leading Brazilian reporter came to me and asked me what was wrong, and since Ayrton hadn't enlightened us, I said, "There was nothing wrong, the car wasn't quick enough and he chose to stop." Hours later, my comments were broadcast on the local radio, and when Ayrton heard them he called me back at the circuit and I had to hold the phone a foot away from my ear in order not to hurt my eardrums, which weren't all that good anyway. Ron Dennis was close to me at the time and when I told him that I thought I'd just lost a friend, he said to me, "Well he deserved it, the way he stormed away like a spoiled child. We all thought the same, but you were the one that said it."

Senna was still mad with me the next day when I saw him. I pointed to my cheekbone and said, "OK, hit me. I may have said the wrong thing but you didn't give us any alternative." We shook hands and the incident was never mentioned again.

What had happened was that the engine was cutting off at high revs. Ayrton had tried to change the fuel mixture to both richer and leaner, but it continued to cut off from time to time, making it quite dangerous to drive, because when it happened in the middle of a corner the car would naturally change direction. All in all, it was a very bad weekend, with Berger also out after only a few laps and another double for the Williams couple, their third in the first three races.

Mansell won again in Barcelona and at Imola (yet another 1–2 for Williams). What a contrast with the year before when, by the time we got to Monaco, only Senna had won a Grand Prix! This season it was not until Monaco that Ayrton saw his first chequered flag, and even then only with a little help from Mansell, who suffered a rear tyre deflation in the closing stages that allowed Senna to take the lead and gave the spectators the best fight to the flag ever seen at Monaco. Mansell tried everything he could to regain the lead, but Senna kept him at bay. It was a very entertaining ending, with Ayrton smiling broadly for the first time since Adelaide the previous year.

We got to Montreal with a little improvement in the MP4/7 and the Honda engine, and Senna's skills at this special circuit enabled us to suddenly break Mansell's monopoly of 1992 pole positions: the McLarens were first and fourth, sandwiching the Williams-Renaults. In the race, Ayrton took care of Mansell, who crashed, and Berger took care of Patrese. Senna then had electrical problems and a delighted Gerhard won, only to find that the scrutineers thought his rear wing might be a millimetre too high! The car was measured several times on different surfaces, with Gerhard getting more and more nervous about the situation, until he just had enough and said to me, "I can't handle this, I'm going back to the hotel. Please call me when it's all over and let me know who won the Grand Prix."

After a couple of hours, the officials finally decided that the rear wing conformed to regulations. It was my best telephone call of the year. The phone only rang once and Gerhard was on it. I didn't have the heart to joke so I just said, "Congratulations!" The reply was a resounding *"YES!"*, and the celebrations began.

From then on it was back to the *status quo*, with Mansell winning the next three races at Magny-Cours, Silverstone and Hockenheim. And as if that wasn't enough to fuel Senna's assault on his own team, he never stopped reminding us that if Alain had been driving (this was the year that he took a sabbatical from the cockpit) we probably wouldn't even have been third.

During the French Grand Prix at Magny Cours, a circuit where Ayrton had never won, he had a close encounter with the newcomer who was to become his number one rival. Senna was Michael Schumacher's idol – the best, and the man he had to beat, much in the same way as Prost was for Senna four years earlier. Ayrton knew that Michael was the next big threat, way ahead of all the other young drivers at the time. But with the respect came the rivalry, and Ayrton used every means possible to maintain his pre-eminence, including a little psychological warfare.

At the start of the race, Michael misjudged his braking and shunted the back of Ayrton's McLaren, putting it out of the running. The race was short but the disappointment was great. After 19 laps, a torrential storm hit the circuit and the race was stopped. When the rain eased off the race was restarted, and just before the start Ayrton told me, "Watch this – I'm going to tell Michael a few things." I didn't hear what he said, I just saw Michael listening very respectfully and intently. Then Ayrton walked back with a grin on his face: "Right, I got him just before the start and hopefully I've spooked him a bit!" Michael had another shunt and didn't finish the race...

On the Hungaroring we still weren't on a par with Williams,

but we were very close, and with Ayrton's skill on a driver's circuit making the difference he beat Mansell to the flag. It was a good race for McLaren, with Gerhard Berger finishing third. But Mansell's second was good enough to secure him the 1992 World Championship five races in advance, which didn't make Ayrton too happy. However, it was a championship well earned, even though he was driving the best car: he used the advantage well and never allowed any driver to challenge him. Still, a win is a win, and Ayrton was pleased about that.

Once again, as every year, I took advantage of the fact that the next race was in Belgium, and as the trucks didn't need to leave for Spa until the Tuesday this gave me a chance to take that week off and go to my house in Cogolin in the south of France.

I normally took a lift straight from the race in Budapest with Ayrton, in his fabulous BAe125 jet, and I was generally able to have *moules marineres* in St Tropez the same evening, after my wife and daughter picked me up at Nice airport – more often than not celebrating a good result!

The first couple of times we took a helicopter straight from the paddock to the airport, but I have to say that these were very scary, and even Ayrton wasn't very impressed with their condition. In addition the price rocketed up once the owners got wise! However, I also used to organise a police escort every year to get the rest of the team to the airport, which was always great fun – although some years it got spoiled by the local 'boy racers' brigade, driving as if they were going to pick up an inheritance!

This year Ayrton decided that he no longer wanted the frightening experience of going to the airport in the dilapidated old egg-beaters that the Hungarians very proudly called helicopters, and he asked me if my escorts worked well. I said they were great, lots of fun and everyone enjoyed them. "Right," he said, "we'll go by road." First I had to make sure that the boss's own escort was going to be secure, so that he didn't accuse me of only looking after Ayrton and myself. As soon as the race was over I went down to the car park to make sure that our own police rider was there, and he was, together with the ever-willing Christine, my personal interpreter (no one spoke a word of English). She'd also made sure that Ron Dennis's motorcycle man was ready.

Then I went back to the motorhome to see that no one had drunk my share of the champagne – we weren't winning as much as in the 1980s, and therefore when we did I wanted everyone to be aware of the fact! After the press conference Ayrton came to the garage to say thank you to the boys – something that he always did – then on to the motorhome for a race debrief with the engineers. Finally he emerged, shouting across to me that it was time to go.

I don't know why, but in Grand Prix racing you always feel guilty whenever you take time off, so I always tried to slide off without being seen, through the back door and into the Honda Legend once the autograph hunters had let go of Ayrton. We started to follow our police rider, who had a smile from ear to ear once he realised who he was escorting. Soon we were driving off-road – cross-country barely described it! Now, if you thought Ayrton was good on the circuits, believe me, he would have made a good rally driver. He went through gaps that were simply not there, and the closer Ayrton came to the biker, the more throttle our man put on his bike. Barry Sheene had nothing on him – he was brilliant!

At one stage we arrived on a winding road under a railway bridge, which had cobbles rather than tarmac, and it was wet right on the corner. Our intrepid kamikaze rider arrived full-on, and Ayrton and I were shouting, "No, no, slow down! We're not in that much of a hurry!" We could just see him splattered all over the wall! However, nothing stopped this guy: he had a mighty spin where the back wheel nearly overtook the front, but he gathered himself back together again, pointing in the right direction. With a tremendous sigh of relief, we continued onto the more open roads closer to the airport. By this stage we'd been joined by some other members from the Grand Prix brigade, including Thierry Boutsen and Domingos Piedade from Mercedes right behind us.

As we got onto the elevated part of the airport express road, our motorcycle guy was gesticulating to the oncoming traffic to move to the left to make more room for us, since the convoy was by now pretty large. As he was doing so, a little old Trabant was approaching: the driver panicked and jammed on his brakes, the right wheel folded under the car, and the left took off, leaving the poor old boy at the wheel completely nonplussed as the guy behind took rapid avoiding action!

Viviane, Ayrton's sister, who hadn't dared to look out of the window during our epic voyage until we arrived at the airport, didn't quite believe that we'd made it with our escort alive. Ayrton told me to open his briefcase and give the police rider the local money that was there. I can't remember exactly how much it was, but I said to Ayrton that in English money it was about £450. "Good," he said, "give it to him! He was worth it, and he probably only earns that in a year!" I can't describe the expression on our Evel Knievel's face when he saw all those *forints*: that alone was worth the money.

Next, shoes off and into the nice high-pile carpet of the 125 jet. Sitting comfortably in the soft leather seats, I was now regretting the champagne that I left at the circuit, as beer was the only alcoholic beverage on the plane. During the flight I took the opportunity to try to persuade Ayrton to stop negotiating with Williams, telling him that we were going to get better; but with Honda not yet decided whether or not they would stay in Grand Prix racing, and Williams being head and shoulders above the rest, he was set to go to Williams for next year if Frank would make a deal. As it transpired later – and fortunately for us – Mansell went across the water, and Frank got a deal with Alain Prost, and elevated his test driver Damon Hill to have a crack as a titular driver.

It wasn't that Ayrton was turning his back on McLaren, but simply that he was looking around to see who might be able to give him the best package for the following year, and believed that Williams would still be just as competitive. Although he knew that McLaren would improve, perhaps he was more certain than Ron Dennis that Honda would be abandoning us at the end of the year, and this was obviously a big factor in Ayrton's view, and quite rightly so. But however many times and however hard I tried to convince him to stay, the one argument to which I never had an answer was when he said, "Look, I've won races with Lotus and McLaren – I've won three World Championships with McLaren. But I want to complement my career as a driver by winning races and championships with other cars. I don't want people to say

'Senna only won with McLaren'. I want to show that I can win with other cars."

Just before the Belgian GP Ayrton had a meeting with Ferrari which wasn't too constructive, and this seemed to put him into a negative frame of mind. During the race it started to rain on lap three, and while everyone started coming into the pits for wet tyres Ayrton insisted on keeping dry tyres on a wet circuit, as he was convinced that it would dry up. But the circuit only became a bit drier towards the end of the race, and stubborn as he was he didn't come in to change tyres. But he did a magnificent job in keeping his McLaren on the road for fifth place, while Michael Schumacher went on to take his first Grand Prix win.

The Italian Grand Prix weekend was eventful in the extreme. Notwithstanding all Ron Dennis's efforts throughout the year to convince Honda to stay in F1, the Japanese giant announced its departure from the sport. This was a very big blow to all of us, and Ayrton felt that he had to make his last push to secure a place with Williams for 1993. Mansell hadn't yet quit, and Frank had had a lot of pressure from Renault and Elf to sign Alain Prost, who was fresh and waiting after a year away from the cockpit, as well as being French. Nigel Mansell, as erratic in his personal business as he was in his driving, was desperate to make an agreement there and then, but Williams weren't offering enough money. Nigel then asked me to arrange an urgent meeting with Ron, which took place on Sunday morning.

I don't know the details of the meeting, but I can imagine the scenario, because Ron was never a fan of Mansell. Finally, just before the start of the race, Nigel announced that he was leaving Formula One at the end of the season to go to the States and race in the CART Champ Car series.

For once, the Williams reliability failed at Monza. Senna won the race from the two Benettons and was reunited on the podium with the great rival of his Formula 3 days, Martin Brundle, and his future Formula One rival Michael Schumacher. Then in Portugal came Ayrton's big blow, when Williams announced that they'd signed Alain Prost for 1993 and elevated Damon Hill from test to race driver. I remember Ayrton coming out of the Williams motorhome with a very grim face. He wondered if Williams had already signed Prost a long time ago, with a clause in the contract from Alain which excluded Ayrton as a teammate. In 1986 Ayrton had vetoed Derek Warwick from joining him in the Lotus team in the same way, although he always maintained that this had been because in those days Lotus weren't able to provide two equal cars, which wasn't the case with the top teams.

This was the last race of the European season and as usual Marlboro gave a big bash. Everyone was there, all the sponsors and associated people. Ayrton made a very emotional speech, and I managed to find a bottle of Dimple Haig Whisky, Ayrton's favourite, and persuaded Kathy McMannon, one of our Marlboro catering girls for whom Ayrton always had a soft spot, to pour the drinks. Ayrton was downing them like water, and I remember Gerhard saying, "Come on, guys, it's not even ten o'clock. At this rate we'll never get to Coconuts." This was the nightclub where we always finished the Portuguese Grand Prix weekend. Ayrton never did make it! Emerson Fittipaldi, who was one of our guests, virtually carried him to the home of a good friend, Antonio Braga, a Brazilian former banker who was then living in Sintra.

The season finished in Adelaide, which was the last race in the team for Gerhard Berger, to whom I remember saying, "A McLaren driver can only leave winning!" And he did. Mansell and Senna were playing at the front, with Mansell brake-testing Ayrton until they collided. Afterwards Gerhard gave me his helmet. He won three races at McLaren and his departure wasn't easy, although he'd been clever enough to negotiate a very lucrative contract with Ferrari for the next two years. After three years working with Senna he was totally exhausted: Ayrton's strength as a driver and a political force within the team was such that Gerhard believed he was suffering from it, and although he loved being at McLaren and got on very well with Ayrton he wanted to try again on his own, out of the shadow of the 'Superstar'. He'd driven for Ferrari before and knew what to expect.

The big dilemma for the 1993 season, of course, wasn't the drivers: it was the engines. Ron suddenly had only a very short time in which to find a replacement for Honda, whose decision to withdraw was one of the biggest setbacks in Ron's history with McLaren. He tried desperately to obtain Renault engines, even to the point of proposing to buy the French Ligier team, which had Renault engines, but I believe that the discrepancies between Renault's contract to run Elf fuel and McLaren's existing Shell contract put an end to the negotiations and thereby the only chance of battling on equal terms with Alain Prost's Williams.

Ron therefore had no choice but to become a Ford Cosworth customer; and our Cosworth HB V8 was not even the top of the range, as Benetton was Ford's 'works' team. However, we hoped that our in-house TAG Electronics system would put the engine at least on a par with those of Benetton. Throughout the whole year there was a political struggle to get the same engines as Benetton, even though we were winning more often than they were.

Because of the events that transpired towards the end of the 1992 season, it looked as if Ayrton might have lost his bargaining power with Ron for 1993, but it wasn't so. Ayrton was the best, and if we wanted him we had to pay for him – otherwise he wasn't interested in driving. At one point he'd also threatened to go to the States, wooed by his friend and countryman Emerson Fittipaldi, and he even drove a Champ Car test with Penske at the Firebird test track in Phoenix. As much as Ayrton knew his value, so did we. I never knew the figures and I didn't want to hear them, because whatever they were, they were obscene. But in business there's always supply and demand, and then value for money, and Ayrton always delivered.

To replace Berger, Ron had signed Michael Andretti, for which he was criticised later as, in hindsight, Michael turned out to be the wrong man for the job. However, at the time he came with wonderful credentials – son of the Formula One and Indy champion Mario Andretti, one of the most complete racing drivers of all time. Michael had won lots of Champ Car races and pole positions, so why should he not do the same in Formula One? Whether or not Ron had some pressure to expand into the American market, he certainly had blind faith that Michael could do the business. For my part, I was willing to welcome any son of Mario – *Il Piedone* ('The Big-footed'), as he'd been called by the Italian *tifosi* when he drove for Ferrari.

Sadly Michael didn't turn out to be all that we hoped, and wasn't at all like his father. Mario was a self-made man who absolutely loved his racing. During his Lotus days I remember sitting next to him on a transatlantic flight, and he showed me pictures of him racing Midgets years ago in Ascot, California – he still carried them in his briefcase! I think that it was Mario who 'sold' Michael to Ron. He wanted to re-live his life through his son, but unfortunately it didn't quite work out that way. Michael was a son of a father: he became a racing driver only because his father was one. If Mario had been a carpenter, Michael would have been one too. The commitment was never there. He had a very cushy life in the USA and wasn't prepared to give it up.

Can you possibly imagine what any other driver in his position would have given for the opportunity to drive a McLaren alongside Ayrton Senna? It would be an unimaginable experience; yet Michael's attitude was take it or leave it. When he was finally sent away, he criticised us for not giving him enough testing opportunities, complaining that Mika Häkkinen was doing most of the testing. This was bullshit, of course. Any other driver in his position would have rented the first house available next to McLaren and when he saw the McLaren trailer driving away for testing he'd have followed it, shouting, "I'll do the test instead of Mika – don't call him, leave him in Monte Carlo." No, not Michael: he spent as much time as possible back home in Pennsylvania. I remember Ron going out of his way to help him find a place in the south of France, even offering him his house in Provence, so that he could bring the family over for the summer, but nothing like that was good enough.

He went to ridiculous lengths in order to be at home, like testing on a Friday at Silverstone, finishing at 17.30 and driving like crazy back to Heathrow to catch the 19.00 Concorde to New York, where he had his own plane waiting to take him to Pennsylvania. He'd then repeat the exercise in reverse on Monday, in order to test on Tuesday! We all thought it was lunacy! Apart from the money it was costing him, the fact was that he didn't fully concentrate during the Friday test, and was totally jet-lagged for the Tuesday one.

One of Mario's selling points for Michael was his tremendous ability to get through traffic – his aggression was second to none. This had perhaps been so in Champ Cars, and maybe he was recognised for it in America, but he soon realised that on this side of 'the pond' the competition was far, far greater. Any aggression had to be measured by Formula One standards and Michael soon found this out the hard way, by shunting race after race. He didn't listen to or follow Ayrton enough, but drove a Formula One car, which is light and has to be driven with finesse and precision, with the same aggression as he handled a Champ Car, which is heavier and could be driven by throwing it hard into a corner.

I remember Ayrton saying, "Look at him, he never approaches a corner the same way as the lap before, he always chooses a different line. He thinks he's still in America." Ayrton, having tested a Champ Car, knew what he was talking about.

Some people have said that Michael was handicapped by the new rules introduced in 1993 which restricted the number of practice and qualifying laps for each driver to 23 in the morning and 12 for qualifying, suggesting that since he hadn't seen many of the circuits before, this was a major factor in his inability to get up to speed. But I really think that a hundred laps still wouldn't have been enough for him to cut the mustard: when he realised the commitment wasn't there he should have just stopped racing in Formula One. As it turned out, his confidence dwindled race by race, and he ended up embarrassing himself.

Our 1993 car, the MP4/8, wasn't a bad car at all. Even Ayrton was quite pleasantly surprised and complimentary when he tested it for the first time after his long off-season winter holiday in Brazil. But it wasn't by any means certain that he'd drive for us the whole year, his demands being far higher than McLaren could meet. However, the arrangement was that he'd be driving on a race-by-race basis, and in between Ron Dennis would be 'robbing banks', begging and borrowing. Different logos of extra sponsors and names kept cropping up on either the car, the helmet or the overalls, and Ekrem Sami, our commercial director and sponsorship co-ordinator, was in overdrive. As always, he was earning his pay!

Before the season, I reminded Ayrton once again that, inevitably, he was going to be sharing podiums and press conferences with Prost, and perhaps it would be a good idea to shake hands with him and bury the hatchet once and for all? He replied: "What, shake hands with the little frog? Fuck him!"

Ayrton was second to Prost's Williams in the first race of the season at Kyalami; then in what became wet and atrocious conditions, Senna won the Brazilian GP, making it clear that although he didn't have the most powerful machine, no one could match him in adverse weather.

1993 was the year that the European Grand Prix was run for the only time at Donington Park in England. If this wasn't Ayrton's greatest drive it was certainly among his best, and those of us who were there were lucky enough to see the best two laps in modern Formula One history. The race started on a wet track and Ayrton, starting from fourth on the grid, was leading by the second lap. His speed was such that it made everyone else look ridiculous. I even thought that perhaps the Williams-Renaults of Prost and Hill had changed tyres at the last minute for slicks and were hoping the track was going to dry, so I went closer to the pit wall to check that they were on the same tyres as us. They were. With weather conditions changing all the time it was an inspired drive by Ayrton, which I'll never forget.

The other thing that I'll never forget about that weekend was meeting Princess Diana. She was the guest of honour and gave the trophies to the winners, but before the race she visited our pits. I must have spent all of five minutes with her and the two boys, William and Harry, showing them the steering wheels, cars and helmets, and they appeared to be intrigued and interested. We spoke briefly about their go-kart experiences and I got the impression that for those few minutes I was the most important person in the world for her: she was so attentive that her magnetic eyes and beautiful face were etched in my mind forever. After they'd continued the tour and gone out into the pouring rain, she suddenly came back and said to me, "I'm sorry, I never said goodbye." She then shook my hand and went back to her group. I was in love from that moment and didn't wash my hands for the rest of the day!

Having won the Brazilian and the European Grands Prix, we (and especially Ayrton) thought that we deserved the latest version of the Ford engine, the series 8, instead of waiting until the British GP as was the original agreement. However, Benetton saw things differently, and as a result Ayrton went into sulk mode and decided to stay in Brazil until the last moment before the San Marino Grand Prix at Imola. By that time he could only get a flight to Rome, so Ron sent me there with the company plane to collect him, with the terse message, "You get back here with Ayrton in time for practice or don't show your face at all." So I set off for Fiumicino airport in Rome with Bob and Jeff (our pilots), only to find that private planes weren't allowed to land there but had to use a nearby military aerodrome, where we spent the night in a hotel.

Next morning I went by taxi to Fiumicino to await Ayrton's flight. I had a great driver and I asked him to wait for me outside, but as in any major airport the authorities wouldn't let him wait, so he had to keep driving round in circles waiting for us to reappear.

Ayrton was off the plane almost before it reached a complete stop and was VIP-escorted out like a flash. As we came out onto the street, my faithful taxi wasn't there. I said that he should be back in a minute as he was going round in circles, but Ayrton was frantic, saying, "Forget him, let's go get another taxi." I said that there was no way I could do that as my briefcase was in the original taxi, but he replied, "Fuck your briefcase, I have to get to Imola." I had tickets, passports, money, agenda and team documents in that briefcase and it would have been impossible for me to just abandon it, but Ayrton said, "Look, he's probably run off with it by now anyway." I was determined not to give in as I trusted my original taxi driver, but by then Ayrton was coming on really heavy. I said, "Look, it's not my fault that you're late – we always seem to be running around in circles because of you." But finally I had to give in and take another taxi: there was more at stake at Imola. As we arrived at the tiny airport, Bob had the engines running.

We boarded the plane, and just as we were taxiing onto the runway I saw my taxi driver running towards us with my briefcase in his hand. My faith in human nature was restored! I was dizzy with relief and Ayrton's smile was as broad as mine. He even said sorry!

In the meantime I'd arranged a helicopter to wait for us at Bologna, and once again, as we landed the chopper blades were already turning, and off we went on the last leg of the journey to the Autodromo Enzo e Dino Ferrari, where a team scooter was on hand to take Ayrton to the pits. I could hear the engines warming-up: we'd made it with two minutes to spare and I still had my job!

It was all to little avail. With his anxiety, nerves, lack of sleep and jet-lag, Ayrton's concentration was less than 100 per cent – after all, he was only human – and a few laps into the session he stuffed it into the earth banking coming out of the Tosa corner. He went on to qualify fourth but went off halfway into the race with hydraulic problems whilst in second place behind Prost.

While all this was happening at Imola, I was also busy with Ekrem Sami, trying to get more money for the team as it was crucial to keep Ayrton. Ekrem once again excelled himself by getting the OK from Philip Morris to have Segafredo coffee back on the car despite the fact that they owned Maxwell House. We had all the branding identification defined, confirmed and agreed on the nose of the car and on the drivers' overalls for $1.5 million. However, Segafredo boss Massimo Zanetti wanted to meet Ron again, just to touch base with him and feel welcomed back to the team.

With this in mind, we invited the Segafredo party to Imola for the San Marino weekend and we were due to have lunch together – Massimo, his two closest associates, Ekrem, Ron and myself. Unfortunately it all went pear-shaped. I don't know what was wrong with Ron, but he was in one of those moods that every now and then got him to where he felt that he could walk on water. It was a disastrous lunch where, rather than welcoming them back into the team, he kept on saying how lucky and privileged they were to be allowed back in the team. Ekrem and I looked at each other in disbelief and tried to cover up and butt in, but Ron, for whatever reason, didn't even finish lunch and left the table. Even Ekrem was lost for words, and at the end of the lunch it was a "Don't call us, we'll call you" situation. It was awful, I felt totally embarrassed. Ekrem and I tried to make excuses for Ron with faxes and phone calls, but it was to no avail: they pulled the plug. Ekrem and I were gutted. It had to be McLaren's must expensive lunch ever.

Later on we were instrumental in getting the Segafredo sponsorship for Williams, as we were no longer allowed by Marlboro and Philip Morris to have Segafredo on our car. Williams had the Segafredo branding on its side-pods for 1994, where it would unfortunately receive so much tragic exposure in the San Marino Grand Prix at Imola, when Ayrton lost his life at the wheel of the Williams – absolutely the last thing Massimo would have wanted. He'd been a Toleman sponsor when Ayrton had made his debut ten years before, and was a great admirer.

In Monaco Prost jumped the start and was penalised, so Senna got his sixth Monaco victory. The next few race wins were shared by Prost and Hill. It was after the Italian Grand Prix that our all-American boy Michael Andretti was finally sent home for more hamburgers. Ironically, it had been his best drive of the year, finishing third despite a spin. However, the decision had been taken earlier, and perhaps it was only through Mario's persuasiveness that Michael was allowed to do just one more race, at Monza.

In Portugal Alain Prost clinched his fourth World Championship, finishing second to Michael Schumacher's Benetton, and announced his retirement at the end of the year. At the same time, Senna announced that he wasn't going to be driving a McLaren in 1994, although neither he nor Williams revealed their future plans.

Mika Häkkinen, our test driver, was promoted to the race job at Estoril and if anyone was ever ready for this it was him. He was desperately eager to jump into the hot seat and what a delight this was to see, for every one of us. The only one who wasn't ready was Ayrton. Having been racing against Andretti the whole year he hadn't had to try too hard, but when the 'Flying Finn' came onto the scene – looking forward to his first chance at a race after having done thousands of miles of testing – he caught the great master with his pants down and out-qualified him in third place behind the Williams. Ayrton wasn't a happy Brazilian, and during the debriefing after practice Mika wasn't able to wipe the grin from his face, and Ayrton was livid: "What are you smiling about? How many races have you won? How many championships have you won? You'll not last the distance tomorrow."

At the drivers' meeting next morning, I remember Gerhard Berger congratulating Mika for his qualifying efforts: "Well done, Mika, enjoy it, because as long as you live you'll never, ever out-qualify him again."

In the race, Senna displaced Mika immediately at the first few corners, but later suffered an engine failure. Häkkinen was tucked into the slipstream of Jean Alesi, dicing for third, when he lost control of his MP4/8 coming onto the main straight – a driver error, but a McLaren debut of which he'd every right to be proud. After the race he said, "I got the message from Ayrton, he put me in my place. But I was amazed to see how he could be so damned quick at the start."

But then again, this was one of Ayrton's personal trade marks: he always approached the first corner as if it was the finishing line. By the time the other drivers had settled down and adjusted their breathing to the racing beat, Ayrton had often vanished.

I first met Mika at the Transamerica Hotel in São Paulo in 1991, when he was racing for Lotus. I'd arrived from London early in the morning and my room wasn't ready, so I went to the pool and waited until I could check in. It was while I was sitting there with a coffee that Mika came across and introduced himself. We spent a good time chatting and I warmed to him, because he was a very open and single-minded young man.

When he was our test driver, Mika was invited to be the guest driver in the supporting Porsche Carrera Cup race before the Monaco Grand Prix. He was to drive a Porsche 911, and he'd never ever driven a Porsche in his life. If you've not driven a 911, believe me, they're not the easiest cars to drive, nor was his car the best prepared, yet he was going to compete against all the specialists in that category who raced them every weekend. He put the car on pole position and won the race! He did the same again at the Hungarian Grand Prix weekend, and I said to myself, "We have one hell of a driver here!" I couldn't wait for him to take over Michael Andretti's place.

Mika qualified one-tenth of a second behind Ayrton at Suzuka, but in the race Ayrton had another mesmerising drive to win his fourth Grand Prix of the season, with Mika finishing third, half a minute behind. He said afterwards that his MP4/8 was brilliant, but he'd just realised what a difference a champion makes: while he could be as quick as him in qualifying, doing the same lap after lap in the race is what makes the difference. From then on he started working on that.

As I arrived at the Suzuka circuit early on the Friday morning before practice commenced, Ron came to me and, pointing to a group of lock-up garages behind the racing pits, asked, "What do they keep in those garages?" I said that they belonged to different Japanese companies like Yokahama, Arai and Shoei. "Why?" Then he asked if I could get some space in one of them very discreetly and quietly, and I replied that I'd try, but why? It was then that he confided in me that he'd just crashed the McLaren F1 roadgoing 'supercar'. I said, "No! Not the new one they sent for the big promotion?" "Yes," he said, "I'm an idiot." I made the arrangements and hid the car, keeping it quiet: I knew how he felt and sympathised with him, having done a similar thing in the past, though in a much less prestigious car. Later I found out that he'd been demonstrating the car to Gerhard Berger at the time – and Gerhard made sure that the whole world knew about it.

Adelaide was the next and final race of the season and probably the most emotional Formula One weekend of my life, as there were so many different milestones: Ayrton's last race in the McLaren, Alain Prost's last ever race, and at the time we were neck and neck with Ferrari with 103 Grand Prix wins each. If we won this race we'd automatically become the most successful Formula One team in history and, of course, we were more than keen to achieve this.

There was no doubt about it – it was never going to be the same at McLaren without Ayrton Senna. Even he was apprehensive about joining another team purely because they had a better car, when deep inside himself he knew we were the better team. He put his MP4/8 on pole, the first for a Ford-engined car in ten years, and at the start line he called me over to the cockpit, apparently to do up his belts, which I thought was strange as he always did the last little pull himself using two hands. As I came close to him I realised this wasn't what he wanted. He said: "It's a very strange feeling for me to do this for the last time in a McLaren." And I replied, "If it's a strange thing for you, just imagine how hard it is for us. I don't need to tell you how important this win is. If you win this one for us I'll love you forever."

Ayrton grabbed my arm very hard and I saw tears in his eyes!

Damn it! I got so worried that I'd made him emotional just before the start, but like a good Latin he was a very emotional man and always coped with it. And he won. McLaren was the most successful Formula One team and Prost was second on the podium.

Two weeks earlier, in Japan, they'd also finished in the same places, and Prost had offered to shake hands at the press conference, but Ayrton didn't even look at him. Alain even thought that they should exchange helmets after the last race of the season, in Australia, which would have been a really nice gesture, but after Ayrton's coolness in Japan he forgot about it.

But in Adelaide they did shake hands, to the smiles of the whole world. Ayrton was pleasant and warm, maybe because it was his idea or because Prost was no longer his worst 'enemy' on the track.

Tina Turner gave a concert after the race, to which we all went, and during her performance she dragged Ayrton onto the stage and sang *Simply the Best* to him. Needless to say, it brought the house down!

That evening we had a team dinner in the Trattoria, an Italian restaurant in Adelaide, to say goodbye to the great champion, and to celebrate being the most successful Formula One Grand Prix team of all time. Ayrton was with his girlfriend, Adriane, and I presented him with a steering wheel from one of his victories. I also reminded him that although he was only second in the 1993 championship he'd won five races in places and conditions where power wasn't an issue, only driver ability. Therefore, he was still the best. I ended up by saying: "Three World Championships, 35 Grand Prix wins, 47 pole positions and 447 championships points with McLaren. If you think you can do better anywhere else, you're welcome to try!"

A truly remarkable weekend – and the end of an era.

CHAPTER 14

THE FRENCH CONNECTION

During the 1993 season Ron Dennis was constantly looking for a replacement engine for the following year. More than that, he was looking for an engine partner who would perhaps persuade Ayrton Senna to remain at McLaren. During talks with Chrysler, the owners of Lamborghini Engineering, it was agreed to fit a Lamborghini engine in the back of a McLaren for a trial at Silverstone. This was a very good exercise, because in a back-to-back test with a McLaren-Cosworth the 'Lambo' car proved to be almost two seconds quicker than the Ford.

Chrysler's intention at the time was to boost its Formula One budget for 1994, and, as result of this very encouraging test, Ayrton pushed really hard to take the Lambo car to the last two races of the 1993 season, or at least just to Japan. This, of course, would had been a bit ridiculous, as there wasn't enough time to prepare everything even just for one car. As it turned out, he won both races with the faithful Ford Cosworth V8 anyway.

The Italian side of Lamborghini were very keen on the project. Having spent the last two very frustrating seasons with Larrousse, Minardi and Venturi, the thought of joining a top team was overwhelming, and this reaction was echoed by the top guys in Detroit who signed the cheques and the contracts. If they were ever going to make it in Formula One, this was their best chance, and they'd already made up their minds to go for broke. Chrysler's new chief, Bob Eaton, was a great believer in Formula One as a means of improving the image of the company, and he was planning a big assault on the European market. However, Ron Dennis wasn't convinced.

Having been the fifth employee of Lamborghini Automobili when the company was formed in 1963, I have to say that I was enthusiastic about the idea, even though this would be a whole new ball of wax. Of course, no one from the 1960s was still working with Lamborghini. The top men were British and American engineers, led by the Formula One project leader and managing director Daniele Audetto, a former Ferrari team manager from the troubled 1970s. The 3.5-litre V12 engine was the brainchild of Mauro Forghieri, who'd designed so many successful Ferrari Formula One engines and chassis and with whom I still have a very good friendship.

Ron met with all the top Chrysler 'heavy-hitters' (as he normally called the power men) during the International Motor Show in Frankfurt, and they believed that an agreement was reached, with everyone shaking hands. The lawyers wanted to prepare a contract immediately, but there was just not enough time for the preparation of the paperwork before the parties dispersed. According to Daniele Audetto, Ron Dennis said, "Between gentlemen, a handshake is more important than a thousand-page contract."

François Castaing, who was in charge of Chrysler-Lamborghini motorsport, had authorised a budget to Audetto to prepare the engines for McLaren, changing the electronics from Magneti Marelli to TAG and developing variable induction trumpets. In the meantime, two engines were modified as suggested by Ayrton, with a lower range torque and more progressive and smoother power. Mika Häkkinen was due to test these at Pembrey, when · Daniele Audetto received a telephone call from Ron. He told him that he had to give him some bad news, but business is business and he had to take care of 500 people at McLaren. Ron said that he didn't feel that Chrysler's commitment was 100 per cent behind the Formula One programme and that's why they wanted him to pay 50 per cent of the engine development. He concluded by telling Audetto that he was in Paris and had just signed a deal with Peugeot, with free engines plus bonus money and a budget for testing. Therefore there was no point in sending the modified engines to Pembrey.

When Audetto broke the news to Detroit, Bob Eaton went berserk. He demanded a stop to everything, even though Daniele had also just had an engine request from Benetton, who had

Michael Schumacher. Eaton told Audetto that he no longer wanted to dive in the 'piranha pond' with the Formula One people and later reduced the business to a minimum, making over 100 engineers and mechanics redundant. Later, Chrysler sold the Lamborghini Company for peanuts to Tommy Suharto, the son of the Indonesian president.

It was all very sad, but we couldn't condemn Ron if he'd reneged on the deal: it would have been the first time and he had good reason for it. It was a known fact that Chrysler didn't have the wherewithal to develop the engine, so it was a risk Ron couldn't possibly take. Nevertheless, Audetto even now remains very bitter about the affair.

We presented our new car, the MP4/9 powered by the Peugeot V10, in January 1994. I, and no doubt everyone else at McLaren, had a good feeling about the new project, as we knew the seriousness of the French company and the fact that they'd succeeded in every type of motorsport that they'd attempted. Hopefully Formula One would be the same, but we were under no delusion that the loss of Ayrton Senna to Williams and Renault wasn't a massive one – he was irreplaceable. In fact, I didn't know how Ron had managed to pull off the Peugeot deal without being able to offer a World Champion or at least a race-winning driver. Ron thought that if only the deal had been struck a few weeks earlier, it might have helped to keep Senna in the house, but we'll never know. As it was, Mika Häkkinen had proved to be quick, but he wasn't a winner yet, we didn't have a second driver, and all the race winners were already taken.

Ron still toyed with the idea of convincing Alain Prost to return to the cockpit, but although he agreed to test the McLaren-Peugeot there was no way that he'd have gone from a strong winning combination like the Williams-Renault to an unproved Peugeot engine, no matter how handsomely Ron was prepared to pay him. He certainly wasn't short of people like myself in the team, pushing him hard to do it, and added to that Alain had enjoyed working with McLaren far more than he ever enjoyed his short spell with Williams. But he felt that he couldn't possibly go back on his word after all the retirement parties which had honoured him all over France. So we still had the task of finding a second driver.

Martin Brundle was among the favourites, even though he wasn't a race winner either. He had solid experience and he'd represent good value for the team. Again Ron kept him waiting until the last minute, and Martin was leaving all his other offers on ice, waiting desperately for the McLaren call which eventually came. A delighted Martin came to Woking for his seat fitting, met all of us and saw our facilities. Needing to find a driver's suit that would near enough fit him in order to mould his first seat, I produced a pair of Michael Andretti's overalls. Martin took one look at them and turned to me, saying, "For Christ's sake Jo, give me a break!" I reflected on that and replied, "Martin – this *is* your break!" Martin was silent for a split second, and then said, "Yes, I suppose you're right."

He was another great team player, with a world of experience, whose only handicap was in qualifying, where he seemed to lose some ground to Häkkinen. But his speed in the race was very much on a par with Mika, although by then he was some places back.

For all our great hopes, the new Anglo-French partnership was almost dead as soon as it was born. The project leader for Peugeot Sport was Jean-Pierre Jabouille, the former Renault Formula One driver, and he and Ron Dennis never saw eye-to-eye. They never felt comfortable with each other, and there was always a strange feeling in the air during their meetings. The team spirit was non-existent and at times you could have cut the atmosphere with a blunt knife. It was just a matter of when, not if, the partnership was going to end.

The engine design was the brainchild of Jean-Pierre Boudy – a nice enough man, but I always thought that he was very slow to react to the needs and changes that Formula One required. Sometimes Peugeot simply refused to recognise some of the obvious faults of their engines, like overheating, high oil consumption and unacceptable vibrations from the flywheel – not to mention the lack of power. Their engine certainly had the most outstanding blow-ups that I've ever seen in my racing life. Once, a con-rod came out of the crankcase with such force that part of it was stuck in the tarmac! However, it's fair to say that every new version of the engine was an improvement on the last, and perhaps if the partnership had continued we'd have won races. But there was no way on this earth that the partnership could continue, and at the end of it all I felt that we had failed to win a race for Peugeot.

A second place in Monaco by Martin was encouraging in only the fourth race of the season, but Peugeot's elation was soon dampened by a hurtful remark from Ron. As Martin and the Peugeot guys were having some champagne, he came along and said, "Remember guys, second is only the first of the losers." "Thanks, Ron," Martin replied, "We always like to learn something new!"

Another second by Mika at Spa, thanks to the disqualification of Michael Schumacher, and six third places between them, was all we had to show for 1994. This was the first year since 1981 that the team hadn't won a Grand Prix, and it was something that was very hard to swallow. Little did we know then that we'd jog along for another two years without a win.

Scarcely ten months after the presentation of our new MP4/9, the parting of the two companies was announced and a new partnership with Mercedes-Benz was disclosed for 1995. It was another good deal by Ron, who managed to pass the Peugeot V10 engine on to Eddie Jordan's team in order to get Mercedes-Benz, who he'd been courting for years.

At the last European race, as was the custom, Marlboro had a good party, and this year in Jerez they wanted to do something different. Graham Bogle and John Hogan, who ran the Marlboro sponsorship programme, were looking for suggestions, and I came up with the idea of having a small *corrida* (bullfight), as we'd be in Spain and it was easy to hire a small *cortijo* with all the ingredients. Everybody was thrilled with the idea and it turned out to be one of the most hilarious parties that we ever had after a race meeting. With Mika finishing third, at least we could celebrate something!

A poster was made for the invitation, using Spanish nicknames. We had six *matadors*: Ron Dennis, Mika Häkkinen, Martin Brundle, David Ryan, Leigh Coleman and myself, all dressed up properly in 'suits of lights' so that we looked the part. I was the only one who, many years ago, had had any sort of experience at a similar party in Mexico, so I felt I had to show the way, and having had a couple of drinks previously I went into the ring very bravely for two *'oles!'* But on the third I was thrown in the air, which left me with a very sore arse and a very damaged ego! From then on we all took it easy: the bulls were, in fact, a little bigger than I'd been led to believe! The girls, particularly Liz Brundle, were really worried, and in retrospect perhaps it was a bit of a crazy idea, but luckily no one was hurt and indeed everyone had a good night.

The year 1994 was one that would stick in our minds, not because we failed to win a Grand Prix, but because we lost the best ambassador of our sport during the tragic weekend of 1 May. The San Marino Grand Prix had been the first that Ayrton Senna had won in a McLaren: sadly, the 1994 race was also the last race of his brilliant life.

The tragic weekend started with the spectacular accident of Rubens Barrichello's Jordan-Hart, which left him with an aching right arm and minor cuts and lacerations of the mouth and nose. He got away with a night in hospital. But the highlight for 'Rubinho' was that his great idol Ayrton Senna came to the hospital to say hello. Rubens had only been in Formula One for a year and he was moulding himself on his great hero and compatriot.

Next day, the second of qualifying, the young Austrian rookie Roland Ratzenberger lost control of his Simtek Ford a few seconds after its front wing had come off in the fastest section of the circuit after the Tamburello corner, and he was killed by the impact when he crashed into the barrier. The motor racing world was horrified. It was eight years since a driver had died in a Formula One car, so we were no longer as accustomed to tragedy as we had been in earlier decades, when such events were more commonplace. Elio de Angelis was the last one who'd left us in this way, while testing at Paul Ricard in 1986.

Ayrton Senna had only just met Ratzenberger the day before and had welcomed him to Formula One, for which Roland had been very grateful. After the accident Ayrton was very glum indeed and spent a long time talking with Professor Sid Watkins, the FIA's chief medical officer, an excellent person loved and respected by all. Even though Ayrton was more than aware of the risks involved with driving one of these cars and often spoke about it, he was very depressed when confronted with the reality. No matter how safe the cars and the circuits were, every now and then the sport claimed its victims. Ayrton had supported Professor Watkins in his campaign to improve the quality of immediate trackside assistance, which nowadays is excellent.

Ayrton had come to Imola with his brother Leonardo, leaving his girlfriend Adriane in his house in Quinta do Lago in Portugal, and even though he always had friends around him, in situations like this he missed having a female companion. On the Saturday after practice he asked me to book him a helicopter for after the race, to take him back to Forli where his aircraft was parked. He wanted to get back to Adriane as soon as possible. He told me that at Williams it was very different from being with McLaren: a driver was treated just like another employee, and no one took care of his needs. He added that it was easier to ask me, as I knew everyone, everywhere. For me it was a sign of our continuing friendship, even though we were now fighting under different flags.

Next morning I went to see him and gave him the details of the helicopter. He still appeared low, but a little bit happier with the car after the morning warm up. He qualified on pole, but it was he and not the car that achieved it, the Williams FW16 not yet being good enough: it was only his almost inhuman determination and desire to succeed that had enabled him to reach so many goals over the years that no other driver could. Added to that was an element of desperation, because his new rival Michael Schumacher already had a 20-point advantage over him after only two races. I saw him again at the drivers' meeting, where he stayed on at the end chatting with Michael about making racing safer.

Later on as I was walking to the grid I bumped into Alain Prost, who was in Imola as a commentator for French TV, and he told me with genuine pleasure that he'd had a good chat with Senna, that he was very friendly, and that maybe after all they could end up being friends. The infamous rivalry and five-year feud between these two great champions finally appeared to be reaching its end.

The race started as the weekend had started: the Benetton B194 of JJ Lehto stayed on the start line with a dead engine and the Lotus 107 of Pedro Lamy crashed into it, destroying both cars and leaving the pit straight full of broken parts, while a wheel flew into the grandstand and injured several spectators. Instead of the race being stopped with a red flag, the pace car was sent out for five laps while the mess was cleared up.

Ayrton, who was leading, realised that the pace car was about to go back into the pit-lane and slowed right down – and then accelerated like mad once on the pit straight, taking his rivals completely by surprise. At the end of the next lap, however, he was half a second in front of Michael Schumacher, but Michael could appreciate that Ayrton was over-driving the Williams, which was bottoming heavily on the ground, and was sure that sooner or later he'd have to slow down. But perhaps not even Michael comprehended Ayrton's will to win: nothing on this earth would have made him slow down. Ayrton simply hated to be second, and perhaps this more than anything cost him his life – his total inability to accept defeat.

At the start of the seventh lap, Michael, behind Ayrton, watched in horror as the Williams hit the ground again as it entered Tamburello – and left the circuit at more than 300kph. Tamburello is not really a corner, it's a bent straight, and nobody lifts the throttle there. There have been endless theories about what really happened, especially because it happened in Italy and under Italian law there are no accidents: someone has to be responsible. An inquiry started immediately that was to last for years. However, despite all the investigations, deliberations and conclusions over the years, I remain unconvinced that the best racing driver in the world could make a mistake at Tamburello.

The race was stopped while Professor Watkins and the medical crew took Senna from the destroyed Williams car and helicoptered him to Bologna hospital. The next hour was horrible. The atmosphere was very cold and silent: everyone kept their heads down, doing their jobs, preparing for the restart, when really what everyone wanted to do was to leave Imola as soon as possible.

I just remember that never before in my life had I had to fight so hard with my own mind, trying to keep it away from all sorts of morbid thoughts and trying to concentrate on the race. At times I thought the worst, but two minutes later I would find myself trusting in Ayrton again, who always got out of tight situations, perhaps with some broken bones but nothing serious.

At the end of the race the atmosphere got worse. Nobody was interested in the results. Rumours kept circulating, but I covered my ears as I didn't want to hear anything, and just followed my post-race routine. At 18.40 Ayrton was finally pronounced dead and Keke Rosberg came and broke the news to me.

The motor racing world had just lost its greatest asset. He'd be missed for decades, not only by those who saw him racing but by everyone who'd ever heard about him. Those of us who were lucky enough to work with him and were proud to be on his list of friends would miss him even more. Next day the entire world realised the enormity of the loss. There was no newspaper in the world that didn't have the tragic news on the front page.

Ayrton Senna died as he had lived: out in front, leading the way, to the limit of his chosen profession. He pushed Formula One onto a new level, and those left behind can only follow. He wasn't just the best racing driver – a real poet in the art – he was a great personality, and we inherit his example and a world of memories.

I'd spoken with Neida and Milton, Ayrton's parents, in the days prior to the funeral in São Paulo and they told me I could stay with them if I decided to go. I had my plane ticket, but at the last moment I felt that I couldn't go through the same pain all over again, this time with his family, friends and the whole country that had just lost its most beloved citizen. I stayed home and went quietly by myself to a nearby church at the same time as it was happening in Brazil, to think of him and say my prayers. Gerhard Berger told me that it was a very moving day, so dignified and well organised that it almost seemed as if it had been arranged by Ayrton himself.

At the last race of the year in Adelaide, where Michael Schumacher and Damon Hill shunted and the championship went to Michael, he was nice enough to dedicate the championship to 'absent friends'. The Benetton team arranged a big celebration party at the circuit bar, which was right on the edge of the Adelaide street circuit, and all the teams were invited. Ron Dennis wasn't very pleased that the championship had gone Michael's way, but felt that he had to take one more shot at trying to get him to McLaren. So he told me to find a room in the pub somewhere and somehow try to get Michael there. This wasn't an easy task in a public bar, but I managed to find a place, get Michael into it, and give the nod to Ron. Although some people saw them going into the room and drew their own conclusions, I stayed on guard outside so that no one would disturb the improvised meeting.

When Ron came out he said, "Maybe I was too late – but time will tell. Nevertheless, it was a positive meeting. Thank you." Two weeks later in England he confirmed that he'd been too late but that Michael would now have much more money in his pockets – and Benetton would have much less in theirs to develop their 1995 car! Well, perhaps that short meeting in Adelaide was something for which Michael's manager Willi Weber should be grateful. Certainly it refuelled some animosity between Ron and Flavio Briatore, the boss of Benetton, but unfortunately it didn't seem to upset the Benetton team too much, as they won the championship again with Michael in 1995.

One big tragedy which resulted from the enormous loss of Ayrton Senna was that millions of fans throughout the world would never get to see what would have been one of motorsport's all-time great rivalries, between Senna and Michael Schumacher. Michael was nine years Ayrton's junior and was getting better and better race by race. They'd already had their disagreements, most notably, as I've described, at the French Grand Prix in 1992, and at a test session at Hockenheim in July of the same year, when Ayrton accused Michael of brake-testing him. He ran to the Benetton garage with the real intention of thumping Michael but was 'dissuaded' by our chief mechanic, Ian Dyer.

The promise of real fireworks between the two of them was well on the cards, but Schumacher's main problem was his lack of public image – there was little about him that would make him interesting enough. Senna, on the other hand, had an excess of charisma. He was already a legend – and a romantic legend, too, because of the mysticism that surrounded him. Some people may not have liked his ruthlessness but they loved his Latin warmth, philosophical intelligence, good looks and magnetic appeal. Whenever he entered a room or a circuit his mere presence was electrifying.

Schumacher would never have been able to compete with Senna outside their cars. Inside a car, however, they were very similar in many ways. Both had the same killer instinct and ability to perform 100 per cent, lap after lap, for the entire duration of a race – a talent only found among the very best. They were both also able to extract the last ounce from their respective teams through devotion, respect and trust, creating a working environment which gave them both the best chance to perform at the highest level. They both shared the same ability to be fast from the first lap, they were both able to keep their concentration at the wheel while discussing tactics and pitstops over the car radio, and were both great masters in the rain – although I think that perhaps Senna had the edge. I also believe that Senna's determination and will to win was greater, although Michael is probably the fittest Formula One driver of all time. And, like Ayrton, he didn't think twice about crashing into a rival when it was necessary.

CHAPTER 15

STORMY WEATHER

There was never really a question of 'if' Mercedes-Benz were going to join McLaren, only 'when'. Ron Dennis had been working on the deal for years, and was a very loyal Mercedes supporter: even when he could have had a free, top of the range Peugeot, he still bought a Mercedes. He'd been following the Stuttgart car giant's progress in competition since the arrival in 1990 of Norbert Haug as its new motorsport manager. Haug was a great racing enthusiast and had been trying to convince the company's top men to return to Formula One after a 35-year absence. In the meantime Mercedes had enjoyed some success with Sauber in sports car racing and with Penske in the Indianapolis 500.

The next logical step for Mercedes was to form a partnership with one of the existing top Formula One teams. Norbert Haug didn't need much convincing, but Ron needed to sell his team to the board, and the deal was finally announced towards the end of 1994.

There was only a very short time in which to prepare for the following season, but working with Mercedes was like a breath of fresh air compared to what we'd been used to during the previous year. German people have always had the reputation of being too autocratic, over-confident, even arrogant, always wanting to have their own way, but it was nothing like that at all. We had a few meetings with all the relevant people and we agreed on most things, one of which was that everyone would wear the same common uniform at race meetings, which immediately identified us as one team, not 'them and us', but a royal 'we'.

An added benefit was that the Mercedes V10 engine was made by Ilmor Engineering of Brixworth, England, a company run by two brilliant former Cosworth engineers, Mario Illien and Paul Morgan. For us this was much better than Paris, for obvious reasons.

It was the team of the 'Four Ms': McLaren, Marlboro, Mercedes and Mobil. This was to be the first year of having Mobil fuel and lubricants on board. After ten years of one of the most wonderful partnerships in the history of our team, Shell hesitated a little bit too much over whether or not to continue the association, perhaps thinking that we needed them more than they needed us. They delayed signing the new contract, not knowing that Mobil were in talks with us and were very keen to join. Ron Dennis, Ekrem Sami, the Mobil people and the lawyers got together one Thursday, and, after a meeting which lasted nearly all night, a deal was announced on Friday morning.

It would have been interesting to be a fly on the wall at the Shell board meeting that Friday and heard the swearing that must have taken place – all because somebody had opted to delay signing the contract. They were very disappointed, to say the least, but they took it like the gentlemen they were. They invited all of the McLaren management and PR personnel to a friendly, informal dinner at the Shell Centre in London, where Lawrie Austin and Mike Brannigan, among others, apologised for their shortcomings and said goodbye to us. They were so upset that they decided to stay out of Formula One for 1995, but in 1996 teamed up with Ferrari, where, of course, they've enjoyed remarkable success.

With the four Ms in place and Mika Häkkinen signed up, we only needed a second pair of hands at the wheel. Williams had opted for David Coulthard, even though Nigel Mansell was available and had only just come back to do the last three races of 1994 with them. He'd won the Australian GP in convincing fashion, but either they'd had just about enough of their beloved 'Nige', or perhaps they genuinely believed that Coulthard, being younger, had more to offer in the long term. They said that Nigel had been wonderful on his return to the team, as well as bringing some comedy and drama back to Formula One. Ron Dennis was under great pressure from the other three Ms to sign him, but he was resisting. I remember that even I said to Ron, "Well, we've tried everyone available and failed to win a Grand Prix last year. Nigel has won races and championships, so he knows how to do it."

Marlboro was the 'M' that put the most pressure on Ron, but he remained insistent that Mansell wasn't the answer, and resisted right up until January. He even kept Martin Brundle waiting until Martin himself realised that he couldn't compete with Nigel's pedigree and went and signed a deal with Ligier. In the end, Ron had to give in to those who signed the big cheques, and we committed ourselves to Mansell.

At the time, Patrick Head, co-owner and chief designer of the Williams team, said to me: "I can't tell you anything about Nigel because you'd never believe me – you actually have to live the experience." Obviously not every member of the Williams team belonged to the Nigel Mansell fan club. A couple of months down the road I told Patrick that he'd never spoken a truer word!

The laughs and smiles at the launch and presentation of the car soon faded and it was trouble from day one. Admittedly the MP4/10 wasn't one of the best McLarens that we'd ever made, by a long chalk, and we realised it soon after the first test and didn't need a has-been former World Champion to tell us. What we needed was a motivated, experienced driver to help Häkkinen to develop the car, and Mansell wasn't interested in that. He wanted a winning car 'out of the box'. Apart from not being a winning car it was also too small for him – or rather he was too big for the car. Perhaps it was the very special way in which he drove, sitting very close to a funny little steering wheel that he insisted should be only 24cm in diameter.

Ayrton always said of him, "No wonder he's always so erratic in the car – with that silly wheel he can't possibly control the car smoothly." Ayrton himself normally liked a 28cm steering wheel, and would ask us to design the car around that.

Nigel's arms were never stretched, but bent, and therefore he needed lots of elbow room and consequently a wider chassis. Rather than try to botch up one of the existing chassis and doing our best to accommodate our *prima donna* as much as we could (if we didn't we'd never hear the end of it), we built the wider chassis in just a month and even Mansell was amazed. In the meantime, Mark Blundell stood in for him in the first two South American races, leaving Nigel to make his debut at Imola in San Marino. This was the first anniversary of the blackest weekend in Formula

One, and our minds were still full of it, so we were hoping for a pleasant and trouble-free race.

As at every race, I arranged courtesy cars from Mercedes for the drivers, to be ready at whichever airport they were flying into. These were top of the range, brand new cars. Nigel was arriving at Forli airport and his car was there waiting for him. As he arrived at the circuit, out of courtesy I just asked him if everything was OK with his car, and he shouted irritably that the courtesy car business wasn't a very good arrangement. "Why not?" I asked, "It's always worked before. What was wrong?" To which he replied, "Do you know what it's like to arrive at a small airport in your private plane, be inundated with autograph-hunting *tifosi*, and then be asked to sign for the car? This is not good enough!"

At first I though he was joking or was winding me up, but he was deadly serious. I was speechless for a second before replying, "No, I wouldn't know what it's like, I don't have my own plane and I'm not famous. But I've made the same arrangements many times for great champions like Senna, Prost, Lauda, Stewart and Rosberg, and they never minded signing for their cars."

I related the incident to Ron Dennis and he said that he'd encountered a similar attitude from him: "But don't take any shit from him, Jo. This is a McLaren team and he has to work with our system. I'll back you up 100 per cent all the time." Thanks, Ron, that was just what I wanted to hear.

Nigel was outpaced by Häkkinen in the San Marino Grand Prix, and even before the next race, in Barcelona, the team was already losing motivation. It was only thanks to Mika, whose enthusiasm it would have taken more than a bad car to dampen, that the team kept going. While Mika was fighting for fourth place in the Spanish GP, Mansell was 14th when he chose to stop and get out, saying that the car was undriveable. This, perhaps, was what was needed to make Ron take action. The following week Ron and Martin Whitmarsh met up with Nigel at his golf club and the contract was terminated. I remember opening a bottle of champagne when I heard the news.

Mark Blundell got back into our second car, albeit on a race-by-race basis, and was a very welcome face. But he struggled like the rest of us with a bad car and an underpowered and difficult to-drive-engine, in what was probably the worst McLaren season to date, with only two podiums (at Monza and Suzuka) and the most embarrassing race I ever remember at Hockenheim. Our cars were always in double-figure positions in front of the whole Mercedes hierarchy, including Roger Penske. At one point Mansour Ojjeh came off the pit wall, gave me his headset and said, "I've had enough," and walked away. I felt awful, particularly as I knew that there was no quick fix for our problems and that the situation was going to get worse before it got better.

But the one thing we didn't lose was our sense of humour, and our ethic was still the same as it was in our winning days: we worked hard and we played hard. This year's traditional party in Adelaide, on the Thursday before practice, was held at Cobo's, a naughty but nice topless restaurant. The gorgeous girls decided to take Ron up onto the stage, where they'd installed a bath, and they set about removing all his clothes and bathing him in front of his devoted employees! Perhaps they didn't like his deodorant! As always Ron played the game, but he made the mistake of inviting along the two Keegan boys (former driver Rupert Keegan and his brother), who swiped my camera and took a roll of film of the evening.

The next day, Ron was a very worried man, and repeatedly asked me if it was I who had the camera. I assured him it wasn't me, even though I did admit to seeing a few flashes (from the camera, not Ron!). He instructed me to make it my business to find out who had the camera and retrieve the film for him. At the time he was having breakfast with Marlboro boss John Hogan, so I said, "OK, how much is it worth to you? Isn't it wages review soon?" I finally got the camera back, but minus the film, and to this day I've never seen any photos of that evening.

To finish our *annus horribilis* Mika Häkkinen suffered an horrendous crash in qualifying, when his left rear tyre was cut and deflated rapidly, making him lose control on a fourth-gear corner and slam into a concrete wall with only a one-layer tyre barrier. Mika's head hit the steering wheel quite hard as a result of the safety belts stretching and he bit his tongue badly, filling his whole mouth with blood, which was stopping him from breathing. It was only thanks to the quick intervention of Professor Sid Watkins and circuit doctors Jerome Cockings and

239

Stephen Lewis, who very quickly performed a tracheotomy, that Mika was able to breathe again.

While this was happening the practice was stopped and the TV monitors stopped showing the scene of the accident. There was silence all round the circuit and an atmosphere of doom. Ron and I tried to get on a second ambulance, but we weren't allowed, and then we both thought the worst.

Mika was rushed to the Royal Adelaide Hospital, conveniently just around the corner. He had serious head injuries but his life was not at risk. He stayed at the hospital for some weeks convalescing, and was joined by his girlfriend Erja Honkanen, who later became one of Mika's greatest assets and ended up marrying him at the end of May 1998. Erja is a wonderful girl who always knew when it was time to be there and when it was time to be somewhere else. She always allows Mika plenty of space and his confidence increases enormously with Erja by his side.

He tested again during the first week of February 1996, and was even then almost 100 per cent fit enough to return to racing. Dr Lewis had been right when he told me not to worry about Mika's full recovery. He'd continue racing, he said, and he'd go on to be even better, "Because when I had his brain open, I fitted a faster 'chip' in it so that he'd go even quicker!" Apart from the normal weight-loss and pallor that follows a spell in hospital, the only change I saw in him was his lack of humour. He was more serious and quieter than before and seemed more thoughtful, but this only lasted a few months and gradually the old Mika re-emerged, a stronger and faster flying Finn!

1996 was the second year of our marriage with Mercedes-Benz, and by all accounts we were bound to get better. Steve Nichols, the creator of the MP4/4, arguably the most successful Formula One car, was brought back into the fold and there were significant improvements on the car and engine. But there were technical improvements in most of the other cars too, and at the end of the day almost the *same status* quo remained.

It was the first season that we had Scotland's David Coulthard on the team, after a long battle with Williams. David appeared to have signed two contracts, and the situation had to be cleared up by the Contracts Recognition Board. McLaren had signed him as early as November 1994, when Coulthard, who had a testing contract with Williams, was occupying Ayrton Senna's vacant place on the Williams team following the tragic weekend in May. However, Williams had given him a contract for only one year (1995) as a race driver – whether or not Sir Frank regretted this later only he'd know. In those days David was very much a Ron Dennis type driver: presentable, good-looking, well-spoken, well-educated and a fast racer, a real asset for the team and sponsors and someone who fitted in very well with everyone, including Mika.

Alain Prost was back on the team too, as a development driver, consultant and drivers' guru, a fact that irritated Mika Häkkinen no end at the beginning: "What the hell is he doing here? Why do we need him? If he wants to race the car again, he's welcome to it and I'll step down."

I couldn't understand why Mika felt like this. I said to him, "Why do you care, he doesn't want to race the car and you're not paying him. He has a world of experience, with more Grand Prix wins and championships than anyone alive. You must keep an open mind. Just listen to him and take on board anything you think will be of any help and forget the rest. He only wants to help!" A few months down the road Mika told me that I'd been absolutely right, Alain had been "incredible, fantastic", and had put him right on a few matters. In a word, Mika said, Alain was great.

In the first couple of years the partnership was very equally balanced: David was quicker in some races and Mika in others. David clearly suffered in coming from a team that had a perfect package into one that was suffering from both car and engine problems. He missed the power and driveability of the Renault engine and couldn't handle an oversteering car. In spite of all this, he almost won the 1996 Monaco Grand Prix, and only lost through an error of judgement in the pitstops. Although at the time our engineers swore that the sequence couldn't have been changed, I still believe that we fucked up. That race should have been ours and not Olivier Panis and Ligier's, but the second place was our best result of the year. Although we looked strong at Silverstone, Spa and Monza, once again we completed the year without a win.

Another era came to an end in McLaren history when, after 23 years of collaboration (probably the longest title sponsorship in Formula One history), Philip Morris decided to put all their eggs in one basket and increase their Marlboro sponsorship with Ferrari rather than divide it between two teams. Luckily, it came at a time when Reemtsma, the German-based tobacco company which manufactured the West cigarette brand, was looking to return to Formula One, a decade after they had sponsored the Zakspeed team. They approached Ron Dennis and Ekrem Sami and a long-term partnership was signed.

Marlboro decided to stage their goodbye party to the team at the last European race, which was in Estoril, rather than at Suzuka, which is not much of a fun place. Unfortunately, work-wise it couldn't have happened at a worst place, since we not only had a bad race and awful performance, but every team's nightmare actually came true for us when our two drivers, Mika and David, put each other out at the 'corkscrew', the tightest bend in Estoril. Well, they say it happens at least once in a drivers' partnership and we looked forward to the fact that it wouldn't happen again.

We tried to book the Coconuts nightclub in Cascais for the Sunday night after the race, but it was impossible because it was the 'place to be' for everyone, and they couldn't close it just for a private party. However, after a little hard bargaining they agreed to close from eight till midnight for our party and then reopen for the public. As always the Marlboro party was a huge success, but by 11 o'clock the first members of the public were already knocking at the door, and the doorman had to look for me to ask if he could admit a fellow by the name of Michael Schumacher! I could hardly keep Michael, his wife, Corinna, and Willi Weber outside, and soon afterwards we had to open the doors and let the whole Formula One circus in.

The club had programmed a wet T-shirt competition for 'Miss Portuguese Grand Prix' later on in the evening, and unbeknown to me John Connor of Marlboro had set me up as one of the judges, along with Jacques Villeneuve, Eddie Irvine, Pedro Lamy, Johnny Herbert and himself. What he *didn't* tell me was that he'd set up Ron Dennis to be part of the strip-show afterwards, but when Ron decided to leave early they grabbed me as a second best.

I had no idea what it was all about when I was dragged onto

the stage for an impromptu performance; at the time I thought that I was going to do alright with these two ladies wearing nothing but very skimpy black leather underwear, but when they started taking my clothes off in front of the whole crowd, with my fellow judges shouting encouragement, I suddenly got cold feet and pleaded not to be made to go through it. However, the girls were deaf to my pleas, so I decided to give in 'gracefully'. I was stripped to the skin, including my Marks & Sparks Y-fronts, tied to a chair, and covered with hot candle wax. They then dowsed me with water – the torture chamber was a little too real for comfort! Although I'm sure that a few photographers were present, much to my relief I've never seen any photographs of the evening. They would have been most revealing!

The party went on through the night, and at seven o'clock in the morning Michael Schumacher came to me a little embarrassed. "Jo," he said, "I'm sorry to ask you, but I lost my wallet. Could you lend me some money to pay my bill?" I burst out laughing: "One of the biggest earners in the world is asking *me* for money!" He promised to pay me back as soon as we got to Japan. After looking at his bill and realising that, being a driver, he'd been given all his drinks free, I found he only needed about £20 pounds. I gave him the *escudos* and told him, "I don't want the money back. Take it as your first payment whenever you drive for McLaren." Good as his word, as soon as we arrived at Suzuka he came to see me with the money, but again I said, "No, I don't want it. Like I said, it's an advance payment for when you drive for us." "OK, maybe one day." He smiled and we shook hands.

Damon Hill in the Williams won brilliantly in Japan and clinched the World Championship. Schumacher was second and Mika third.

There have been a few anecdotes like this about Michael Schumacher, the man that has set and broken more records than anyone else in the history of the sport, that show the kind of person this superman really is: human, down-to-earth and enjoying life to the full. However, he never settles for second best and has to win at all costs.

I will always remember, with a smile, a time when we raced each other in Montreal, Canada, just after practice. I was leaving

243

the circuit with three of our engineers, and at the same time we saw Michael getting into his car with Willi Weber, his manager, and Corinna, his wife. They were staying at the Vogue Hotel, the most glamorous and expensive place in Montreal, while we were at the Hôtel de la Montagne, the most popular place in town, which during 'happy hour' was packed with Montreal's young and beautiful people. Both hotels were on the Rue de la Montagne, opposite each other.

From the circuit Gilles Villeneuve to the hotel is normally a 20-minute drive when there's no traffic; however, during race weekend traffic is always heavy. To reach the hotel there are two straights on Ile Notre-Dame, leading on to the freeway for a few kilometres and then the city. After a few blocks left then right, you get to the hotel.

As we left the car park Michael winked at me and took off, leaving behind a spray of mud and stones on my windscreen, so setting a challenge to reach the hotel first. So, as soon as the road was clear I passed him on the straight – only because my courtesy Mercedes had more power than his courtesy Fiat from Ferrari – but when braking at the corner before the freeway he passed us sideways and almost touched the concrete wall.

My passengers started getting nervous, but – like all of us in this line of work, addicted to the drug of competition – they began shouting "Go, go, Jo! Don't let him catch you!" Not that I needed any encouragement. The superiority of my Mercedes soon enabled me to pass him again on the freeway, but the size of his Fiat had the advantage when we reached the city. We exchanged places a few times until we arrived at the last corner in Saint Catherine, just a block from the hotel. At the traffic lights we were in front, and my passengers were already singing victory songs and gesturing with their fingers at Michael.

When the lights jumped to green, I had covered both my left and my right – my car was the widest Mercedes in production – so I have no idea how on earth, with the next hundred metres covered in cars, Michael managed to get in front! To this day I still can't work out how, when, or where he passed us. I swear his car must have had wings!

This was certainly a big lesson in competitiveness and in never giving up, right to the last minute. This describes the type of man that Michael Schumacher is. My only consolation was that after parking his car in front of the hotel, I stopped just a centimetre from his door so that he had to climb out of the passenger side whilst trying to wave two fingers at us, with an even bigger smile on his face than the ones we'd had 100 metres earlier!

Another year gone and again we didn't have much to show for it. There were also political (and financial) problems on the agenda when McLaren, Williams and Tyrrell refused to sign the new Concorde Agreement of the Formula One Constructors' Association and therefore wouldn't be getting their share of the TV money. Ron Dennis, Frank Williams and Ken Tyrrell were adamant that the terms of the agreement weren't right and that the 'players' should receive a more equal percentage of the commercial income. The rest of the team principals didn't have the same vision as these three musketeers and at the time Ron Dennis was anxious to justify his decision. He even made a fool of himself by mentioning the problems during his speech at the presentation of the award for the McLaren/*Autosport* Young Driver of the Year at the December *Autosport* party in London. But although it was tough for a while, in the end the agreement was changed and the teams enjoyed a much better distribution of the funds.

For 1997, it was going to be strange to see the cars in a different colour scheme: the popular red and white classic Marlboro livery had been an inseparable feature of McLaren. Also we'd have to deal with the new management of the principal team sponsor, and naturally they would have new ways of promoting their products which we'd have to accommodate within our racing schedule. This proved to be a lot more hectic than Marlboro's way, as was to be expected, since they were new on the scene and they'd a lot to catch up on. But they were a great group of people, from top men Dieter Weng, Conrad Pollit, Manfred Häussler and Axel Dahm to Tom Ehman and Pavel Turek, who were the Formula One co-ordinators.

There was only one small incident about the changeover that bothered me. Some days prior to the signing of the contract, when all the top guys from the Reemtsma group were due to come to our factory for a meeting, Ron Dennis ordered us to remove all the Marlboro livery from the seven cars that we had in our reception trophy room. I was very much against this, and stormed into Ron's office to show my discontent. "This is wrong, those cars won those races and those championships with the Marlboro logos, and that's now a part of history that you can't change. It's McLaren heritage, and should be left as it is." But Ron was adamant that they should be removed. I said, "But our new partners will think that in years to come, when they're no longer with the team, their logos will also be taken off the cars!" I felt that this could be a delicate issue on the first visit by the Reemtsma executives.

We used to go to great lengths to ensure that all of our heritage cars were preserved with their original engine, gearbox and brakes, and even the wheels and tyres. But even now, eight years later, the cars on show at the new £350 million McLaren headquarters have no Marlboro livery. Either Ron had parted company with Marlboro on anything but friendly terms – though it certainly didn't feel like that at the time – or there were other reasons why he preferred not to have the cars in their original form.

There was a competition to define the team's new colour scheme, which gave Ron an opportunity, at last, to introduce his favourite colours – black and grey, with the other colours naturally being Mercedes silver and a hint of red for West. Three complete cars were painted in the best of the proposed liveries to decide the final version, while in the meantime we presented the real car in the original 1968 McLaren orange – not with the intention of confusing people, but simply to make a double presentation and get double exposure. The car then appeared in its chosen colour scheme at a lavish, all-singing, all-dancing, completely over the top ceremony at Alexandra Palace. Participating in the whole shindig were the then extremely popular Spice Girls and Jamiroquai. I remember thinking that we'd better start winning races soon to pay for this lot! But whether we won races or not, the colour scheme was absolutely gorgeous. To this day, I never get tired of looking at those cars.

After initial testing we felt that the new MP4/12 was a bit better than the previous year's model, but when we got to Melbourne for the first race we were totally stung when Jacques Villeneuve got pole position a staggering 1.8 seconds faster than teammate Heinz-Harald Frentzen. It looked like another Williams year, but apart from them we perhaps didn't look too bad, with David fourth on the grid and Mika sixth, which meant that if the Williams had troubles we could still be in with a chance, and that was good enough to keep our hopes up. I said to Mika and David: "If we don't win today, it will be our 50th Grand Prix without a win, and I'd hate to have this on the McLaren record – so go for it!"

Jacques was put off at the start by 'our friend Irvine' with his Ferrari, and Heinz-Harald had brake troubles at the end, so David won and Mika was third. We were ecstatic. The taste of winning after so long was a lot sweeter than the taste of the champagne, although that was pretty good too.

The late George Harrison, a good friend of the team and indeed of Formula One, always came to the Australian Grand Prix, and he was there this time with his wife Olivia (a fellow Mexican) and son Danny. They came for a drink after the race and asked me where the party was that night. I said, "I don't know yet, but we're working on it. It's just that we haven't won for so long that we were unprepared." He insisted on providing the champagne as soon as we knew where it was going to be, and I promised to call him at his hotel, which he told me was the Hyatt.

The party was arranged and I had to go through the razzmatazz of calling a hotel and trying to talk to a VIP. "Oh no, we don't have anyone in the hotel by the name of George Harrison," said the operator. "I thought you might say that. OK, please tell Mr Harrison that I'm on the line because he's waiting for my call." Finally I got through and told him that the party was at the Crown Casino. And what a wonderful party it turned out to be. Dieter Weng from West started the speeches, introducing himself to the team: "I'm Dieter Weng, the one with the cigarette." I think Norbert Haug resented having been two years with McLaren chasing a victory, and the minute West arrived – *bang*! They scored! The party finished in the early hours with George at the piano, singing a song that he'd written for Formula One, called 'Because Bernie says so', as well as some of his classic songs. It was a very special celebration, and as one of the guys in the team said the morning after, "I thought I'd died and gone to heaven."

But when we woke up and confronted reality again we seemed to lose our momentum pretty quickly, as once again we struggled for the entire first half of the year. Our lowest point was in Monaco, where our 'weather expert' told us at a wet starting grid that the rain would only last five minutes at the most – and I guess if you don't believe him why employ him? We started one car on slicks and one on intermediates and on the second lap both McLarens were in the wall. The race was wet from lights to flag and the weatherman lost his job.

But my personal best weekend was the Canadian Grand Prix, where I was invited by *Autosport*'s Peter Foubister to take part in a forum, including commentator Murray Walker, journalists Alan Henry and Nigel Roebuck, and saloon car driver John Fitzpatrick, to accompany a group of Formula One fans to New York on board the *QE2* on the way to Montreal. All we had to do was give a series of talks on Formula One on each of the six days of the journey, one hour in the morning and one in the afternoon, and to be honest we were amazed at the number of people who filled whichever room they decided to give us, even when the weather was good and the punters could have been sunning themselves out on the top deck. I took my daughter Vanessa with me, and together we partied every night and met a host of interesting people. I can now boast that I'm one of the privileged few to have travelled in both the original *Queen Elizabeth* and the *QE2*.

The trip was almost sealed with gold, but when David Coulthard – who was leading the race comfortably – stopped to change a blistered tyre with plenty of time in hand his clutch refused to engage, and he lost precious seconds while Schumacher took the lead. Then the race was cut short because of a high-speed accident involving Olivier Panis's Prost. If DC had only done one more lap before he stopped he'd have won!

Meanwhile, back in the office, it was finally certain that Adrian Newey, the Williams technical director, would be joining McLaren in August in a similar position. This was something that Ron Dennis had been working on for some time in his never-ending determination to get the best for the team regardless of cost. Although it wasn't easy working with Adrian, there was no doubt that he was a genius, a real artist. He wasn't the most systematic person in the world and was very absent-minded at times – he frequently lost his FIA pass, his passport or his notebook; nor, perhaps, was he the leader we needed. But he certainly knew how to make a quick car, and there was no doubt in anyone's mind that our new car would be a winner.

Adrian had had a good working relationship with Damon Hill and it had been partly because Williams didn't re-sign Hill that Newey fell out with them, and he suggested to Ron and Martin that they bring Damon into the team. McLaren made what I thought a very good offer to Hill, based on performance, especially since Hill knew how good a car Adrian could make. However, Damon thought that a performance-related contract wasn't in keeping with his position as a World Champion and rejected the offer.

We battled on for five more races with nothing to show for them, and then Coulthard and the team achieved a wonderful victory at Monza. I say "and the team" because in fact the race was won in the pits, as David and race leader Jean Alesi, in a Benetton, both came into the pits together for fuel and tyres. Our pitstop was 7.8 seconds and Benetton's was 8.7, enough for David to shoot out in front and the race was won. This type of win is very satisfying for a team, and equally very depressing when you're on the losing side.

David made second place in Austria after Mika had blown his engine. One amusing little incident here, which always makes me laugh when I remember it, happened when one of our guests for the weekend was the actor Michael Douglas, who was a close friend of Mansour Ojjeh. Michael was a keen racing enthusiast and often came to Austria and Spain, and this time Bernie Ecclestone asked him to present the winners' trophies on the podium.

After the race, Michael had to rush out to the airport by helicopter, but an accident had blocked the roads and no cars could get to the heliport. Mansour Ojjeh was worried about how to get Michael out, but I said, "No worries, there's an underground passage through the grandstands that gets you out of the circuit, and then it's only a 300m walk and you're at the heliport. Mansour was extremely worried about walking Michael through the crowd, thinking that they'd pester him, but I was confident that no one would expect to see a Hollywood icon among a crowd of German race fans, and Michael agreed with me. He was happy to walk with me to the heliport.

In any case, Michael is a very level-headed guy and very approachable. Earlier on in the day he'd been recognised by a punter in the pit-lane, who'd chased him for an autograph before one of the officials stopped him. Michael turned round and said to the official, "No, don't stop him – these people sign my cheques, I don't mind signing their books." I was so delighted to hear that, and I told Michael that a few of the big-headed, overpaid drivers could do with a lesson from him!

We started walking down to the heliport and once we were out of the underground passage and into the crowd, a punter recognised me and came up to ask me to sign the back of his T-shirt. Trying not to laugh, I said to Michael, "Oh, sorry Michael, I just have to give this gentleman an autograph!" We both laughed our heads off all the way to the heliport, and I said to him, "OK Michael, I'll have this one on you! But I bet in Hollywood no one would recognise me."

In the new Luxembourg Grand Prix at the Nürburgring, Mika and David were running away with victory when both their engines blew up almost together, once again in front of all the top guys from Mercedes-Benz. It was another tough day in Germany, but at least this time we'd been at the front.

At the last race of the year, in Jerez, the championship had to be decided between Ferrari's Michael Schumacher and Jacques Villeneuve of Williams. The fight started from qualifying, where the two Williams and Michael's Ferrari did exactly the same time – 1m 21.072s (something never seen before or since). The championship was decided on lap 48, when Jacques made a long and brave attack inside a surprised Schumacher on a right bend and, when both cars were side by side, Michael desperately and blatantly turned into Jacques. The cars collided and the Ferrari ended up in the gravel, but the wounded Williams continued leading the race with a damaged left side-pod, with Jacques pacing himself carefully. All he needed to win the title was a single point.

In the closing stages our two cars were running second and third with David in front of Mika, when Patrick Head from Williams came to our pits to say that Jacques wasn't going to put up any resistance – third would be fine, because he just wanted the championship. We radioed this to our drivers and at the same time we asked David to let Mika pass. This was a long and colourful conversation, with David not happy at all, but early in the race we'd had to reverse the pitstops and this had given DC an advantage. Even so, David was adamant that it wasn't right, but he was finally pushed to the point where his job was put in jeopardy and he unwillingly moved over and let Mika pass. I think Ron mainly felt that on many occasions the car had let Mika down, as it had, so he felt justified in giving Mika his first overdue win. In addition it would be psychologically better for the team to start 1998 with two race winners.

So Mika had his first win, David a disappointing second place, and Jacques his World Championship, but we and Williams were heavily criticised for conspiring together and fixing the race result. The whole radio dialogue was published in the *Sunday Times*, who'd got it from a tape sent to them by Ferrari – who thereby revealed the fact that they listened in to other teams' conversations during the race. No doubt they released the tape in an attempt to divert attention from the fact that a mortal sin had been committed by their beloved Michael Schumacher. In the end the FIA ignored Ferrari's accusations and punished Michael by taking away all the points he'd scored during the season, and therefore his second place in the championship, and forcing him to do some road safety work on their behalf.

CHAPTER 16

EVERY CLOUD HAS A SILVER LINING

As the autumn and winter of 1997 got under way, so did our new 1998 car, the MP4/13. There were some suggestions from the superstitious among us that perhaps we should jump straight to producing number 14, but it was thought that this could create adverse results and it was decided to make a 'lucky 13'. This was the first car from the pen of Adrian Newey, and there was soon no doubt that it was Ron's convincing 'pitch' which had lured Newey from Williams. Ron had boosted the capabilities of McLaren: anything Williams can do we can do better, anything Williams can make we can make faster, and so on. From day one, it was as if Adrian was testing to see whether or not this was all true, and there were some very hard times for the drawing office, which was increased in size, and likewise for the fabrication and carbon departments, which had to work around the clock.

Adrian certainly pushed very hard, but in his own way he motivated people to do their best. He was a good listener and always considered any suggestions which could be incorporated into the design. It was Adrian who first urged us to have two tests simultaneously at different locations in Europe. But in spite of it all we survived to tell the tale, and we had a super car from the word 'go'. The team had also switched tyre suppliers for 1998, from Goodyear to Bridgestone. We won the 'winter testing championship' and we were ready for the real one, and what a wonderful feeling that was!

Come March, we were in Melbourne for the first race – and both McLarens were on the front row, seven-tenths in front of the rest headed by Michael Schumacher's Ferrari. It looked as if we had the first Grand Prix under our belts and there was no point in throwing away the first race by having our two drivers race against each other, so an agreement was made. Echoing the 1989 arrangement, the deal was that whoever got out first after the first corner would be allowed to lead.

Coulthard normally made better starts, but this time, when it counted most, he failed. Häkkinen led, but a misunderstanding during radio communication brought him into the pits – a legacy of his Adelaide crash was that his hearing wasn't 100 per cent. We couldn't believe it when we saw him in the pit-lane; we rushed him out again, but by then he was half a minute behind his teammate. In his anger he promptly carved 17 seconds off that, but three laps before the end DC was told of the radio mix-up. In a very obvious manoeuvre David slowed down and moved to one side right in front of the main grandstands and let Mika through.

It was a great result for McLaren, especially because we lapped the rest of the field, but one for which we were heavily criticised by the press and especially by the Australian Grand Prix promoter, who took the part of the many fans who'd put their dollars on Coulthard to win and were 'robbed' of their winnings. He urged FIA's Max Mosley to punish McLaren, but the plea fell on deaf ears, with the FIA saying that team orders were as old as the sport itself. However, Max did make provision for future Grands Prix to penalise those who interfered with the competition results and reminded the teams that it was a championship for drivers and not only constructors.

There was another victory for McLaren at Interlagos in Brazil, with this being a very satisfying performance indeed after a fiasco about our special secondary braking system. This had been fully approved by FIA technical man Charlie Whiting from day one of it's conception, and had been used on our cars before, but this weekend Ferrari had suddenly decided to object to it, saying that it was a primary steering system rather than a braking one. They started getting support from other teams and tried very hard to have the system banned, although Williams and Jordan were also using similar systems. It was clear that Ferrari, who'd been trying for some months to have a system of their own in place but had failed to get it ready in time, were taking advantage of their immense power and influence, and had decided that it was easier and faster to have the system banned than to continue their work.

We disconnected the system for practice while we waited for clarification from the stewards, who no doubt had had their orders from above, and we weren't very hopeful. The stewards agreed with the Ferrari theory and the system was banned, so we removed all traces of the 'braking/steering aid'. But we still qualified a full second in front of the Ferrari F300s, and won the race in style, finishing 1–2 a whole minute in front of them!

Schumacher beat Häkkinen in Buenos Aires, Coulthard beat Schumacher at Imola to keep his bid for the championship alive, and Häkkinen led another team 1–2 in Barcelona and won in Monaco – but then Schumacher pulled off a hat-trick by winning in Montreal, at Magny-Cours and at Silverstone. McLaren responded with another two 1–2s at Austria's A1-Ring and Hockenheim, but at the Hungaroring we were beaten by Ferrari and Schumacher in what was certainly their best race of the year and probably one of their best ever.

With a third of the race gone it was clear to Ferrari that they wouldn't beat us unless they tried something different, and they changed their strategy from two to three pitstops, which meant that Michael had to do a string of about 25 laps virtually at qualifying speeds – which he did! Häkkinen had mechanical troubles and slowed down, and we failed to keep David ahead with our own strategy, which should had been enough to win the race. But mistakes on our part or not, it was a remarkable win by Ferrari and 'Schumi'.

Then came Spa-Francorchamps in Belgium, where DC, from the front row in a wet start, triggered one of the worst pile-ups in modern Formula One history. In the restart he was hit from behind by Michael Schumacher, who, although he had an enormous lead, was still not slowing down but was actually opening the gap further. It was completely unnecessary: if he hadn't hit Coulthard he'd have hit someone else. As he came up behind DC we advised David that he was just about to be passed, and David replied, "If you see Michael, please tell me where he is – I can hardly see anything in my mirrors." He tried to move out of the way but Michael hit him, losing his right front wheel. Both cars came into the pit-lane and Michael jumped out of his car and stormed into our pits, shouting at David, "What were you trying to do? Were you trying to fucking kill me?"

It was a pretty disgusting display, hardly worthy of a World Champion, and an incident that cost Michael a lot of 'brownie points'. He certainly went down a lot in the estimation of all of us who witnessed the confrontation.

At Monza, it was Ferrari's turn for a 1–2, to the delight of the noisy *tifosi*, but then on the Nürburgring, Mika Häkkinen was at last able to bring a smile to the faces of the Mercedes-Benz bosses with one of his best drives, ensuring that he'd be going to the last race at Suzuka with a four-point lead over Schumacher.

There was a whole month between the races rather than the normal two weeks, so the agony was drawn-out for everyone. The pressure was on! Mika was always very good in these situations, but even he admitted to being nervous on race morning, and he did look a bit preoccupied. He was second to 'Schumi' in the front row, and having driven an almost flawless year he was determined that today wasn't going to be any different. Even if he only took second, that would be good enough to win the title he believed he was 'programmed' to win.

At the start Michael stalled his Ferrari and had to go to the back of the grid. Needless to say, Mika felt 'gutted' for him! The race script was almost as if it had been written by McLaren, except that Coulthard didn't quite manage to beat Irvine to second. 'Schumi' produced another memorable drive, which put him in third place after the first stops, only to suffer an exploding rear tyre which forced him to abandon the race. He took the defeat graciously, congratulating Mika and the team and saying that we all deserved the championship. But he added that without the problems he suffered the race today would have been his. I felt he was almost as disappointed at not winning the race as he was by losing the championship!

I walked to our pit with Mika after the press conference and he was totally overwhelmed and delirious with joy. He couldn't quite take it in, even though he'd known that he was champion for the last 20 laps once Michael had his tyre failure, and he'd started singing in the cockpit.

Just as I'd told Ayrton Senna a few years back, I said, "You'll believe it in the morning when the room waiter brings you the morning papers." Mika said that Damon Hill had told him on the podium in Japan in 1996, "When your turn comes you'll find out what an unbelievable feeling it is." "After my crash," Mika added, "my life changed a bit. I think I became a better person. Will it change again now?" I said it would only change for the better, that he was going to be a very busy person now, but to make the most of it, take full advantage of it. "It's your moment – you deserved it and you worked hard for it." But Mika never really made the most of it, he wasn't that type of person, not even when he did it again the following year and the climate in F1 was right. He wasn't a super-ambitious person, just a very uncomplicated man with a wonderful nature, a revealingly nice smile, and a very marketable name.

After the race there were the normal group photos, drinks, handshakes, embraces, telephone calls, and so on. Champagne was brought to all the mechanics, who were sitting by the cars and toolboxes chatting, reminiscing and generally unwinding, not just from another hectic race but from the mounting pressure of a seven-year drought which had now, suddenly, been relieved. We'd gone three years without a single victory, but now we'd conquered the world – with the best result and nine wins in the year. The feeling is indescribable unless you've done it. There's nothing quite like it.

At this moment the team manager came along and shouted at everyone to get off their backsides and start working to prepare a car for a tyre test the following Tuesday! We were testing tyres with just one car and we had the whole of Monday to prepare: the work could have been done standing on our heads in half a day! It was the most over-the-top show of megalomania that I've ever witnessed – some of the boys threw their champagne glasses on the floor in disgust. I was pretty horrified when I heard about it and tried to counteract the order, but it was too late – the damage was done. The mechanics felt justly aggrieved: was this all the thanks they were going to get for seven years' hard work that had culminated in the greatest achievement in motor racing?

I wonder if incidents like this explain why McLaren has always given the impression to outsiders of being a very military type of organisation, where discipline is imposed regardless of emotions and human feelings? But I can assure you that this is not how it always was. Far from it, it had always – with a few notable exceptions – been a very close and friendly working environment where human values were of utmost importance.

The 1998 Japanese Grand Prix was such an important race for Mercedes-Benz that all the top people involved were there, and that evening they went completely out of their way to book a wonderful room at the Suzuka Circuit Hotel with a very good dinner to celebrate clearing the final hurdle. It ended up looking like a funeral wake. None of the team mechanics were there and I was feeling pretty pissed off. Ron Dennis came up to me and said, "What's the matter with you. This isn't like you on an occasion like this, and where are all the boys?" I explained the circumstances to him and he felt that our sentiments were justified, but he pointed out that it was too late to do anything about it so I may as well forget it and have fun. Nobody knew more than Ron what a party animal I've always been. I sat and started lubricating myself to get in the party mood. The boring speeches started and Bob McMurray, Peter Burns and the boys and girls of marketing urged me to get up and make a speech explaining the reason for the bleak atmosphere and the absence of the mechanics. I was tempted, but realised that I was likely to say something that I'd have regretted the following day. So I stood up and left the room.

I went to the Log Cabin (usually known as the 'Rog Cabin' because of the Japanese difficulty in pronouncing the letter L) to join the mechanics and the rest of the circus. This is the place where everyone ends the night drinking and singing *karaoke* in the various booths around the main bar. At the time I thought it was a good idea to gate-crash the Ferrari booth singing 'We are the Champions', but as soon as I finished the first sentence I was wrestled to the floor by the two Schumachers, Ross Brawn, Nigel Stepney, Eddie Irvine, Stefano Domenicali and others, and my shirt was torn into little pieces! But the satisfying feeling was well worth the price of another Boss shirt.

The 1999 season started with McLaren and Ferrari as the main contenders for the title, with Mika facing the hard task of defending it – which, as all champions will tell you, is always tougher than the first time and only a few have accomplished it. So as Mika was embarking on his biggest test, our design and management team decided to build a brand new car, which always gave me the shivers. The MP4/13 had been our best car for years and surely all that was needed was to develop it more, improve its good points and take out its bad ones? But no, McLaren never did anything by halves. They always made bigger changes, and I knew that sooner or later this policy would catch the team out. Fortunately, 1999 wasn't one of those years.

When we got to Melbourne we were flabbergasted to find that our new MP4/14 was a whole second quicker than the Ferraris, and we once again filled the front row. However, our excitement was short-lived: both of our cars had problems and handed Eddie Irvine his first win after Schumacher had to start at the back after stalling on the parade lap. At Interlagos, as in Melbourne, our qualifying times were a second quicker than the Ferraris, but this time local hero Rubens Barrichello sneaked his Stewart-Ford in between. DC was left standing on the grid with clutch problems, 'Rubinho' disappointed the crowd with a broken engine, and Mika won the race, with Schumacher trailing second.

Returning to Europe, all that Michael Schumacher could see in front of him again at Imola were McLarens, although not as far away as before. Häkkinen opened up a big lead in the first 17 laps before he made the first of his two big mistakes in 1999 and shunted the McLaren in front of the pits, a stupid accident that could also have been a very costly. Schumacher won, David was second, and the Ferraris were leading the championship fight.

As we went to Monaco we heard the sad news of the loss of a friend and a great character in the Formula One circus: Harvey Postlethwaite had died of a heart attack at a test in Barcelona. At the time, Harvey was leading the preparation for an all-Honda chassis-engine entry in the World Championship, which after his death was aborted. He was one of motor sport's great designers who covered many eras. 'Doc', as he was called, had designed James Hunt's first winning Hesketh 308 and the Wolf WR1 in which Jody Scheckter had won the first race of the 1977 season. He was also the man behind the Ferrari Constructors' titles of 1982 and 1983, before moving on to Tyrrell, where he invented the high nose which everyone copied from then on. During his spell at Ferrari, he asked me several times to join him. He'd say: "We'll make a deal for you so that when you leave you'll never work again!" I never knew if he meant I'd be so rich that I wouldn't need to, or that I'd be so worn out that I wouldn't be able to!

At Monaco, Häkkinen resumed his customary pole position, with Schumacher and Coulthard following. In the race Schumacher made a better start and later Mika lost time at the Mirabeau corner, and both the Ferraris got ahead. But at Barcelona we were untouchable and finished 1–2, so at least Häkkinen was second in the championship.

Back across the Atlantic, in Montreal Michael crashed while in the lead and Mika won, putting him ahead in the championship. At Magny-Cours wet/dry conditions made qualifying a lottery, with the two rivals, Michael and Mika, finishing sixth and 14th. Mika drove a fantastic race, which was dry/wet, until he led, but we got caught out by a brilliant one-stop strategy from Frentzen's Jordan, which saw him win the race. Mika nevertheless increased his championship lead with a second place.

At Silverstone Mika was once again on pole with Michael alongside. Michael made a poor start, and seeing the two McLarens plus Irvine pulling away in front he made a desperate attempt to overtake on the inside of Irvine's Ferrari. Eddie didn't make it easy for him, possibly because he knew that his days at Ferrari were numbered, and Michael locked everything up going into Stowe corner, finishing up on the tyre wall with a broken leg. Ironically, while all of this was happening the red flag was showing, because some cars were stalled on the grid. Whether Michael was seeing too much red on Eddie's Ferrari and didn't see the flags, or the Ferrari team forgot to pass the message, whatever it was, he was going to be out of action for a few weeks.

However, this only gave us a little bit of a breathing space because Eddie Irvine was on top form and already second in the championship, with the same number of points as Michael. Mika withdrew in the race, and David Coulthard won, to the delight of the British crowd – and the team. As usual at Silverstone, DC gave a great party around his motorhome for the team and friends. This time he'd made an ice sculpture of a woman with different perforations through which flowed a constant supply of Finlandia Vodka (one of our sponsors). There was a prize for the naughtiest and most ingenious way of drinking the spirit!

There was almost a disaster for us at Austria's A1-Ring, as the two McLarens touched starting from the front row. David kept the lead but Mika dropped right back. A better strategy by Ferrari got Irvine a first with Coulthard second, while a good drive from Mika got him the last place on the podium, perhaps not too happy with his teammate!

The disaster that didn't happen in Austria did happen in Germany, when Mika led from his customary pole but later had a massive rear tyre explosion which caused him to crash heavily. Coulthard then ran into Mika Salo (replacing Schumacher in the Ferrari). David had to pit for a new nose and Salo eventually led the race before allowing Irvine to pass him for a Ferrari 1–2. Irvine now led the championship.

Many people thought that perhaps McLaren were relaxing a bit while Michael was in hospital, but they couldn't have been more wrong. You never relax in this business because you don't know what's around the corner, and everyone at the leading edge would tell you so. Irvine's Ferrari hadn't won the last two races: McLaren had lost them.

We recovered nicely with a 1–2 in Hungary, although Eddie wouldn't go away and was there in third. At Spa, a McLaren favourite, Mika again took off from pole, but in a close-call situation at La Source hairpin DC got the best of the situation and ran unchallenged to the flag. Mika was second, but this time he was really unhappy, thinking that since he was clearly McLaren's best card team orders should have prevented David from winning. David saw it differently and had already proved in Austria that he meant business and was ready to take up the challenge. He'd never been the world's best qualifier, but in race conditions he's as good as they come – and with this win he was also back in the running for the title.

The press was also very critical of McLaren's policy, but refusal to favour one driver over another has always been a very strong point throughout McLaren, and Ron Dennis was adamant that it should always be that way. The moment that you favoured one driver, you would demotivate the other half of your team, and Formula One is about motivation. Without motivation you will not be committed. Without commitment you will not achieve. In any case, there were still four races to go.

Monza, the second race in Italy, was the scene of the second big mistake of Mika's title defence. When he was clearly in the lead on lap 29, he selected the wrong gear at the first chicane and, in an instant, his MP4/14 was off the track. His disappointment was such that tears came out of his eyes in front of millions of TV viewers. Ironically, he only made two mistakes during the season, and both of them were in Italy, as if the Ferrari jinx was with him! Coulthard couldn't take advantage, however, as the best he could manage was fifth; but happily neither could Irvine, who came in sixth.

At the Nürburgring, the rain came to disturb proceedings and it was a very interesting race, with an unexpected winner in the shape of Johnny Herbert's Stewart-Ford. I was delighted for Jackie Stewart, who'd worked hard for it, and with Barrichello finishing third in the other car it was a great day for the new teams, with 'my' other ex-driver Alain Prost's new team finishing second with Jarno Trulli. Coulthard crashed in the lead and Mika rescued fifth place in the closing stages, and I remember how we all cheered so much for those two valuable points that gave Mika back the lead in the championship.

Then came the first ever Malaysian Grand Prix, on the new Sepang circuit near Kuala Lumpur, and top man Michael Schumacher was back with the sole purpose of helping his teammate (for a change), and this he did quite admirably. It was painfully obvious that he didn't have anything to prove by putting his car on pole, but he was making it very clear that he was there to help the team – not Eddie Irvine. One had to believe that he must have been under a lot of pressure to come back, as I don't believe that after investing so much time and effort with Ferrari, and wanting to be the one who brought back the championship to Ferrari after more than 20 years (since Jody Scheckter's 1979 title), he was about to give it to Irvine on a plate.

The race went like a dream for Ferrari, with Eddie winning, Michael second, and Mika third, turning the tables upside down in favour of Irvine and Ferrari. However, Michael's tactics in holding up Häkkinen weren't acceptable and Mika was a very angry loser. He said, "I knew what he had to do and I accepted it, but he wasn't being fair. He was very inconsistent and unpredictable." But then again, as Ayrton Senna always said, "Nice men don't win Grands Prix", and we know that Michael hasn't always been the most ethical driver in the world. But in lots of people's eyes he's the best there is, and he wanted to make this very point.

The race in Malaysia didn't go without a hitch: the Ferraris won, but the aerodynamic devices – known as 'bargeboards' – fitted just ahead of their sidepods didn't conform with the rulebook by about 10mm, and the result was therefore put on hold. While we were all waiting for the case to be heard at the FIA Court of Appeal in Paris, Mika Häkkinen went off on holiday, not knowing whether he was champion again or not. The whole affair was really bad for the image of the sport, but then again we were getting used to this kind of nonsense. As was expected, the bargeboards were said to be within the rules, Ferrari was again on top with McLaren losing both events, on the track and in the court! So it was do or die at the season's finale in Japan for the fourth consecutive year.

At my retirement party in Indianapolis in 2001, I was presented with a bargeboard from Ferrari mounted on a very smart carbonfibre plinth, with various annotations from the management, and Ross Brawn wrote on it 'Malaysia 1999 (Joke)'! It's always nice when eventually, as time goes by, you can talk and laugh about contentious things. That's why I loved Formula One, and the people in it, so much.

Going to Japan, Mika was four points behind Irvine. It would have been almost impossible to take a guess at the amount of pressure he was under that weekend, as he always responded to it well. He was second to Schumacher on the grid, and from the start he pulled away from everyone. Meanwhile David Coulthard did his best to hold Schumacher up, repaying the compliment from Malaysia. Mika won the Japanese Grand Prix, with Michael five seconds behind and Eddie a distant third. After the finish, Michael attacked Coulthard's weaving and blocking, which cost him precious time, but this was really just a bit of showmanship. I reckon that Michael was very happy that Irvine lost the championship. Privately he admitted that the best man had won, and that was really the view of most people in the paddock and among the public. We and Mika probably made more mistakes throughout the year than Irvine and Ferrari, but there was no doubt about it, the quicker driver won the championship and perhaps the best compromise was reached by Ferrari winning the Constructors' Cup and Mika the drivers' championship.

At the end of 1999 we took the holiday of a lifetime. Bea, Vanessa and I went to Acapulco for a family reunion, celebrating the end of the century and our second consecutive World Championship of Drivers.

The year 2000 was, in many ways, a great year. We led every race, but broke down more often than not in a year with many 'ups' and many 'downs'. In the end, the 'downs' outnumbered the 'ups', and we finished as the bridesmaid to Michael Schumacher and Ferrari. The message was loud and clear: to finish first, first you have to finish. The fragility of our cars let us down, but we did have our moments.

We dominated the practices for the first three races, but failed to finish in the first two before getting a 2–3 at Imola. Michael Schumacher and Ferrari won all three and opened up a tremendous lead in the championship, but we then pulled out all the stops and reacted quickly, with an inspired David Coulthard winning his local race at Silverstone with a great drive. Mika was second and Ferrari started to take notice. We did it again in Barcelona, with Mika in front this time. David drove this race with three broken ribs as a result of surviving a private plane crash in which both his pilots were killed. We thought that perhaps the accident would affect his much improved driving, but this wasn't the case.

If there's one single thing that could possibly change a person's life, this would have to be surviving a plane crash, as not many people do, and David was no exception. He became a better man – simple as that. He gained new perspectives of what was important in life. He was more charitable, understanding and caring, and his driving also became more focused, and as the season went on he was outqualifying Mika more than he ever did before. He also beat him in Monaco and at Magny-Cours where he was supreme.

Montreal was to be the scene of McLaren's 500th Grand Prix, and I was very keen to do something special, as were our marketing department and our catering company. Surprisingly, Ron Dennis wasn't so enthusiastic, so I said to him, "What's the point of creating a successful company if you don't celebrate the milestones? You celebrated McLaren's 30th anniversary two years ago in Monaco, so we must do something here." He finally agreed, as long as it was tasteful and not too expensive. Lyndy Woodcock and her team from Absolute Taste spent nearly all Saturday night making a wonderful cake and blowing up 500 white balloons to form an arch over our paddock by the Olympic lake. It was a great occasion, appreciated by all and commented on by our rivals.

People outside McLaren had started to think that perhaps it was Mika who was losing his spark rather than David who was undergoing a renaissance, but it wasn't so for us in the team: we on the inside knew the reasons for the turnabout. But it's true to say that Mika was very demoralised at the start of the year, having had the best car and throwing wins into Michael's hands, and unless you were there it was hard to understand. However, he went for his summer break and came back like the old Mika to head a 1–2 for the team at Austria's A1-Ring. At Hockenheim, another certain 1–2 result was prevented by the appearance of a lunatic spectator, who got onto the fastest part of the circuit and forced the clerk of the course to send out the pace car. Barrichello, who'd replaced Irvine at Ferrari, got his first win instead, although we still took second and third. Apparently the track invader was a sacked Mercedes-Benz employee making some kind of futile protest.

Then came the Hungaroring our best race of the year, not just in terms of the result – Mika first, Michael second, David third – but because we'd turned the points tables round. After San Marino, Mika had been 24 points down on Michael Schumacher, and McLaren 29 points down on Ferrari in the Constructors' Championship. But now Mika was two points ahead of Michael and the team only one point behind Ferrari. I was ecstatic, singing and dancing and spraying champagne over everybody, when Ron Dennis came and said to me, "Slow down, calm down, we could lose the next one!" I replied, "Who gives a shit? We won this one, we turned the tables round, this is a time for celebration. Tomorrow we'll kick ass and see what we can do to win the next one, but today we celebrate!" Ron said, "Oh no, oh no you can't. It's the championship we want. A race win means nothing!"

Imagine if we were second and third at every race – I'd say that there was every chance that we'd win the championship, but what a hollow championship it would be without a win! It really went to show just how much times have changed: in the old days winning a Grand Prix was just such a fantastic thrill. There were five or six teams that were capable of winning a race during the season, but now there were only two or three because of the enormity of the budgets needed to create a winning team.

The sport was changing, and at times it was hard to change with it. That day in Hungary I struggled, but I kept drinking champagne on Mika's plane all the way down to Nice for my summer break in Cogolin. This time, on the journey to the airport we 'beat' our own police escort, which pleased me no end!

As usual in Hungary, we arranged all the courtesy cars in line for the convoy run to the airport, putting Ron Dennis's car at the front. When everyone was in place, I went back to the truck to get my briefcase, only to find on my return that Ron ("I'm alright, Jack") had told the police to go. I got back in less than a minute and only Mika's car was there, so we took off trying to catch up with the convoy, but once we got to the bottom of the hill we couldn't see which way they'd gone. I said to Mika: "The police use a different route which I don't know, so we'd better go the way I do know and hope it works." While I navigated, Mika continued his Grand Prix Sunday drive and got us to the airport without seeing any sign of the police convoy. We returned the car, went through passport control, got in the plane and took off, and it was only when we were in the air that we spotted the convoy arriving. Yes! Two wins in one day for Mika, and two fingers for Mr Dennis.

At some stage during the 2000 season I had another hint of the way that Formula One was changing. I was asked to stay close to the Ferrari pit and take note of all the changes that were made on the cars, even to the extent of measuring the time it took to refuel the cars during practice and qualifying – in plain words, to spy on the enemy! Why me? Because I was the friendly face, the one that had friends in all the teams, and wouldn't be suspected of using this friendship to spy on them. Only the week before, when we were testing at Mugello, I'd needed road permits for the trucks to circulate in Italy over the weekend, and my friends at Ferrari had used their influence to get them for me. Now I was supposed to spy on them? No way! I wasn't just totally and utterly opposed to it on principle, it also made me feel bad and ashamed that we (and Formula One in general) had to resort to this type of underhandedness. If this was the future, I no longer wanted to be part of it.

I spoke with Ron, Martin Whitmarsh and Adrian Newey, not only refusing to spy for them but saying I'd rather leave if I was forced to do it. I was accused of being a puritan, and maybe they were right, but life is too short to create enemies. I enjoyed racing in the 'classic' way – and I wanted to keep it that way for as long as I could.

After Hungary came the Belgian Grand Prix, which was another great race for us at the fabulous Spa-Francorchamps circuit. The race started on a wet track and it was agreed by all concerned to start behind the pace car, to avoid a similar pile-up to the one the previous year. Mika led from pole and opened up a little gap, but spun in the 13th lap and lost his lead to Michael Schumacher. He regained it briefly when Michael pitted but lost it again when it was his own turn to pit. The rain had now stopped, and from then on it was a tremendous fight between them on the best circuit in the world.

Mika was unable to pass, as Michael kept closing the door. Four laps from the end, as they were coming out of Radillon into the long straight, Mika was slipstreaming behind the Ferrari, and as they got behind and ready to lap Ricardo Zonta's BAR, Michael went to the left, while Mika got another little push in Zonta's slipstream and squeezed the McLaren between the BAR and the grass on the damp, right-hand side of the track at 330kph! As they both passed Ricardo they arrived at the right-hand corner, Les Combes, neck-and-neck – but with Mika on the inside. The race was his.

This had to be the manoeuvre of the century: everyone in the pit lane just went "Wow!" Afterwards, Ross Brawn from Ferrari came along to offer us his congratulations, and said, "If Mika wins the championship again this year, he won it today – that was a breathtaking move."

Unfortunately we didn't win the championship, even though after Belgium Mika was leading Michael by six points and McLaren were leading Ferrari by eight. Michael went on to win the next four races, and while Mika finished second in Italy, his engine gave up as he was well placed for a win at Indianapolis and this completely unsettled his battle for the title. In a fine race at Suzuka, the old and new champions fought like a pair of lions and 'Schumi' just got the advantage – and the championship. The Ferrari celebrations went on all night in Japan and (no doubt) in Italy, and so they should have done: it was their first driver's World Championship for 21 long years, and it was a deserved one. But as I congratulated them I told them that it wasn't going to take McLaren 21 years to get it back!

With the start of a new century, things were starting to change more rapidly at McLaren. The new McLaren Technology Centre in Woking was well under way, the wind tunnel was already operational, and the Team was growing even more than usual. I always loved every minute of my job but maintained that the first morning that I woke up and found it difficult to go to work, that would be the time to stop, and a couple of mornings during the latter part of the year I'd felt a bit lazy as I woke up. It was mainly the feeling that we were no longer a racing team – we were more like a big factory, with far too many personal interests and not everyone pushing in the same direction.

2000 was also the year in which our partner engine company, Mercedes-Benz, as part of the Daimler Chrysler Group, had taken 40 per cent of the TAG-McLaren Group, which meant that the company would only be getting bigger. This is fine if you're a young man, as the security of one of the biggest European companies would certainly be a plus, but I didn't feel that I needed the security and I was concerned that the team spirit could be diluted.

At the end of that year and the beginning of 2001 I took some days off to unwind and to gather my own thoughts for the future. When I came back I found that a few changes, systems and procedures had been put in place at McLaren while I was away, some of which directly affected me. This was a sign of the syndrome of a bigger company taking over, and I wasn't happy that these changes had been made during my absence. After 18 years with McLaren I was offered a different job. It was a nice, cushy number which should have suited me fine, because I was getting ready to slow down. But it really held no challenge and I didn't even look at or consider the details of the offer. Instead, I presented Ron Dennis with my resignation.

Ron, who had for some time had very little to do with the day-to-day running of the company, was completely shocked. He probably believed that I'd die at McLaren! He was totally unaware of any of these new changes and they'd been none of his doing. He apologised to me and promised to put things back as they were, as far as he was able. But by then there were other people involved and I didn't want the whole affair to get completely out of proportion – which it very nearly did. I was very disappointed that my beloved company, for which I'd given the best part of my life, was changing so much, and in a way seemed to be betraying me. I thanked Ron again for his offer but I said that even if I stayed I no longer had the same feelings and motivation for the company, and it was therefore time for me to go.

But once again Ron bent over backwards trying to keep me, and I could see that it was almost going to be another 1990 – and again I appreciated it very much. This time, however, we agreed that I'd finish the racing season working alongside my replacement Michael Negline, and Ron would sponsor my farewell party at Indianapolis and I'd walk away from McLaren's door at the end of October.

As the Formula One circus got to hear of my premature retirement, I was surprised and flattered by the number of job offers that were made, but the one that I have to admit I was very tempted to accept was the one offered by Ross Brawn. He said to me, "Jo, you're too young to be retiring – you just need a change of air. You've been at McLaren's too long. Come to Ferrari, we'll design a very interesting and challenging job for you. I guarantee that you'll like it." And Jean Todt followed it up by saying, "Jo, you started at Ferrari, you must finish at Ferrari."

Maybe it was the thought of having me back at home that made Bea urge me to take the job: either that or she wanted to see McLaren's reaction when they saw me in Melbourne in a red shirt! Michael Schumacher signed a picture for me saying: "Jo, you look much better in red". But I couldn't have done it. Everyone at McLaren, and especially Ron, would have taken it personally. Some of my counterparts at Ferrari told me that as much as they'd like to have me at Ferrari, they couldn't possibly imagine me there, because, to them, I was McLaren! And perhaps they were right. Even now, I still feel very attached to my old team.

CHAPTER 17

THE FINAL LAP

Most of us at McLaren wanted to see David Coulthard emerge as a strong contender for the World Championship over the course of the 2001 season. He'd greatly improved his act in 2000 and we felt we'd have failed if we didn't make him champion this time. But judging by the way in which Ferrari had been improving, it was going to be a tough task.

Come the Australian Grand Prix in Melbourne, and the tables had turned 360 degrees: now it was the Ferraris on the front row, almost a second quicker than us. However, in the race we were well placed for a win when Häkkinen had an horrendous high-speed accident because of a front suspension failure, sending him to the circuit hospital for checks. This accident left Mika pondering for a few races whether or not the suspension was going to fail again! At Melbourne, meanwhile, David recovered second place for the team.

DC won at Interlagos after a brilliant drive in a dry-wet-dry race, passing Michael Schumacher and beating him fairly and squarely when 'Schumi' had been expected to be the master in those conditions. This race did a lot for David's confidence and hopes for the World Championship. He had another strong second at Imola behind Ralf Schumacher and was neck-and-neck with Michael in the championship.

This was the year that the controversial issue of 'driver-aids' was going to be out of the closet, and there would be a free-for-all from the Spanish Grand Prix on. Until now, traction control was officially 'forbidden', but it was well known that a few teams had been tinkering with one method or another of cutting the power to the wheels electronically. This was easily appreciated if you stood in a tight corner and listened to the engines. However – and this is something that has always bothered me – even in this day and age, with all the fantastic technology at our disposal, we really can't police the use of traction control. Therefore the FIA effectively gave up and declared it legal. All electronic aids were to be permitted: launch control, traction control and fully automatic gearboxes were back.

My reaction to this, obviously – second to the sad fact that we were no longer going to see these 'supermen' controlling these wonderful cars with their feet and hands, but yet another driver aid would be helping them – was the fact that I had blind faith that, with the help of our sister company TAG Electronics Systems, we would come up with the best control devices in the world. I was wrong!

In the very first race DC was left standing on the grid at Barcelona with a malfunction of the 'launch control'. He started at the back of the grid but, with a tremendous drive, recovered fifth place. Mika Häkkinen responded to his critics (who were saying that he was 'spooked' after his Melbourne crash) with a great drive which saw him leading the last lap until, 500m from the flag, his clutch blew up and left him on the verge of the track. 'Schumi' won, and genuinely felt sorry for Mika, to whom he gave a lift back to the pits.

At Austria's A1-Ring it was the turn of Mika Häkkinen to stall on the grid, while David made a starlit performance to win, beating the two Ferraris. But this race marked a very sad weekend for the West-McLaren-Mercedes team. Back in England that Saturday afternoon, Paul Morgan, co-founder and owner of Ilmor Engineering, which designed and made the Mercedes racing engines, tragically crashed to his death as he tried to land his vintage Sea Fury aeroplane at Sywell airstrip near his home.

Paul was one of the greatest innovating engineers of our times, an extremely practical man when it came to the laying out of projects and the realisation of them, while partner Mario Illien was the brains behind the engine. Paul created the wonderful factory and all the manufacturing processes and systems. He was worshipped by his entire 450-strong workforce and he knew them all by their full names. But as his wife Liz said, "The men and the boys are only separated by the price of their toys." The enormous success of the company that he created enabled him to feed his lifelong hobby of buying, restoring and flying old aircraft – a passion and love that ironically took his life. His death was an incredible waste, which was to inflict a knock-on effect on the future of Ilmor racing engines.

We were still very subdued in Monaco, and our mood wasn't improved when, once again, David Coulthard's launch control let him down, but this time he was on pole for the Monaco Grand Prix, the 'jewel of the crown', in front of the *crème de la crème*. I can't think of a worse thing that could happen to a driver!

I couldn't print the words or the tone in which they were delivered out of David's helmet when the car stalled, but Ron Dennis made a joke remark to the VIPs around him like. "Oh yes, my wife sometimes does that when she goes shopping," thinking that it was David's mistake, but he later apologised for having spoken before knowing the facts.

DC had to start from the back and was stuck for 30 laps behind the Arrows of Enrique Bernoldi, who was under instructions from his boss not to let the McLaren pass. It was a ridiculous situation – even Bernoldi's lap-times were slowing, as he was driving on his mirrors! Despite these handicaps and his understandable anger, when Coulthard was finally free of the Arrows, he set the fastest lap of the race and finished in a very respectable fifth place.

By then we'd become the laughing stock in the pit-lane, and the press were taking the piss by saying that McLaren had a 'stop control' instead of a launch control. In Ron Dennis's own words, "We made a meal of trying to optimise our launch control." In effect he was admitting that, as always, our system was far too complicated to operate, but he told the media that we were making the necessary adjustments to simplify the mechanism into a foolproof aid. This was no consolation for David Coulthard, for whom it had already cost two potential wins. With an engine failure next time out in Montreal, his challenge for the World Championship was rapidly disappearing.

At about this time of the year another incident involving McLaren came out in the motor racing media in a very exaggerated manner, due to the strong friendship between our technical director Adrian Newey and the then team principal at Jaguar Racing, Bobby Rahal, dating from the days that they worked together in Champ Car racing in America. Adrian, who felt let down and upset at the team's failure to get to grips with the launch control, accepted an invitation from Rahal to join Jaguar Racing when his McLaren contract ran out in August 2002. I heard that the deal would have paid Adrian enough to put a small African nation back on it's feet! Encouraged by his wife, Marigold, it was easy to see why Adrian had made this decision. In joining a team whose car was two to three seconds slower than ours, it would have been reasonably easy for him to design a car capable of going one or two seconds quicker than before, thus keeping his reputation topped up and considerably increasing his bank account at the same time.

Ron Dennis, who hadn't been informed beforehand, was devastated that Adrian didn't warn him and went completely over the top trying to rescue the situation. I remember going into Ron's office saying, "Ron, this is completely out of order. You were the one that got him out of Patrick Head's shadow to lead our design team and recognised his value by paying him a driver's salary! He can't do this to you. But what good will it do to keep him against his will?" But Ron's commitment was greater than his pride, and he very calmly answered, "We're better off with him than without him, so I must keep him."

Statements were issued from both sides, McLaren saying that Newey had changed his mind and would stay and Jaguar claiming that they had a signed contract from Newey, and therefore the matter was with their lawyers. A few days later at a meeting with Ron, Adrian, Bobby and Niki Lauda (the future Jaguar team principal), the whole affair was settled out of court with a financial settlement between the two teams.

It was a very bitter affair, but, as I said before, it was totally blown up out of all proportion by the media. Yet it showed what life is really like in the 'piranha pond' today. To survive at this level you really need to have a very thick skin.

But the thing that really upset me was that after this unpleasant episode took place, when the dust had settled, Adrian didn't have the common sense to gather all his design staff and apologise to them personally, as well as reassure them that he was still 100 per cent committed to McLaren. He chose to do it through a company statement, which cost him a lot of 'brownie points'. Few people in the design office ever looked at him through the same eyes again, which was a great shame. He was a brilliant designer who needed only to apply a tenth of that gifted talent to his personal dealings and he'd have been a far better man. I always got on very well with him, but this chapter of his life at McLaren really bothered me.

In the meantime, not only were Ferrari coming together very strongly with a foolproof car, but Williams were also starting to outqualify us, which could possibly have been due to the confused state of Adrian Newey's mind at the time. In this business if you don't improve, you never stay put but actually fall backwards.

In France we suffered another embarrassing moment when Mika Häkkinen was left standing on the grid before the parade lap, totally motionless. His MP4/16 was pushed away from the starting line, and although Coulthard finished in fourth place this was no consolation to anyone. At least at Silverstone Mika was able to show that he could still provide good drives and get results, on a day when we seemed to have the edge on the competition. It was a shame that DC collided with Jarno Trulli's Jordan at the start, as it would have been a certain McLaren 1–2 otherwise. At Hockenheim we didn't take advantage of a rare mechanical problem in Schumacher's Ferrari and once again both of our Mercedes engines failed on German soil – and to add insult to injury, Schumacher junior won in his Williams-BMW.

At Hungaroring, David trailed the two Ferraris for third place, while Mika definitely seemed to be off-tune for the weekend. But the highlight of this race for me was my 60th birthday and leaving present from Mika and David. The Hungarian Grand Prix always fell around my birthday, and this year I had one of the most wonderful days of my racing career, not only because of the gift, but also for the way and the style in which it was presented.

Late in the afternoon after qualifying, as I was doing some paperwork in the race car transporter, I was told to go to the motorhome – which I did, but found it empty. I therefore returned to the truck thinking I'd been given a bum steer. Shortly afterwards, our PR lady Ellen Kolby came and insisted that I go back to the motorhome straight away. I returned to the empty seating area to find Mika coming out of one door and David out of the other … then it clicked that something was going on. Maybe they knew that I was having a 'big' birthday, I thought, and I got ready for a defensive move, as I could feel a cake coming straight for my face! And they did have a cake. But they just put it down on the table, and produced a superb leather jacket, by which time dozens of photographers had gathered at the edge of the motorhome.

"Do you like leather jackets?" they asked me. "Sure I do!" I replied. As they slipped the jacket on to my back, I noticed the Harley-Davidson emblem on the front and across the back. Not having the slightest clue what was about to happen, I said jokingly, "Oh, Harley-Davidson, great! – All I need is the bike!" At which point they lifted me onto their shoulders and carried me back out of the motorhome. I then heard the unmistakeable vrooom-vrooom-vrooom sound of a Harley engine almost at the same time as I saw this monster of a shining motorbike coming towards us. They put me down and said, "Do you like it?" The emotion was taking over as I replied, "Do I like it? I love it!" Mika and David were smiling broadly: "It's yours!"

My eyes were watering and I was absolutely lost for words as I had my first ride across the paddock, with all the Formula One photographers taking pictures.

It took over 24 hours for it to actually sink in that I was really the proud owner of a Harley-Davidson Road King. The dream of a lifetime – sitting in the Café Senequier in St Tropez admiring my Harley parked with all the other Harleys at the port – had become a reality. I had to pinch myself and make sure that I wasn't still dreaming. I'd been given the ultimate present for a 60-year-old swinger! Can you just imagine me on my Harley in Puerto Banus, with all those rich middle-aged women queuing to have a ride on my crossbar?

This, without a shadow of a doubt, had been one of the greatest moments of my life, for which I'll be eternally grateful to Mika and David. So much for those who say that racing drivers never put their hands in their pockets! Even now, and I guess for the rest of my life, whenever I feel low I just have to think of that August day to have a smile across my face again.

At Spa-Francorchamps, David drove a hard race to finish second to Schumacher, who'd just beaten Alain Prost's former record of 51 wins, which at the time seemed unbreakable. And now Schumacher's own record is a joke!

The Italian Grand Prix at Monza took place just five days after the tragic events of 11 September, and even in Italy there were rumours that the race would be cancelled. However, sad as we all were, everyone was determined not to give in but to continue life as normal. It was nevertheless a very subdued weekend, during which Mika Häkkinen announced that he was taking a sabbatical year and the team had signed Kimi Räikkönen as his replacement.

At Monza, a different winner made a change when Juan Pablo Montoya scored his maiden victory for Williams-BMW in a race that saw neither McLaren at the finish. It's always hurtful when the cars break down and you don't finish a race, but at Monza it's really painful, especially as history shows that we've always been Ferrari's most determined rivals. So leaving the race amidst the whistling crowd of *tifosi* is not a pleasant experience at all.

The following Grand Prix was going to be in the United States, and of course the question now was even more intense: should the race be cancelled? For me personally it was very sad, as it was my last race and my big farewell party was to be held at Indianapolis, on the Thursday before the race. I wasn't sure whether or not I should cancel the party, but various media people said to me: "Don't do anything – it will be cancelled for you." But the race wasn't cancelled, which was good sense, otherwise we'd have been doing just what the terrorists wanted.

My party was held at the Eiteljorg Museum in downtown Indianapolis, although – because of 9/11 – some of the key people in my life who were due to be there weren't able to make it: Mansour Ojjeh, Dan Gurney, Jackie Stewart, Alain Prost and several others had to cry off. However, about 300 people from the past and present Formula One days were there, including six of my brothers and sisters, who arrived as a surprise. It was a truly memorable occasion, Ron Dennis said a few words and then I made a little speech, which had worried me beforehand because, being an emotional Latin, I was afraid I was going to fill up. Bea was looking at me all the time miming, "Don't you start crying," but I guess a couple of *tequilas* beforehand had done the trick – I was fine. The marketing people had made a small video of the high points of my motor racing career with a soundtrack consisting of Carly Simon's song 'Nobody Does It Better', which was great. I'll be forever grateful to everyone from McLaren who was involved on the day, and especially the marketing girls Diana Kay, Caroline Sayers and Lucy Smith, and Lyndy Redding of Absolute Taste.

There was Mexican food and Mexican music, with a band of *mariachis*. I was presented with all sorts of presents, like a full golfing set of clubs, bag, trolley and clothes from Mercedes-Benz, and a carbonfibre water ski from McLaren. However, *la pièce de resistance* was a silver/gilt 1:12 scale model of the 1991 MP4/6 McLaren with removable body shell, very detailed engine, and working suspension and steering. This model had won several prizes in silver craft exhibitions. As Ron and I posed with the silver model for the photographers, he said to me from the side of his mouth: "This is really too good, I didn't want to give it to you but Martin [Whitmarsh] insisted that you should have it. But it's too valuable!" I remember going hot and cold but I managed to kept smiling at the cameras. I felt like saying, "Ron, have it back, I don't want it! I didn't ask for anything, please have it back!" But I thought, no, to hell with him, I won't let him spoil my day, and just thanked him very much, very politely: "It's lovely, thank you, I really appreciate it!"

In spite of whether or not Ron wanted me to have the model, the little car sits proudly in my sitting room and I never tire of looking at it.

The weekend continued to be good. It was Mika Häkkinen's birthday and also the last Grand Prix for commentator and friend Murray Walker, 'The Voice of Formula One', who after 50 years had decided to hang up his microphone for good, so there were various gatherings at the track to celebrate the man who was going to be missed by all in the paddock – and in the armchairs of many English-speaking fans throughout the world.

We qualified second and seventh, but we were looking good in race trim. I remember that as I was entering the circuit on Sunday morning, the car radio was playing Tina Turner singing 'Simply the

Best', and as always it reminded me of Ayrton Senna. I decided that this was a good omen and we must win today, and I said as much to Mika, who was also feeling good. However, in the morning warm-up Mika went through a red light in the pit-lane, a light that was a bit obstructed and not very visible and it was obvious that he didn't see it as it gave him no advantage whatsoever to ignore it. Nevertheless, the stewards decided to give him a very draconian penalty for what was an unimportant offence, and they took off his best qualifying lap-time, replacing it with his second best. This meant that he moved to fourth on the grid instead of second, leaving the two Williams-BMWs in front.

This was totally unprecedented. Normally a fine would have been imposed, and everyone in the paddock was wondering how they could penalise Mika's Saturday qualifying for a fault committed on Sunday morning? I was furious and I urged Mika to mention it on every television interview that he gave. This was yet another reason why I was so disappointed in the direction that the sport was taking and didn't feel so bad to be turning my back on it.

Even Michael Schumacher thought that it was disgusting and hoped that Mika would pass the two Williams at the start and get some justice. As it happened, our strategy was brilliant on this occasion, and Mika ended up winning the United States Grand Prix, with Michael second and David Coulthard third. I couldn't believe it: my last weekend ended up almost as if I'd planned it myself.

A few years back when I was approaching my hundredth Grand Prix win, my good friend and travel broker Lyndy Swainston said to me: "I think you should ask Ron to let you pick up the Constructor's trophy from the podium when you get your 100th. It would be a nice gesture." I don't really know why, but in a weak moment, when Ron was in a good mood, I did ask him. He then gave me a very long-winded lecture about so many people who should be there before me – Mansour, Norbert, Adrian, and the rules, this and that, so immediately I said, "Sorry, Ron, forget it – it was very stupid of me to ask. Really, I don't want to do anything that compromises you or the team." And I left it at that.

That afternoon at Indy, as we were running out to the winner's circle, lots of people asked me if I was going to collect the trophy, and in fact the officials let me in, as they thought I was on the way to the podium. I congratulated Mika, David and Michael, and then Ron appeared, and as he was walking to the podium he stopped and walked back towards me, and for one second I had the silly, stupid thought that he was going to ask me to go up instead. He looked at me with a sarcastic grin on his face, knowing what I was hoping to hear from him, but he said, "Oh, could you hold this for me?", and handed me his radio and headset! I really felt like throwing it at his feet, just like he'd thrown the Constructors' cup at Prost's feet at Monza in 1989. Ron was really crucified by the Italian and Brazilian television journalists, who said that I should have collected the cup, and later by the British press too, but I guess I understood the point that he was trying to make.

It was a great afternoon with all my brothers, Emerson Fittipaldi, and lots of friends from the past, including my hero Placido Domingo, gathered around our hospitality suite, drinking champagne. Later on I was given a proper send-off by the McLaren boys, tied onto the tyre trolley and pelted with eggs, soup, tomato sauce and all the leftovers from the kitchen, a real messy affair! But I enjoyed it, as it's traditional for anyone that's leaving the team, and if you don't get it, it means that they don't like you.

I couldn't have asked for a better end to my working racing life.

CHAPTER 18

AFTER THE
CHEQUERED FLAG

After my party at Indianapolis and my wonderful send-off by McLaren and the sponsors, I didn't think it was appropriate for me to go to the Japanese Grand Prix, the last one of the year. Nevertheless, I have to admit that I was dreading the thought of missing the first Grand Prix for God knows how many years, and I didn't know how I was going to cope.

However, I was lucky enough to have been invited to the charity go-kart race in Monaco run by Prince Albert and organised by my good friends Mauro Serra and Beppe Gianotta, so I spent the weekend enjoying Monegasque weather in the company of many ex-colleagues from Formula One, such as Emanuele Pirro, Gianni Morbidelli, Beppe Gabbiani, Alex Caffi, Johnny Herbert, Thierry Boutsen and Stefano Modena.

In my race there were 15 of us, including motorcycle champions Giacomo Agostini, Troy Corser, Stefano Tilli and various other sports personalities. Our go-karts had bodywork and gears, and although I never got used to the gears in the limited practise time, the feeling of racing at Monaco, on a short version of the track that included the hairpin at La Rascasse and the swimming pool complex, was absolutely wonderful. I probably spent more time watching the scenery than the course, and perhaps that was the reason why I spun on the first lap! I just about recovered to finish seventh. What a superb weekend.

My last day at McLaren was on Friday 26 October 2001. I enjoyed a champagne send-off organised by Martin Whitmarsh at the restaurant, with all the workforce, and left the factory for the last time. As I drove off, with the McLaren factory shrinking in my rear-view mirror, I felt very emotional, asking myself if I was doing the right thing and replying that yes, it was the right timing – I should make room for the younger generation. After all, I'd lived through the golden era of the sport, from the 1960s through to the 1990s. I'd had a very good run and it was much nicer to be asked "Why are you retiring?" than "When are you going to retire?"

If I'd been able to live my life all over again, I'd have done exactly the same. Having said that, normal people retire from their work and then get on with the rest of their lives, but for me Formula One was never a job, it was my life, and I wasn't tired of living!

Come the start of the 2002 season, I realised the truth of Ron Dennis's words the previous year, when he'd told me that I'd feel as sick as a parrot not being in Melbourne. In order to ease the pain I took Bea on a trip to California to visit old friends from my earliest days in Formula One, Dan and Evi Gurney and other stalwarts of the old AAR days. With the influence of a good mate from BA we were upgraded to First Class, which set the tone for the whole trip. We watched the Grand Prix over a barbecue at the house of Marcelo Gaffoglio, the nephew of Juan Manuel Fangio and owner of Metalcrafters Inc, builders of prototype cars for the rich and famous and companies such as Daimler-Chrysler and General Motors. We had so much fun over the ten days that we nearly missed the flight home!

Forty years at the sharp end of motorsport wasn't going to be easy to shake off, and I wasn't under any delusions about not missing what had been my life and my love. I found that I didn't miss the work at the factory (except for some of the people). I certainly didn't miss the politics and the sudden rule changes. But I desperately missed the racing – the competition, the people and the buzz, the problems and the challenge of fixing them, the adrenaline, the parties, the women and the joy of winning: all the things that kept me young. And that was what worried me at times.

David Coulthard had once said to me: "At the moment you're always working with younger people, doing the same things as they do: swimming, waterskiing, playing football or just messing around, and no one would ever think of you as older than the rest. But when you retire, the people that you'll mix with will be your age, and it'll be then that you start getting old!"

That really hit me once we moved to a little village just south of

Oxford and were invited to lunch with some old friends, and the conversation was about eye deterioration, rheumatism and hip replacement operations... Yup, I guess I'd passed middle age and arrived at old age in a hurry!

Once the racing season moved to Europe, I just had to visit my old team in action, and I decided to go to Monaco – the obvious choice. This was the first Grand Prix of 2002 that I went to see live, and naturally I was looking forward to it, although with some reservations, as it would be the first time in 40 years that I was going to be on the outside looking in. However, I was invited to take part in a round-table forum that was to be part of a Grand Prix package tour, and I therefore had at least one commitment and so didn't feel a complete 'anorak'.

The Monaco Grand Prix is ideal to visit for someone like myself who's been involved in the sport for so long. Being the most prestigious event in the Formula One calendar, every personality from motor racing past and present would be there, including the now late Cliff Allison, the legendary Ferrari and Lotus driver of the 1950s. The Grand Prix is run over four days, so you have more time to see and chat with your friends, and there are parties galore night and day.

Apart from this, I think all of us who love the sport and have been associated with it are, deep in our hearts, frustrated racing drivers, and in our youth probably terrorised our neighbours by screaming our tyres around the block. So the fascination of Formula One cars running on normal streets still appeals to us and fills us with excitement.

The whole week was filled with invitations to different parties, presentations, lunches, dinners, or simply getting together for a boozy evening. It started on Tuesday evening with the charity football match between the 'Nationale Piloti', against the 'Start' team of Prince Albert. The former was headed by Michael Schumacher and Giancarlo Fisichella, and they ended up as the 2–0 winners. As you can imagine on the eve of the World Cup, it was a fantastic atmosphere with which to start the weekend – particularly as it was followed by a great dinner at a superb restaurant by the sea in Menton, with dozens of former Formula One drivers.

The following day I was given a great ego boost that told me that I was still welcome on the scene. I'd just arrived at the entrance of the F1 paddock when I suddenly remembered that I had no pass, no credentials; nor I was wearing team clothes. To collect my pass from the FOM office, I had first to get in! I thought that there was no way the Monegasque guards would let me through, since they have a reputation of being the most strict and unsympathetic guards in the world, and I approached the gate wondering what on earth I was going to say to the guard on duty to persuade him to let me through. But as soon as he saw me he said *"Bonjour, Monsieur Ramirez, bienvenue encore,"* and raised the gate. I was speechless, but just managed to say *"Merci beaucoup,"* and kept walking with a big smile on my face, thinking that my 40 years in the sport had at least accounted for something!

It was great to be back. Every other step I took brought me face to face with a friend to say hello to. But there were also some new faces in team uniforms that I hadn't seen before. For some years now we've had an injection of new people into the sport, and there are two reasons for this: the teams are getting bigger and the workers don't last so long in the sport, especially the mechanics, some of whom get involved for the excitement rather than the passion and soon afterwards decide that there are better ways of earning a living.

The thing that really caught my eye was the dreadful new uniform of my old team, McLaren: the tight black T-shirts and the silly tight shiny trousers didn't do anything for anyone, male or female. They looked more like petrol station attendants than Formula One crew members, and for the life of me I couldn't believe how on earth, having Boss as one of their partners, they couldn't see that they were the worst-dressed team in the pit-lane – a team like McLaren, who'd always set the standards. The boys used to call the shiny one-piece mechanics' overalls the 'gay-suits'. Ron Dennis may not be the world's best-dressed millionaire, but he's always smart, so how come he'd decided on such an ugly and unpopular choice? However, Ron and the hierarchy wore smart trousers and impeccable normal white shirts, which was totally against his principle of 'teamwork', which he'd normally supported so strongly. It was apparent that there was already a 'them and us' demarcation. McLaren is not a football or a rugby team: T-shirts are for the beach or DIY at home, but definitely don't belong in the high-profile world of Formula One racing. This alone would have been a good reason to change teams!

A confession: the foregoing paragraph was written in response to requests from many team members who said to me, if you write about McLaren, include something about these uniforms we have to wear. They felt that somebody had to tell Ron how ridiculous they looked, and ask him why, if he thought they looked 'cool', he didn't wear them himself? Since I thoroughly endorsed their comments, I had to mention it. Having said all of this, I'm now happy to see that the uniforms have been vastly improved.

I was a guest of Juan Pablo Montoya and was staying on his boat, a state-of-the-art, beautifully designed 20m Italian Azimut, and therefore I was going to see the Grand Prix from a totally different angle. This was an entirely new experience for me, and I was ready to see how the other half lived! I couldn't have been in better care. Juan Pablo's family are the most unassuming, uncomplicated and delightful people, and therefore I felt at home from day one; every detail was taken care of, including a fantastic Italian cook.

On the Thursday night there was a dinner organised in memory of Gilles Villeneuve, to mark the occasion of the 20th anniversary of his death. This was held on board the boat and hosted by Beppe Gianotta. The guests included Joann, Gilles's widow, who was there alongside old friends Pierre Dupasquier, Christian Tortora, Pino Allievi, Peter Windsor and Nigel Roebuck. It was a night of reminiscences and anecdotes from us old codgers who knew this charismatic man at his best and at his worst!

I spent Saturday evening with Mika, Erja and Hugo Häkkinen, playing billiards at their home, looking at his trophies and reminiscing about the old times, chatting about the Harley-Davidson, and then eating out at their favourite restaurant, just by the main palace square, until the early hours. I had, of course, spoken with Mika a few times since last November, but I was curious to see him, as many people said he'd put on weight and that his hair was black (!), but none of this was true. He looked as if he could just step into that McLaren and put it on pole again.

I've never seen him so relaxed and happy as now. Hugo is the most fabulously happy young chap you could ever see, and was at an age when he'd started to be interesting and good company, so I wondered if we'd ever see Mika prepared to forsake all this and get back behind the wheel.

Formula One definitely misses him, but did he miss Formula One? No, I didn't think so, at least not at that stage. Since then, of course, Mika has returned to the cockpit, but in a DTM Mercedes-Benz, racing against the likes of Jean Alesi and Heinz-Harald Frentzen and all the young hotshoes of touring car racing, and winning again.

The Monaco race was, without doubt, the best of the year – although the lead never changed, it was action-packed behind Coulthard. I was delighted for DC and had everything crossed for him, hoping that justice would be done today to redeem what happened last year, when he was on pole and the team electronics let him down.

I watched the start and the finish from the pits and the middle from the boat with Pablo Montoya Sr. We were all disappointed when JPM's engine failed, and I commiserated with Pablo and Lydia for only having one horse in the race, whereas I had two and my second was still leading! This was a great win for DC – good for McLaren and good for Formula One at a time when the sport is losing some of its credibility because of Ferrari's superiority. We all hoped it would continue.

When JPM returned to the boat he said that he was annoyed with his engineers, because when he'd practised starts in the morning the traction control wasn't working adequately, and he'd requested a manual start without the software. However, he was told that they'd found the trouble, and that it was going to be OK for the race, which clearly it wasn't. Mind you, it hardly mattered since the engine called it a day a few laps later.

I left Monaco after another great party celebrating David's win, and the circus prepared to move on to the next fly-away race, in Montreal, yet another favourite of the Grand Prix brigade. In the meantime, I'd once more experienced that feeling of standing on the grid when the engines are roaring ready for battle, the ground vibrating through your legs and up to your heart. There are only a few places that this feeling is so much alive, and Monaco is certainly one of them. That weekend brought back so many memories and reminded me of the fact that I really still miss the sport a hell of a lot.

The British Grand Prix at Silverstone was my second visit of the year to the F1 circus, and naturally I was looking forward to being back in the 'real world' again and getting my racing 'fix'. Silverstone being the home of British motorsport, and Britain being one of the dominating nations in this particular sport, the emotions and adrenaline always run high.

To think that at some stage the FIA and Bernie were threatening to scrub the one and only Grand Prix in this country makes one shiver, but I never thought that the threat was really serious – just a typical push for a 100 per cent improvement, and you perhaps get 50 per cent done. One of my good friends in the course of my racing life is Brian Pallett, a former Silverstone director, who is a 'doer' rather than a 'talker', a man who's devoted his life to Silverstone. When I spotted him on race day, I went across to say hello, without realising that in front of him was Bernie Ecclestone – and at this particular time he was giving Brian an almighty bollocking for things that were wrong.

It all started when Bernie, who arrived by helicopter, wasn't able to land at the normal helipad because of low clouds. He then landed on the other side of the circuit and got a lift in a car whose driver didn't know his way around. He called Brian for directions, but failed to convey his whereabouts, so Pallett and his men were running round in circles over the 850 acres of Silverstone trying to find him, without success. Naturally enough, Bernie wasn't amused. I believe his main complaints were the lack of signs and directions throughout the perimeter of the circuit, the lack of proper parking places (just muddy fields), and to add insult to injury there were queues in the very few toilets available.

Basically I don't think that Bernie has forgiven the British Racing Drivers' Club, who own the circuit, for spending several million pounds on their own lavish clubhouse but not enough on the circuit facilities. It's not difficult to understand the old racing boys, having spent all their time and money on their racing cars, wanting some luxury and comfort in their old age! But they were accused of having only petrol in their veins, lacking business acumen, and being short-sighted and unaware that racing is a business that has moved with the times. It's only thanks to the efforts of Ron Dennis, Frank Williams, Jackie Stewart and Martin Brundle that Silverstone kept its entry.

But it wasn't only Silverstone that was in trouble. As I was riding my Harley out of the circuit on Thursday, I saw the big unmarked Arrows transporter (the one that transports the racing cars) pulling away, and it suddenly dawned on me that the rumours I'd heard during the day were true – that Arrows had failed to pay their engine bill and therefore Cosworth weren't giving them any more credit. Earlier in the day I was ignoring the rumours, as I was sure that Tom Walkinshaw would be more than capable of bailing the team out of trouble. However, if he wasn't prepared to do that, then the problem was more serious than I thought. But we were all very happy to see them back on Saturday for qualifying, and very sorry to see Heinz-Harald Frentzen come from 17th to seventh only to have his Cosworth engine give up on him.

Having been a member of no fewer than five Grand Prix teams that no longer exist, I get particularly sad when another team fails to make the grid. Not only do you lose people who were at the leading edge, and are unable to join another team, but the sport also loses the team's name, and with it its history. So many big and small teams have gone – Lotus, Brabham, Ligier, Fittipaldi, Shadow, Tyrrell, Prost – and now Arrows was going the same way. Nobody likes to see this, not even the teams that are running behind them.

But I guess one has to be realistic: Formula One is getting more expensive every year, and cutting costs unilaterally would only make you slower. Added to this, the big corporations are cutting their advertising budgets, and with the financial market being at its lowest for years the chances for survival of the smaller teams are very slender. Unless you have a car manufacturer as a partner, the writing's on the wall that you won't make it. Sadly the days of the small racing enthusiast Formula One teams have gone – those wonderful scenes we saw in Melbourne 2002, when Minardi's Formula One 'rookie' Mark Webber scored two points by finishing fifth in his home race, seem too long ago!

Bernie Ecclestone is already talking in terms of asking the top teams to enter three rather than two Formula One cars in order to make up the numbers, but sad as it may be to lose the small teams, the racing and the competition will certainly improve, as more drivers will be able to race the same cars as the stars and will undoubtedly be eager to make their mark in the sport.

With all the rumours flying around the Formula One circus regarding the future of the Belgian Grand Prix due to the government ban on tobacco advertising and the possibility of the circuit being chopped and converted into another short and boring race track, I decided that I had to go. If Spa-Francorchamps did disappear from the scene I'd never have forgiven myself for not taking the chance of being there one last time.

I was also trying to get Mika Häkkinen to come and spend a weekend at Spa, a place that he also enjoyed very much. We always stayed at a wonderful guesthouse owned by a friendly Belgian family with whom, over the years, we've developed a close friendship. But unfortunately Mika decided not to come to a race this season: perhaps he felt it was too soon to show his face.

Spa has hosted some of the greatest races in the history of our sport and every one of us has a particular recollection of the Belgian Grand Prix. For me there have been more than most, purely because I've been to more races than the average. The one that will always stay with me is having achieved 'my' first Grand Prix win there in 1967. Dan Gurney's victory in his AAR Eagle was the first and only time that an American had won a Grand Prix event with a car bearing his own name. For me it was 'my' first out of 116 wins in 479 starts, a record of which I was always very proud, although I'm sure that if it hasn't been broken already it must be very close to it.

One of the things that I was most looking forward to doing in Spa, which in 40 years of the sport I was never able to do, was to get close enough to Eau Rouge corner to see qualifying from there. This was 'the' corner of the year, the only corner left in the calendar where the men get separated from the boys now that corners like the Curva Grande at Monza and the Curva Uno at Interlagos don't exist any more. It was great to be close to this corner and hear who was lifting and who took it 'flat'.

I was, however, somewhat disappointed this year at Eau Rouge, where a new surface and obviously more grippy tarmac had been laid down. There was also extra tarmac on the run-off area outside the corner instead of gravel – and, of course, the dreaded traction control! All the drivers went flat-out: some cars almost seemed to be on rails while others were merely a little bit twitchy. I watched the start just outside La Source, which I think is the best place to see the top 20 drivers in the world trying to miss each other without losing ground and more often than not managing to. It's always great viewing.

I was very glad that David Coulthard was able to show that he'd made the best choice of tyres for the race, and that McLaren's rising star Kimi worked so hard to keep his position after such a tremendous show in qualifying before his engine expired.

Having completed my racing 'fix' for the year, I was also able to spend some real quality time with some of my old colleagues from McLaren over the weekend. But I also had a very strange feeling of being on the outside looking in – much stronger than I'd had in Monaco and Silverstone. Perhaps it was something to do with a very strange conversation that I had with Ron Dennis on the Saturday in the pits.

Having spent at least two hours with him and all of the senior personnel of McLaren and Mercedes, drinking and chatting the night before during a very friendly evening, in the morning we reminisced about my farewell party at Indianapolis, where he was very detached from my wife and daughter over the whole weekend. This and another couple of unexplained quirks in Ron's attitude towards me and my family over my very last weekend had left me wondering. Before my days at McLaren, we had all been friends: he used to come to my parties and we used to go to his. Vanessa, my daughter, came to several Grands Prix, and often we had dinner together. Ron always used to make a fuss of her. But for some reason he had decided to be very distant, and I was very hurt about it as I could not figure out why or what point Ron had meant to make.

During all the time that I worked for Ron, he'd always been very supportive, very complimentary about my work. He'd often valued my opinion and, if I made a decision, he usually backed me up. Whenever I was wrong, he showed me a better way. Luckily I never had any major personal or health problems, but if I had, I'm sure he'd have helped me out, as he has countless McLaren employees who've had misfortunes. In 2001, he convinced me to stay as long as possible. And he'd thrown a wonderful farewell party for me.

So I'm still puzzled as to why he behaved so objectionably towards me on my last weekend. What was the message that he wanted to convey? Had he actually wanted me to walk away with a sour taste in my mouth?

Ron Dennis is one of the greatest creators in the sport. As a leader he's inimitable. He has the strongest vision for the future that I've ever seen in anyone, and one is constantly learning from him. As a friend you couldn't have a better one; as an employer, the McLaren record of staff retention speaks for itself. Is it the job that has turned him into someone that he'd probably rather not be?

Tyler Alexander summed it up on one occasion, as Ron Dennis walked through the pit garage looking straight through people without moving a lip or blinking an eye. Tyler commented: "Hah, why does he have to say good morning? He pays us, doesn't he?"

In the run-up to Christmas 2004 I was invited by Neil Trundle and Peter Stayner, two of my best friends of the many I still have at McLaren, to have lunch and visit the new McLaren Technology Centre. This emporium is now the headquarters of McLaren Racing as well as the production centre of the Mercedes-Benz SLR sports car, the luxury 'supercar' made by McLaren. I wasn't sure if I should accept the invitation, having been taken off the list of invitees to the old McLaren drivers' reunion on the occasion of the opening of the MTC – one of those events where every McLaren employee felt particularly proud to be part of the company, and having devoted the best years of my life to McLaren I'd have loved to have been asked. However, I did accept the invitation while I still had some friends there.

I was completely flabbergasted. Even knowing that the MTC building was going to be magnificent, I never imagined that it was going to be so grand.

I believe Ron Dennis and Norman Foster, the architect, were extremely proud and satisfied with their creation, and they have every right to be. The most cynical of cynics in the world could only agree that it's by far the most wonderful building ever made for a working environment. It's not surprising that this was the recipient of The Building of the Year Award from British Sky Broadcasting and the Royal Fine Art Commission Trust. As Her Majesty the Queen said when she opened it: "Very impressive." Although there may be far too much white, grey and black, there's elegance and perfection shouting at you from every corner. Perhaps there are too many empty corridors and the feeling of space is a bit over the top, but I could sit in a corner and look at it all day long. As an engineering and architectural accomplishment it's nothing short of superb. I can imagine Ron sitting in an office that would be envied by the president of any nation, looking at the MTC's peaceful lake and feeling very proud of having fulfilled all of his life's dreams.

But my impression of the place was that it had no soul. It was far too quiet and a bit depressing, had no atmosphere, and everyone spoke softly and seemed very serious. I knew that no one was allowed drinks at their desks, that there's no public address system, and that there should be no papers on your desk unless you're there. But are they also forbidden to laugh? As much as I'd have felt proud to work in that stupendous building I just couldn't see myself there at all.

So much water has gone under bridge, as they say, since I walked out of McLaren's front door. Since then, they have produced a new World Champion and a new approach to F1 racing car development. In December 1996 a young boy called Lewis Hamilton was at the *Autosport* Awards to collect his trophy as the Cadet Go-Kart champion. He thought it appropriate to come and meet Ron Dennis to ask for his autograph – and also to say he wanted to be signed up as he intended to become a future McLaren World Champion! Ron, far from laughing at this approach, thought the youngster had flair and real belief in himself, and told him to come back to see him in ten years' time when he had more to show on his CV.

Rather than waiting for Hamilton's further success, Ron followed his progress closely and, two years later, decided to sponsor his career in exchange for a long and profitable contract with McLaren. I very much remember Ron's words to me at the time, pointing out how much money we spend on engine development, wind tunnels, electronics, aerodynamics, suspension, testing, etc, and then sign proven drivers like Senna and Prost, paying them millions for their skills. Now we would instead spend the money developing a driver and if he comes good we will have saved a fortune.

Once again, luck was on Ron's side and he did indeed create a World Champion, but it wasn't always an easy ride. For his first year, Hamilton was paired with double World Champion Fernando Alonso who, because of his status, demanded favouritism, something that has never happened at McLaren. The young rookie proved to be far too quick for the Spaniard, who had never before been beaten by a team-mate, and the relationship became tense – a situation not helped by the fact that another scandal had broken within the sport.

The origin of the mistakenly named 'espionage' between Ferrari and McLaren was the theft of information by a dishonest Ferrari engineer who, with a McLaren engineer, planned to offer it to other teams. However, their carefully laid plans went awry and the McLaren engineer was caught with the drawings and information at his home. As the recipient of the information, McLaren was blamed and consequently penalised with the loss of all of their constructors' championship points and a fine of $100 million – yes, you read correctly, one hundred million dollars.

The outcome may have been different if the relationship between Ron Dennis and Max Mosley had been more harmonious. The team's focus on the drivers' championship suffered, Lewis made the inevitable rookie mistakes, and Alonso raged at his own inability to deal with his team-mate in or out of the car. The consequence was that McLaren lost the 2007 drivers' championship to Kimi Räikkönen and Ferrari.

Lewis Hamilton clinched the title in 2008 at the last corner of the last lap of the last race, by seizing an all-important fifth place in the Brazilian Grand Prix just as Ferrari were about to crack open the champagne for Felipe Massa, who won the race. For Felipe triumph lasted only 16 seconds!

The 2009 season was without a doubt one of the more problematic years for our sport. As I see it, the writing had been on the wall for several years but the team principals had been too wrapped up in themselves and their own affairs to see it. In my opinion it was clear that sooner or later the dominance of Max Mosley might jeopardise the whole show and this is almost what happened in a year of wonderful racing, where the usual winners became backmarkers and the backmarkers won races.

The summer of 2009 brought some moments of real crisis to the sport and there was a genuine threat that it would split into two series, as almost occurred back in 1980–81, in the infamous FISA–FOCA war. The difference was that in those days FOCA (Formula One Constructors' Association) was not quite as powerful as today's FOTA (Formula One Teams' Association) and the big teams were somehow closer to FISA (Fédération Internationale du Sport Automobile) than they are today to the FIA (Fédération Internationale de l'Automobile). The outcome of the FISA–FOCA war saw FOCA eventually rendered meaningless and it soon dissolved, confirming FISA's role in the control of the technical and sporting rules while the commercial affairs were given to Bernie Ecclestone, who later formed FOM (Formula One Management).

Later, in 1991, Max Mosley was elected President of the FIA and for a few years it seemed to do the sport some good. At the time we welcomed Max, an intelligent and approachable man, with open arms. We had all had enough of the dictatorship of his predecessor, Jean-Marie Balestre, but as time went by we began to discover the rough edges of Mosley and he became a changed man, perhaps one he may not have wanted to become. Perhaps it is something that comes with the job. I would have preferred that he hadn't remained in his position for as long as he did, but he always managed to get re-elected by cleverly inducing the smaller Automobile Clubs of the world to vote for him, even though the larger clubs mostly wanted him out – but there are many more of the smaller clubs.

Mosley even managed, to the annoyance of much of the automotive industry, to keep his position after the well-publicised sex scandal broken by the *News of the World*. After winning his lawsuit against the British tabloid for invasion of privacy, the man must have felt that he could walk on water.

During his time in charge, Mosley tried relentlessly to bring the big manufacturers into the F1 family. This brought much more image and exposure to the sport, but inevitably made it far more expensive, and so one by one the smaller teams disappeared. When the world economic crisis hit the automotive industry hard, the big manufacturers started abandoning ship. Mosley then tried to lure small teams back into F1 and offered them ridiculous advantages as well as forcing them to use a prescribed engine – the now-defunct Cosworth. For 2010, his wish was that the new, smaller teams and the established teams would race against each other under two different sets of rules, and all the teams would be held to an annual budget of 45 million Euros – for some that would have represented a budget cut of more than 75 per cent.

Needless to say, the newly formed FOTA, the international media and F1 fans worldwide were up in arms at his suggestions, which were completely and utterly against the very principles of F1. However, Mosley remained oblivious to the outside world, merely postponing the date when the teams would have to sign their entry into the 2010 World Championship. Unfortunately the Williams and Force India teams couldn't stand the heat and left FOTA by lodging their entry in the FIA books.

FOTA didn't wait until the FIA date, announcing – the day before – that they wouldn't participate under the new rules dictated by the FIA, and instead would set up a new championship. This was the touchpaper that the F1 world was waiting for and the World Motorsport Council immediately called for an unprecedented meeting, in which all of the points and issues that the FOTA presented were granted. Peace was once again restored with the assurance that Max Mosley would no longer seek his own re-election in October.

This is just a brief résumé of what has been happening within my beloved sport, but there has been a great deal more, some for the good of the sport and some that, at times, has made me feel ashamed to have ever been part of it. However, at least it shows that the latest union of the teams, never previously achieved, is now here to stay and will fight for their own rights, for more stability of the rules, and for transparency in the management of the sport.

However, if I'm honest, I was looking forward to the new FOTA series. If it had happened, the other teams would have soon joined and the FIA series would have disappeared. There would once again have been races in countries where there is a culture for automotive sport, such as France, Canada, the United States and South Africa. No-one wants to race in these new places that get a government injection of money to bring F1 to town, then after couple of years, once the novelty has worn off, they eventually have to pull out because tickets won't sell. FOTA lost a great opportunity to go its own way.

In the meantime, the FIA continues to impose its authority in a dictatorial and patronising manner, showing no consistency when issuing fines or penalties, and taking the fun out of the sport. There are no longer 'racing accidents' and in their eyes there always has to be a culpable party, someone to be punished. They want to take the excitement away from the scent of the sport and aggression will soon be prohibited – when that happens we might as well have any Tom, Dick or Harry driving these sophisticated F1 machines.

While 2009 was a very heavy year for the offices of the FIA and the teams, as well as their respective lawyers, it was eventful on the track and saw some very exciting racing. This was a season in which we saw the World Championship won by a team that hadn't existed a year before. Previously called Honda, it was the first of three big manufacturers to be lost within 12 months, as BMW and Toyota were to follow.

In December 2008 Honda decided that they could no longer spend so much money on F1 racing when they were closing factories. Only a couple of years earlier, Honda had lured Ross Brawn – the man who masterminded Michael Schumacher's seven World Championship wins – out of a sabbatical year. Sadly they didn't have the patience to see the car created under Ross's management and pulled the plug just as it was completed. Nonetheless, they behaved like gentlemen and bent over backwards to help Ross form a new team, Brawn GP, which debuted in Australia and swept the floor with a 1–2 for Jenson Button and Rubens Barrichello, thanks to a controversial new rear diffuser.

Ross Brawn had warned the teams several months before that the new rules were somewhat vague with regard to the rear diffuser and that they should be seeking clarification. The teams didn't listen and seven of them put up a protest against the Brawn cars in Melbourne, but the FIA declared the rear diffuser legal and everyone else had no alternative but to develop their own versions of it. Clearly, Ross's interpretation of the rules was correct, although many suggested that the outcome of the World Championship might have been different without this 'unfair advantage' at the beginning.

We also saw the first of the season's interminable off-track problems in that first race, this time created by McLaren when Lewis Hamilton, having finished third, lied to the stewards over an incident with the Toyota driver Jarno Trulli while following the safety car. Unfortunately, Hamilton and team manager Dave Ryan didn't work out their strategy carefully enough and they were caught. Sadly, this was to cost the head of Ryan, one of the most senior and long-standing members of the team. Ron Dennis, who had earlier in the year handed over the reins completely to Martin Whitmarsh, wasn't to be seen again at a Grand Prix for the rest of the year.

As the year progressed, the Red Bull team became more and more capable of fighting for the drivers' crown thanks to the efforts of F1's supreme boffin, Adrian Newey, and the new German star Sebastian Vettel. Ferrari and McLaren also improved through the year and managed one and two victories respectively. Smaller teams also had moments of glory, none more so than Force India, with Giancarlo Fisichella starting from pole in Belgium and only losing the race because KERS (Kinetic Energy Recovery System) gave Räikkönen's Ferrari the advantage off the line.

Changes in rules, of which KERS is one example, brought many fascinating aspects to 2009. Qualifying times across the whole grid, for example, were closer than ever before, although the closer racing and increased overtaking we hoped to see – thanks to the role of the FIA's 'overtaking group' in the implementation of the new rules – wasn't really evident after the early races of the year. When I went to the European GP in Valencia, I noticed at first hand all the new winglets that had been developed on the front wings, causing an increase in the air turbulence that stops drivers following each other close enough to overtake.

At the Hungarian GP a suspension spring, by a one in a million chance, fell out of Barrichello's Brawn car and hit Felipe Massa's helmet. This freak accident could have cost Felipe his eye or even worse, but thankfully it looked likely that, as I write this, he would be racing again in 2010. As a result, Ferrari showed the world how to waste a good car for the next two races by giving it to Luca Badoer, the test team driver who hadn't raced for ten years. Michael Schumacher had applied for the seat, but sadly his neck was not fully recovered after a motorcycle accident earlier in the year; Michael was bitterly disappointed, as well as all of his fans.

Then we had 'Crashgate' – one of the most incredible affairs in the history of the sport. When I first heard about it, I completely refused to believe it could be true that Nelson Piquet Jr had deliberately crashed his Renault at Singapore in 2008 so that team-mate Fernando Alonso could win the race, even though the circumstances showed this to be perfectly feasible. Nelson Piquet had already crashed a Renault 17 times, but by this stage the Renault car was much improved and this was confirmed a week later in Japan when Alonso won again without any help – and rumours of a fake accident in Singapore were soon gone.

However, a year later Piquet was fired from Renault. With his father, he decided to spill the beans to the amazement of the world, and all the pieces of the puzzle began to fit in place. The only thing that was never clear was who came up with the idea in the first place: Nelson himself or Flavio Briatore and engineer Pat Symonds. The deal was that if Piquet performed his stunt and Fernando won the race, Nelson would automatically secure a seat for 2009, but this was not fully honoured by the team and they sacked him halfway through the season. The fury of the Piquets, father and son, towards Flavio Briatore was so great that the truth came out – but at the cost of ruining the reputation and racing future, if he had any, of Nelson Jr.

The FIA punished Briatore with a lifetime ban from the sport and Symonds received a five-year ban. Renault got away with a suspended sentence while Piquet Jr got off scot-free because he co-operated with the FIA. That was disgusting: the man who actually pulled the trigger didn't suffer any penalty – a terrible state of affairs. This pre-planned crash shows how desperate for success teams and drivers can become in order to keep their places in this highly competitive sport.

Jenson Button won six Grands Prix in the first half of the year and although he didn't win again those early successes were enough to fulfil his dream of becoming World Champion, in the process answering those who criticised his lack of performance in the second half of the year. But the World Championship is the sum of all the races of the year and Jenson was a worthy winner.

CHAPTER 19

LAP OF HONOUR

Having, during 2004, decided to write this book in English and Spanish almost simultaneously, the English hardback version was launched at the Goodwood Revival meeting on Saturday 17 September 2005, as the most appropriate place to promote a book covering the last 40 or more years of the sport. I will always remain very grateful to Lord March for all the help he gave to make this possible. However, the launch coincided with the saddest period of my life, the illness and subsequent death of my beloved Bea.

As well as building our beautiful house in Spain, we had so many other wonderful plans and things we wanted to do, including lots of exciting trips abroad. Sadly we only managed three. I have always been very keen on opera and I wanted to take Bea to Verona to attend the open-air classics, something I used to do while I lived in Italy and something I think everyone should do once in their life. We also took a trip to Egypt and were both fascinated by its culture and history. Our final trip together, which we had always talked about, was a journey on the Orient Express. This was scheduled for May 2005, but by this time Bea was already starting to feel unwell and had to make several trips to the hospital for various tests. At one point I contemplated cancelling the trip but Bea said no – no way was she cancelling her holiday for anything.

We flew to Bangkok, and the holiday of a lifetime began when the Peninsula Hotel, for whatever reason, upgraded us to a fabulous suite overlooking the river. We had four nights there, doing lots of sightseeing and the obligatory shopping, before boarding the Eastern and Oriental Express to Singapore for the most idyllic and unforgettable four-day experience. The variety of nationalities aboard was fabulous, the evenings in the bar were truly memorable, and the food was of the highest standard. Unfortunately, however, Bea could only manage an appetiser or half a main course because she had so little appetite. Needless to say, I was rapidly putting on the weight she was losing!

Four nights in Singapore followed. Naturally we did all the tourist things, and apart from her waning appetite Bea thoroughly enjoyed the whole trip (which has to be another of those things I think everyone should do once in their life). Bea was without doubt the most wonderful travel companion anyone could wish for. Besides speaking and writing six different languages, she was also so eloquent and knowledgeable, and one of those infuriating people that could answer every TV quiz-show question. I always threatened that I would enter her on Who wants to be a Millionaire? because I was sure that she would easily win the million. However, her reply was always "Don't you dare!" She was convinced that she would completely embarrass herself by freezing in front of the camera, and probably wouldn't be able to speak. A great shame, as that was the only way that we would ever have become millionaires!

On our return home Bea resumed her visits to the hospital for more tests, and a couple of weeks later she was finally diagnosed with pancreatic cancer, one of the most aggressive and inoperable cancers. I will never forget the day we sat in front of the consultant who told us the bad news. I had this horrific feeling of emptiness and of hot and cold flushes running through my body, and even though I tried to remain as calm as Bea I couldn't stop my tears.

Not knowing the first thing about medicine, I quickly became familiar with all the terminology and the course of this dreadful disease, but in spite of all my friends in medicine (including Sid Watkins, the Grand Prix doctor) assuring me that nowadays cancer was no longer the death sentence it used to be, we knew it was very serious and we didn't know how to break the news to Vanessa. She was about to travel to a friend's wedding to be bridesmaid, but she had to know and would not have forgiven us if we hadn't told her. I remember both of us bursting into tears, but Bea quickly and firmly told us to stop because this was not the way to help her and she accused us of burying her before her time. She said that this was just like a tough bout of flu and that it wasn't going to kill her. "I will fight it and I will beat it," she promised.

I will always admire the strength, courage and dignity that Bea showed throughout her illness. She never ever at any point shed a tear, and she never lost hope – she was a truly remarkable lady who taught me a lot in her last six months. I was glad that I was no longer working and could look after her and try to make her life more bearable.

After a few months of not eating and just taking fluids and drugs she was very thin and weak. The chemotherapy had not worked and the doctors were trying different treatments, but she did not want to miss the book launch. Vanessa brought her down to the Sussex coast, where we stayed in a hotel by the sea and she was able to come to Goodwood on a beautiful late summer's day to hear all the flattering words that Sir Jackie Stewart and Murray Walker had to say about the book.

Murray was working for the BBC at Goodwood, while Sir Jackie was the motor racing ambassador for the RBS, who were taking an active part in the weekend. Jackie told me that he would be delighted to launch the book but that he had to clear it with Sir Fred Goodwin, as he was paying for his time, so we therefore agreed on a convenient time to suit the RBS. Jackie asked me afterwards to send a signed copy of the book to Sir Fred to thank him for making it possible, and soon afterwards I received a very nice thank-you note in the post, handwritten by Sir Fred himself, undoubtedly one of the most renowned and influential people in Scotland. Little did we know then that his banking career would end so publicly and controversially a few years later.

The Spanish edition was scheduled to be launched on 5 November in Mexico City. By then Bea was far to ill to even contemplate the trip, and I was in two minds whether to go or not, but thankfully Vanessa had come home for a while to spend some time with her Mum and to help look after her, so I felt able to go. Needless to say, it was a very sad launch, as all my family and I missed her very much; but it was an unbelievable success, with 500 copies sold on the day and 2,000 in the first two weeks. Sanborns and the Telmex group, who promoted the launch, had ensured its success by organising lots of TV and radio coverage during the preceding week, which no doubt contributed to how well the book was received.

On my return Bea was even more fragile, although, as was

typical of her, she showed great interest in hearing all about the event. Sadly, a week later we were told that she probably had only a week to ten days left. However, on the Saturday before she died she felt well enough to come downstairs and sit in her chair. Her voice was strong and her conversation extremely lucid. She was even making plans for the future, to the extent that Vanessa and I hoped that perhaps a miracle was about to happen.

But we knew this was too good to be true. I am told that people who are terminally ill often seem to have a brief burst of life just before it is extinguished forever, and this is exactly what happened to Bea. On the Sunday she didn't come downstairs and only managed short conversations, and on Monday she only acknowledged our voices by squeezing our fingers. Early on Tuesday morning she died in our arms.

In my line of work I have lost many close friends and colleagues, but I had never before lost someone so important in my life, and therefore I did not know how I would react. But there is no truer saying than "you don't know what you've got until it's gone". Being in love with motor racing is not the ideal basis for a good marriage, and although ours was perhaps not always the best in the world our friendship was second to none, and everyone knows that more marriages collapse through lack of friendship than through lack of love. We always shared everything and I never made any major decisions in my life without consulting her. She was my north, my south, my east, my west, my everything.

I felt totally lost in the world. Never for one minute had I imagined that it would come to this – she was the healthiest person I knew and I thought she would have buried me ten times over. She always told me that when I finished playing with racing cars and was happy to stop and grow old, she would take care of me. For the last 25 years of my working life I used to live away from home during the week, near to the factory. However, without fail, my last call of the day was always to her. Among all her qualities, she had the most beautiful voice and it was always a pleasure to talk to her about anything.

Time has a way of healing, but the longer the bond you have with someone the longer it takes to mend. Even now, not a day goes by when I don't think about her. During the first years those thoughts always brought tears, but now they are slowly bringing smiles. I find myself still talking to her every night, and asking her views and seeking her advice, just as I always did. For the first year I felt like a zombie, and kept thinking that without her my life was incomplete. It was difficult for me to get excited about anything. I had no incentive to do anything and it was very hard to sort out her belongings. I held on to some things that were very close to her, but having done that time just went by, and slowly I started spending more time in Spain.

Finally I decided that I really did not want to keep the house in Dorchester-on-Thames any more. It was Bea's house; she had chosen it and it was furnished just as she wanted it, so I could always feel her presence there, which I found very difficult. But she did not spend as much time in Spain, which made it easier for me to settle there. So Vanessa and I agreed to sell the house and her flat in North London and buy a larger house with the proceeds, which would be convenient for her work and to see her friends. My only stipulation was that it should have an extra bedroom, which would be my London pied-à-terre, a place to hang my hat whenever I came to England.

We were lucky enough to find a lovely old Victorian terrace house in Fulham – naturally more expensive than our budget allowed, but perfectly located. The house had a professionally built loft conversion with two little rooms and a bathroom, which ideally suited my requirements; so I have the penthouse and Vanessa has the rest of the house.

Vanessa finally found the man of her dreams eight months after losing her Mum, and in August 2008 Vanessa and Paul got married, in the most wonderful wedding I have ever seen. It took place in a small Catholic church in Marlow-on-Thames, with the reception at the Compleat Angler hotel, the perfect location. The only problem was that the date fell on the same day as the European GP in Valencia, which I had plans to attend – just like when she was born and I was due to race in New York. Things never change!

The wedding ceremony was short and wonderful and then the newlyweds were taken to the hotel by a small boat. The scene was like a Metro-Goldwyn-Mayer romance! On arrival they were greeted by a mariachi band while the guests sipped their first glass of Champagne. Every single detail was scheduled minute by minute with meticulous precision by Paul and Vanessa, and it was a joy to see how everything unfolded exactly as they'd planned. Ron Dennis and Lord March would have been proud of the organisation, just as the father of the bride was.

Needless to say, it was one of the happiest days of my life, with my only regret being that the most important person in our lives was not there, as she would have been absolutely ecstatic with joy. Bea and Vanessa had the most wonderful mother and daughter relationship that I had ever seen, so it was a great sadness that she was not there; but I am sure she was looking after her from above and will continue to do so. As for me, despite having had the most amazing life I'd often had the feeling that there was something missing, without knowing what it was. But when I walked Vanessa down the aisle, it dawned on me what had been missing, and then, of course, I had a great feeling of satisfaction.

After a wonderful honeymoon, Vanessa and Paul are now happily living in their Fulham home, and I join them from time to time between trips or whenever I need to come to the UK. Thankfully they seem to quite like me being there – perhaps it has something to do with the fact that I often take the opportunity to make home improvements. After all, what is a father for?

Nearly four years after the publication of the first edition of this book and the loss of my beloved Bea, life is again very much worth living. I am having a lot of fun doing the things I always wanted to do but never had the time to do – a big difference from when I left McLaren and Formula One. During the first couple of years I must have been hell to live with, because I missed my work and my former life so much, but now I have learned that in fact there is life after F1 and, thanks to having made so many wonderful friends all over the world, I am never short of places to visit and things to do.

One of the wonderful friends I mentioned in my earlier chapters is Bruno Flückiger, who now devotes the majority of his time to his Swiss car dealership but, in one way or another, keeps up his competitive spirit and every year enters the Ennstal-Classic 'old-timer' rally in the beautiful countryside of Austria. He has a team of four cars: a 1972 Porsche 911 Targa, a 1962 Chrysler 300, a 1956 Jaguar XK140, and a 1962 NSU TT, and I am lucky to be invited every year to be the privileged driver of the Porsche, which is really the only car in the team capable of winning.

The rally is organised by the legendary Austrian motor-racing journalist and author Helmut Zwickl, and Michael Glöckner, who are both great enthusiasts. It is a very serious and prestigious old rally which, in its 16 events, has attracted legends of the calibre of Walter Röhrl, Rauno Aaltonen, Björn Waldegård and Christian Geistdörfer, to name a few from the rally world, as well as Formula One heroes including the likes of Stirling Moss (who has only missed one year), Derek Bell, Mario Andretti, Marc Surer, Hans Hermann, Gerhard Berger, Alex Wurz and Adrian Newey. The competition is therefore always very intense and most of the serious cars are fully equipped with the latest rally navigation systems, so that finishing in the first 30 of over 200 cars is quite an achievement, and even gets recognised with a bronze medal.

My navigator for the rally is Johnny Wyssmuller, a Swiss ski instructor to the rich and famous, as well as a first-class co-driver. He is also totally fearless of my driving skills, which helps enormously! He has a firm, no-nonsense approach, so we get along fine, and we have been improving every year – from 69th in our first rally, to 41st in our second, 26th in our third, and last year we were absolutely amazed to be in the top four in all stages except one (when we took the wrong route and had maximum points added). To think that we could have finished fourth overall made us sick. However, we still managed a very creditable 21st, despite the 1,000 penalty points we were given because of our mistake.

The rally has easily become one of the most special and eagerly anticipated weeks of the year for me, not only for the great hospitality shown by Bruno's team (who really are a 'laugh-a-minute' crowd), but also for the unbelievable array of fabulous automobiles, the coming together of all these crazy and rich car collectors from all over the world, and, of course, the welcome that we all receive from the host country, Austria, and its wonderful people. The roads that Helmut and Michael choose have to be some of the greatest drives in Europe. Wherever you look there is a picture postcard scene, and you could swear that at any minute you'll see Julie Andrews singing The Hills Are Alive.

The other event that I have been lucky enough to be invited to since my retirement (and one that has always been one of my life ambitions) is the Carrera Panamericana, which is widely regarded as one of the two greatest road races in the world (the other being the Mille Miglia in Italy). The Panamericana was originally held from 1950 to 1954, but then – as a result of a horrendous accident during the Le Mans 24-hour race in 1955 (a catastrophe in which over 80 people where killed) – the rules for road races changed drastically. The new rules required the compulsory fixing of protective guardrails along the entire 3,500km course, which therefore made it economically impossible for the Carrera to continue.

In my very early teens my greatest ambition was to compete in the Carrera when I was old enough. I also had an uncle who became my hero when he competed in it, and even back then Ricardo Rodriguez and I dreamt of racing in it. But of course, we would have been laughed at. However, in 1988, thanks to the enthusiasm of entrepreneur and Carrera fanatic Eduardo 'Lalo' León, the event was revived in its present format, half race and half rally. The rules are very simple: the fastest driver is the winner in each of the nine categories.

In 2006 I was lucky enough to be invited to race by Señor León, who also arranged the loan of a car, a Volvo P1800 (as used by Roger Moore in the TV series The Saint), from lawyer Luis Barona, who is a keen Mexican Volvo enthusiast and collector. He also provided me with one of the Carrera's most experienced co-drivers, Alberto 'Beto' Cruz, who has not only taken part 15 times but also survived one of the biggest accidents in the history of the Carrera at the hands of Clay Regazzoni, the F1 legend who fell in love with the Panamericana.

With the car, and help from Telmex, we were up and running and I was ready for the dream of a lifetime to come true. Words really can't express the Carrera experience: a whole week of racing, rallying, partying and generally having a fantastic time. The atmosphere of enjoyment and camaraderie that prevails throughout the event are something that I have not experienced for a long time. It is, without doubt, motor racing's best-kept secret.

In my first year I decided to take it easy and just find my own rhythm, to finish all the stages and not do anything silly, and then return to all the towns and wonderful hotels to make sure I didn't miss any parties and to just generally have fun. We had engine problems in the first stage and came nowhere, but we got to the finish so we were happy. On the second day the car ran fantastically and we won the stage! With that the goalposts suddenly moved, and we began to believe that we could actually win our class; so we only had one drink at the evening's party and then went to bed early, to ensure maximum concentration for the following day. We went on to win another two stages, which moved us to second, but unfortunately we broke an oil pipe during the last stage, which relegated us to third as we just pushed the car over the finish line. Señor León said to me, "It's good that you didn't win, because now you have to come back..." And he never spoke a truer word.

Of our second year there is not that much to say, because everything went like clockwork. Whether this was because we had a perfect car (although rain at a crucial stage helped us no end), or whether it was because we didn't face such strong opposition this time, we managed not to put a wheel wrong and ended up winning every stage. We were then told that no one had ever managed to achieve this in any category, and so a special trophy was made for us, which we were delighted to receive.

The 2008 Carrera Panamericana was harder than it had been in previous years. We were in the Historica A+ category with our familiar 1962 Volvo P1800, and there was fierce competition, mainly from an Alfa Romeo, three other Volvos and a couple of Porsches. The route had also been changed and we were back to the original start in Tuxtla Gutierrez, as there were no longer any political issues in the Chiapas region.

All the teams and drivers stayed in Tuxtla for two or three days for last-minute preparations, medical checks and testing of the cars. The day before the start we had to qualify in order to determine the starting order. The main stars present this year were Stiq Blomqvist, legendary driver of the famous Audi Quattro, winner of the 1984 Rally World Championship, who was driving a Studebaker in the Turismo Mayor category; and Jan Lammers, ex-F1 racer and accomplished prototype car driver with many victories and championships to his name, including the 24 Hours of Le Mans. Jan started his F1 career with my team, Shadow, in 1978 and remains one of my greatest friends from my F1 days. He was driving an old Porsche in the original Panam category and I was very much looking forward to us racing together as drivers rather than working as driver and boss.

The qualifying stage, as usual, was on the first stage of day one and we qualified 36th out of 108 cars – one second faster than Jan! This was to be the highlight of my Carrera, although I was under no illusion that I was going to keep that place in front of him for very long. Nevertheless, I enjoyed saying "Wait until I tell Vanessa that I had you in my rear view mirrors!"

So, day one was from Tuxtla to Oaxaca, and just as we were leaving Tuxtla on a long straight road, lined with thousands of bystanders and led by police cars, I overlooked one of those ghastly speed ramps that seem to suddenly grow out of Mexican roads. It wasn't painted or signposted like some of the others and our little Volvo just took off and landed on its back-end with a horrendous noise, but we had no time to stop and assess the damage. Not that we could have done much about it anyway, given that we didn't have any tools.

We arrived at the start of the speed stage and just went for it, but the car felt very loose at the rear and had very heavy oversteer, which needed over-correction of the steering almost before entering the corner. As soon as I got used to the strange handling we started gaining ground, and even reached the Ford Mustang in front, which gave us a false sense of confidence that we were fast, rather than that the Mustang was slow! We soon passed it and arrived at a mountainous section with cliffs at every corner, where a Cadillac, a Sunbeam Rapier and a Volvo had gone off. Beto and I were talking about the accidents when suddenly the car's back end almost overtook me and this time I could not catch it. Thankfully it was just a spin on the black stuff and we hadn't touched anything, but we did end up sideways on the road and feared being hit by the oncoming Mustang. So we let the car roll backwards into the ditch, leaving just enough room for the Mustang to pass – which thankfully it did.

I started the little Volvo, and with the clutch and rear wheels spinning I heaved it out of the ditch. As we started to go, Jan Lammers overtook us in his Porsche, and, as expected, he had a big grin on his face and a pointing finger. We weren't to see the back of that Porsche again, although it was nice to follow him for the rest of the stage, and we both caught up with the Mustang again. On arrival at the service point we discovered that the left-hand damper had snapped off the rear suspension when we went over the speed ramp, and was now hanging loose, which explained the car's behaviour. Traditionally, most of the cars that crash in the Carrera do so in the first two stages, and this year was no different. Therefore once we arrived in Oaxaca we were happy that we had survived the first day in one piece, even though our overalls needed to go to the laundry. The other surprise of the day was that at the prize-giving ceremony that evening we found out that we were second in our class, a minute behind the Alfa Romeo, and had a good lead on the third-placed team. We figured that we had only lost about a minute during our spin.

Day two was Oaxaca to Mexico City via Tehuacan. This time, unlike the previous two years, there was no stage in Puebla. This was a shame, because stopping in front of the magnificent cathedral in Puebla town square was really something special. It would appear that the fraternity of the Carrera Panamericana were not supporters of the Governor of the city, and it was therefore decided that we would not visit Puebla. However, we did stop for an hour in Tehuacan, which, as always, offered one of the best welcome receptions on the whole route.

We finished the second day in Mexico City, for the first time, as they wanted to show the cars in Alameda Park, which is one of the best spots of the newly revamped Centro Histórico of the Ciudad de México. The arrival of the cars was programmed to coincide with the end of a huge parade of massive papier mâché characters, and was a great success. We finished the day in second place after again chipping away at some of the Alfa Romeo's lead and increasing our own lead over the third-place car.

The next day we had an earlier start with a speed stage in the Periferico, 5km from one of the busiest ring roads in the city, which was closed off to salute the cars on their way to Querétaro – an indication of the tremendous popularity that the Carrera Panamericana has achieved in recent years. In this stage, which is virtually an immense gradual curve with no corners, the big V8 Turismo Mayor was reaching speeds of 290kph (we probably just touched 190kph). On arrival in Querétaro, the last stage was six laps of the local racing circuit. However, we arrived when the sun was about to set, and as we were facing the end of the straight I was completely blinded by it just as we reached the breaking point – which, needless to say, I missed, and we finished up in the sand. I managed to keep it going and get back on to the circuit to continue, but as a consequence of the accident I managed to acquire a hole in the radiator.

By the end of our laps the service mechanics had already arrived, and they promptly changed the radiator. However, the spare they had was bigger and didn't quite fit in the available space, so they had to patch it in place with no ventilator fan, just so that we could reach the control in time and without penalty. We managed this by virtually freewheeling, thanks to the fact that it was almost all downhill. This time the Alfa had a commanding lead and we therefore resigned ourselves to finishing in second place (or first of the losers!).

The fourth day was a new stage for everybody as we headed to San Luis Potosi. This was a replacement for the Morelia and Mil Cumbres stage of previous years, which had been, without doubt, the best and most exciting stage for us, and where we had excelled. It had comprised about 60km of the most twisting and winding roads you could ever encounter – a real favourite of the old Panamericanos! However, 'Lalo' León, the Carrera promoter, had been pressurised by the government of San Luis year after year to include their city on the route, as it had been part of the original Carrera event back in the 1950s.

Coupled with this were the frequently catastrophic accidents that happened each year during the Mil Cumbres stage, which were always at the forefront of Lalo's thoughts. It had claimed several lives in the past, so this year Señor León gave in. However, he promised the real racers that they wouldn't be disappointed by the new stages in San Luis, and I have to say that they were indeed wonderful – not quite as tight as Mil Cumbres, but with better road surfaces and beautiful landscapes. I personally never felt that Mil Cumbres was that dangerous, because in comparison to other stages the speed was relatively slow. However, if you were unlucky enough to come off the road there was very little except trees to prevent you going over a steep precipice.

The city of San Luis went really overboard in welcoming us, by closing the main road. I felt very sorry for all the people who were working and trying to carry on with their normal lives, as they had to wait for the grown-ups to finish playing with their racing cars! We finished third in this stage.

The fifth day was to be our worst. Our alternator packed up on a long transit route, leaving us with a dead battery, stranded at the roadside on a long straight while 40 or 50 Panamericana cars passed us. Only one of them stopped to see if they could help in any way. This was car number 333, a Porsche driven by Emilio Azcárraga, president of the Televisa group and one of the richest and most influential men in Mexico, who had to have a car full of bodyguards following him. He was, however, the most normal and down-to-earth person you could ever come across and was having the time of his life. It was his first Panamericana and he was like a child with a new toy, and remarked that he had already booked his entry for the next 20 years! Beto and I were surprised that he stopped, but we certainly appreciated the gesture.

After all the competitors had passed we waited for the service car to arrive. We were pleasantly surprised by the entrepreneurial skills of the Mexican mechanics, who threw themselves into the job wonderfully. The alternator was dodgy and they didn't have a spare, so the only way to keep us going was to replace the battery, which was well and truly dead. So they left their rent-a-van's engine running and removed its battery, which they then ingeniously adapted to the Volvo. Unfortunately this battery wouldn't be able to last the day or even get us to the next stage, but it did enable us to get the car as far as a garage, where we stopped to buy a replacement. As expected, it didn't fit our Volvo, but the guys soon adapted it and reunited their rent-a-van with its own.

We got our helmets and belts on and drove like crazy to the next stage. We passed the control a bit late but we were back on track. Sadly this lasted for only a few minutes, because once again there was no power to the Volvo's electrics and we had to stop in the middle of the speed stage. We again waited to be rescued by the service van, but this time we only got as far as the service point in Aguascalientes, where the alternator was replaced. However, there was no time to check the behaviour of the engine, which was not working at all well.

The next stage was uphill and our engine was misfiring like crazy, but we just made it there, amongst the backmarkers. We lost precious seconds, but we were delighted to beat the Alfa by two seconds on the way down, even with a misfiring engine. However, we were very disappointed to learn that cars passing any control after ten minutes (as we had done) were automatically given the slowest time of their category, plus a ten per cent penalty, regardless of results. So we could have stopped and gone directly to the hotel for a break. What a shame.

Day six was the famous stage of the Bufa in Zacatecas, a mixed stage of uphills, downhills and long straights. Our car was still misfiring, although a lot less than the day before, and we thought we had a reasonable day. However, we were not in the first three at the prize-giving party that night... This was a very painful reality check. Thank goodness we had accumulated enough of an advantage earlier over the third-place car, as we had no chance in hell of beating the first one!

A brighter note regarding this stage is that it finished in the wonderful city of Zacatecas, one of the oldest in Mexico. We arrived right in the main street in front of the incredible cathedral and were greeted with a wonderful display of hors d'oeuvres and drinks. This was followed by the now famous 'Callejoneada' – a donkey running around the callejons (small cobbled streets) with a barrel of Mezcal, the local drink, to be served out to the Panamericanos. We then followed the donkey and danced in the streets before arriving at the five-star Quinta Real Hotel, converted from what used to be the oldest bullring in Mexico. The entrance was truly breathtaking in such a wonderful and unexpected setting. This was the start of the prize-giving ceremony and, without a doubt, the best party of the Carrera.

Day seven, the last of the Carrera Panamericana, is generally the only dull day of the week – 700km of transits, with some speed stages that can send you to sleep, as they're all flat whichever category you're in. Thank God we felt safe in our second-place spot! The problem is that in the north of Mexico it is practically impossible to find any twisty roads; they just don't exist. When we arrived in the main town square of Nuevo Laredo we were greeted by the Governor and given the obligatory beer as the party started. Later on the prize-giving and closing ceremony took place in a very warm and friendly atmosphere, and we were more than pleased to receive our second-place trophy.

In the top class, American Bill Beilharz and his Mexican co-pilot Jorge Ceballos took the honours in a Studebaker. Doug Mockett and Angelica Fuentes were second in an Oldsmobile, and Stiq Blomqvist was third. Jan Lammers won all the stages in the original Panam except the first, when he ran out of fuel. This relegated him from first to second place, but he was still able to entertain the fans with his wonderful driving. I would love to have exchanged cars with Jan just to see if I needed a stopwatch or a calendar to check our time difference! So ended the 2008 Carrera Panamericana, and we were left with the dreadful thought that we had to wait another 12 months to come back to this wonderful and unique event that nothing will ever come close to matching.

To say that it is one of the best events in which I've ever had the fortune to participate would do it no justice. It is simply the greatest week of the year for the competitors and the thousands of fans who follow it, not only in Mexico but all over the world. It is surely unique. What other country on Earth would close its public roads and allow a load of vintage cars to go racing on them? It is said that, on average, men think about sex 19 times a day, but I can honestly say that during that week it never crossed my mind at all. You participate in the Carrera once and you're hooked! As my fellow competitors and I reflected over breakfast, the morning after the event in Nuevo Laredo, "It's a damn shame we have to wait another year to come back to Heaven." Long live the Panamericana and the spirit of the Carrera.

Meanwhile, between rallies, Carreras and Harley-Davidson bike rallies I have managed to finish my house in Spain. My last project was the swimming pool, which is actually more of a lake than a pool, with rocks, waterfalls and an infinity edge that looks out on to the ocean. It's a place that I will never tire of looking at, and I feel enormously proud to own it.

For 2009 there was a little more of the same. I went to the British GP thinking I had to be there because it could be the last one at Silverstone, but mercifully the long-running saga about the future of the British GP ended happily when a 17-year deal with Silverstone was announced a few months later.

As I live in Spain, I also wanted to visit the European GP in Valencia. For the first race, in 2008, the organisers had failed to create another Monaco, as they had intended, because they were far too greedy and asked far too much money for boats to moor in the harbour, which was therefore empty and without atmosphere. In 2009, with the economic crisis and also the experience from the year before, not many boats showed up. Although Valencia is a great city, it isn't on the Riviera and will never have the style, glitz and glamour that Monaco has commanded for decades.

Attending these Grands Prix also gave me the opportunity to follow the progress in the GP2 supporting races of one of our Mexican drivers, 19-year-old Sergio Perez from Guadalajara. Together with Scuderia TELMEX, we are trying to bring him into F1 in the near future, and these were probably his best two races of the year.

Except for my annual trip to Austria for the Ennstal-Classic Rally, I spent most of the summer in Spain and made several trips on my Harley-Davidson to the white villages of Andalucia. The more time I spend at my place, the less I feel like travelling the world.

Apart from the Carrera Panamericana in Mexico, which has become a compulsory part of my life these days, I haven't had any inclination to arrange other trips. As well as being the best week of the year, the Carrera gives me the opportunity to visit my family and friends in Mexico. My mother, at 94, is still the pivot of the family and it's a joy to see her every October, even if I always have the sad feeling as I leave that perhaps I won't see her again.

The Carrera of 2009 seemed to ignore the economic crisis as it attracted 100 participants in its eight categories. It was as enjoyable as always, perhaps even better than usual, although it was also by far the hardest Carrera ever. The race started at the fabulous city of Huatulco, south of Oaxaca and one of Mexico's most beautiful seaside resorts, and we had six to eight speed stages each day, with some of them up to 30km long. With temperatures in the 40s and with 80 per cent humidity, the cars were like portable saunas.

Our category was well-subscribed and full of Porsches, Alfa Romeos and BMWs weighing 200kg less than our Volvo, so Beto and I soon discovered that we were going to have a tough time. We held our own, however, running second to a Porsche in the first stages and in third place by the time we got to Mexico City. However, as soon as the fastest stages arrived towards the end of the week, there was nothing to do but sit back and watch a BMW steal our third spot. Even though it was our lowest position in four Carreras, it was perhaps the most enjoyable because of the tough conditions and strong competition. It was certainly the most rewarding because we kept out of trouble and got to the chequered flag in Nuevo Laredo in one piece.

So there has indeed been life after Formula One – and hopefully there will continue to be.

INDEX